SALLY Bateman ☮

Once More from the Beginning

ONCE MORE
FROM THE BEGINNING

ROBERT MERRILL

with Sandford Dody

THE MACMILLAN COMPANY · NEW YORK

FIRST PRINTING

The Macmillan Company, New York
Collier-Macmillan Canada, Ltd., Toronto, Ontario

Library of Congress catalog card number: 65–25062

Printed in the United States of America

This book is dedicated
To the memory of my beloved parents
And a happy future
With my Marion, David, and Lizanne.

Sincerely

[signature]

OVERTURE

I SAT CAPTIVE in front of my dressing-room mirror—helpless like a man getting a haircut—while George, the makeup man, worked on me silently. *There he goes again,* I thought, as Robert Merrill slowly disappeared in the glass. *So long, kiddo!* Slowly emerging in his place was Sir Henry Ashton, greedy and conniving Laird of Lammermoor, Lucia's brother.

"This is the lousiest baritone role ever written. You know that, George, don't you?"

I was certain that George's silence meant consent. Ashton! Singing the role tonight was hardly going to bring me any glory, no matter how well I did it. But Rudolf Bing had asked me to open the Metropolitan season opposite Joan Sutherland, and my inclination is to please the gentleman—always. I had only recorded with the great soprano, and we had always wanted to appear together onstage.

What an artist she is! I mused. *And what a hell of a cold she's had all week.* A raw feeling was barely discernible between my nose and throat. *My God! If I caught it, I'll die. With my first Scarpia coming up in a few days, that's all I need. Oh, hell, we're more durable than we think. I've been worrying for a lifetime. And I'm pretty lucky. Twenty years, tonight! Most firms give you a gold watch and your walking papers after twenty years. I'm just beginning to warm up.*

A flick of George's wrist, an additional pencil line, and I was changed completely. I watched his artistry with fascination. *What a parade of characters I've played these many years. More than my hairline recedes when I look back at a lifetime in front of this magic glass. I've watched George use more and more makeup for Escamillo and less and less for Germont. But that's natural enough.*

He now placed Ashton's wig on my head, and I tried to assume the inner qualities of the villain. *How great it is to hide behind another's identity. And how marvelous that I can lose myself completely in another character.*

Are we all cowards in the theater, with our string of roles and our wardrobes filled with masks and costumes? You'd certainly think so from the sweat on our palms and the butterflies in our stomachs.

I stood and stared at this guy who was going to go out onstage and drive his sister batty. Before the dresser helped me with my costume, I pulled in my gut as only a student of Yoga can.

"You've become quite slim, Mr. Merrill," George volunteered.

"Have I?" I asked, pretending surprise.

Yes, Mr. Merrill was quite slim, but at my age it is never a surprise. It is because you've worked at it.

You look pretty good, kiddo, I decided as I got into the Lammermoor tartans. *You could have looked like the biggest Plaid Stamp in New York. What a stupid role this is!* Nonetheless, for whatever the combination of reasons that prompted my being there, I now stood in my dressing room sweating like a workhorse in my magnificent costume. I played with the tartan scarf, which was fastened by a large brooch to my left shoulder and draped over my arm, testing my freedom of movement. The costume was certainly beautiful; but my twentieth season had symbolically brought Indian summer to New York City, and it was hot and muggy. Fussing with the jabot, I noticed that the gauntlets were nowhere in sight. The dresser, in a panic as great as mine, scurried off to find them. I wondered whether my wife, Marion, was out front yet.

Alan Lerner was escorting her to the opening and to the party Johnny Carson was hosting for me at Voisin later. What with the diners at Sherry's and the party being given in the private dining

room next door to it and the colorful mob of first-nighters vying
with one another on the stairs, in the aisles, and on every tier, I
doubted that anyone was seated yet.

In an attempt to revive the dignity of past openings, Mr. Bing
had forbidden admission to anyone dressed too outlandishly. It
was true that the audience was becoming more bizarre every
year, its costumes competing with the most ornate onstage. I
knew what must have been going on out there, with what was
left of the old guard mingling diamonds and martinis with the
new money, the horizontal sables outstaring the vertical chin-
chillas, the blinking rubies and emeralds acting as stop-and-go
signals that would keep traffic around the bar completely out
of control.

*What a performance they're all giving! I can't wait until this
is over and we're off to the party and Marion can tell me all
about it.*

There was a rap on the door. "Five minutes, Mr. Merrill."

My heart sank—as it always does at this moment. *Five minutes?
Am I really expected to sing in all these plaid bandages and this
ridiculous headgear! And where the hell are those damned gloves!
The whole thing's absurd.*

Ashton is *such a bore!* And, what's more, he disappears completely in mid-opera. Sutherland had insisted that the scene be
restored in which Ashton sees the fruits of his machinations and
watches the mad scene in remorse and wretchedness. This would
be the first time in years that Ashton reappears to witness Lucia's
death. God knows the restoration does nothing to improve the
role, but it does make sense.

I appraised myself in the mirror again. *Ashton is through, with
or without the scene. He might be the catalyst for Lucia's death,
but she'll tear the house down with bravas before she gives up
the ghost; and as for the tenor, God bless him, he has the whole
last act to himself. There's your Donizetti! What am I going on
about? It's poor Sutherland who's had the cold all week, and the
evening is going to stand or fall on her performance. This is her
ball game, not mine.*

I knew that she would be magnificent. At rehearsals, although
she saved her high notes and didn't even sing full voice, I mar-

veled at her musicianship and authority. Many singers have
beautiful voices but do not know how to sing. Unlike many
others, Sutherland will sing superbly for years. She has real
respect for her gift.

Our duet in the second act has got to go well. The gloves!
Marion! Traffic! Are the kids asleep? My eight-year-old, Lizanne,
had given me a red *corno*—to ward off evil—she had gotten in
Rome last summer. My son, David, who is nine, lowered his eyes
to the floor before I left home and, in his tough and funny voice,
wished me "bonner fortuner," then added, "You're the rat again,
aren't you, Daddy?"

"The baritone is always the rat, my boy," I had answered,
wondering to myself why the pitch of a man's voice should
determine his virtue. Being a baritone has given me a repertoire
of villains to play, and I love them. But if you're going to be hated
by the audience for all your dirty work, then at least you should
have a few great arias.

The gloves! Where the hell are those gloves! How can a man
be expected to sing without gloves?

"Two minutes, Mr. Merrill."

It didn't matter about the part or the gloves, because I couldn't
sing anyway. It was now obvious that I was coming down with
laryngitis, a strep throat, and double pneumonia. Thumbing
through the score, wiping my face, it seemed I was in a fever.
Opening nights! I cleared my throat now. "Mi-mi-mi-mi!" The
mirror shook as my voice blasted the air.

The dresser burst into the dressing room with my gloves. I
could hear the whole floor alive with the disjointed vocalizations
of tenors and bassos. It was the operatic countdown.

With one last look at myself and a final fling of the tartan over
my shoulder, I went into the hall and paced to the door that
opens onto the fire escape. We all sounded like inmates of a zoo
at feeding time as we tuned up like a human orchestra. "Mi-mi-
mi-mi-mi!"

"Break a leg, Mr. Merrill."

"*Merde, amico.*"

"*Bocca lupo.*"

"Good luck, Bob."

Did Marion get here safely? I worried.

Mr. Bing, our keeper, had stopped at our cages. "Thank you, Bob. I know you'll be wonderful."

How could he possibly know that, when I'm dying? I looked down into the street, to the corner of Thirty-ninth Street, and remembered the very first time I entered the Met.

"Okay, Mr. Merrill, the opera is about to begin. Everybody."

I started down the stairs in a daze. *I've walked this last mile for so many years. Twenty years. My God! How did it all begin?*

CHAPTER ONE

I'M AFRAID THAT my parents' marriage was not made in heaven but in what used to be called the old country. My mother, Lotza Balaban, was the daughter of a Polish tailor who had a little store in Warsaw. My father, Abe Millstein, came to that store as an apprentice when he was six years old. The pale little boy sewed away in a dark corner of the store, his legs folded beneath him, his fingers bleeding as he learned his trade. My father spent his whole life like that—hunched over a piece of cloth, his eyes on his nimble fingers, his whole body twisted into a kind of devotion. Work was my father's religion. The world passed him by, and he sat, quite satisfied, sewing, as if he were recording history in his own way. There was something classical about my father. I adored him.

His fate was sealed at the age of six. After that he just grew older. His betrothal and eventual marriage to his master's daughter were simply the next logical steps in the sequence of events. It had nothing to do with love or romance. Marriages were "arranged" in the ghettos too.

My mother was a pretty child with a beautiful soprano voice —her rightful inheritance, since Grandpa Balaban was the only merchant in a family of cantors, and even he had an excellent tenor voice. Music was an important part of the Balabans' life, and Lotza was particularly gifted. In a less rigid environment, she would have been encouraged to build her life around

music; but for a female, that was impossible. One day a noble-
man heard my mother's voice in the street and was so impressed
by its beauty that he sought out Grandpa Balaban with an
offer to subsidize her training for opera. The Polish nobility was
never famous for its love of the Jews, so the gesture was doubly
impressive. My grandparents, with suspicions and fears, refused
his offer. I don't think my mother ever forgave them. She was a
woman born to sing and to die dissatisfied with her lot. But she
never stopped trying, never stopped battling the Fates. In this,
she also was classical.

Promised to each other, my father left my mother in Warsaw
and emigrated to the United States. In New York City, Momma's
older brother Looey, himself a tailor, had promised to help him
find work. With this lofty contact in the New World, Poppa
crossed the ocean and landed in New York Harbor. At Ellis
Island, when he tried to sign his last name, he could not get past
the first four letters, and an impatient official ended his struggle
and changed his name by adding an *e* and an *r*. So my Poppa
set out on his new life as Abe Miller.

After beginning his career with some piecework that Uncle
Looey brought home for him, he luckily got a job in a sweatshop. Encouraged by his good fortune, he sent for Lotza, then
eventually for his parents. Momma kissed her family good-bye,
packed a few photographs and some colored fabric and beads,
and boarded a ship that took thirty days to separate her from
everyone she had ever loved. She was on her way to Abe Miller.
That was what it was like to be a teenager in 1910.

My mother and father were married according to plan. They
rented a room in some remote relatives' railroad flat, where they
acted the roles of a married couple. He went out to work, and
she cleaned and cooked. They must have been bewildered. They
had nothing in common except want—until they brought two
children into the world, a beautiful little girl and then a round,
handsome boy. They were devoted to their babies, each of whom
could sing and dance at the age of fifteen months.

"They're not going to be deprived of life like I was!" my already
bitter mother announced; but both babies died of the flu—as
did a hundred others on the block. This tragedy was something

my parents could share, and they were never again to be so close. My mother, especially in the death of the girl, felt cheated of of a second chance at life.

But God gave Lotza Miller a third try. I was born on top of the kitchen table in Williamsburg on South Second Street. Lotza— now Lillian—clasped me to her breast as no Jewish mother had ever clasped any Jewish boy before. It seems I looked just like the talented infant girl who had died. I was a treasure so dear that I might just as well have been named Ruby or Diamond instead of Moishe. No boy was ever loved with such a vengeance, smothered with so much devotion, and weakened by such strength. By the time I was conscious of what was going on in my world, Momma and Poppa were engaged in a war of attrition, and home was an armed camp. My arrival and subsequent survival in this world demanded that the Millers do better. My mother's dissatisfactions became greater by the day, her ambitions wilder. Her contempt of my gentle father was to know no end.

Sadly enough, my father was never to do any better. He was then a sewing-machine operator in a factory and was earning more money than he had ever earned before. His salary was about twenty-five dollars a week. For a man with no ambition, this was a fortune. He had never dreamed he could bring home so much money. Actually, Poppa had never dreamed at all. If Momma had only gotten off his back, he would have been the happiest of men—with his little son and all the cloth he could ever sew in a never-ending assembly line.

Pop would have been satisfied to live in one room forever without steam heat, without air, without a view, without hot water. To my father, life was a gift that needed no extra wrappings. You worked and you ate and you washed it down with some cold seltzer. And you listened to some good music on your Victrola—like Cantor Rosenblatt, maybe, or that great opera singer Caruso, who had a Yiddish throb in his voice and sang those minor Italian melodies that so attracted Jewish immigrant listeners. And Pop did love to hear his Lotza sing at local affairs, although her ambitions were a source of irritation to him.

Pop was a peasant philosopher. Life was supposed to be a

struggle. You worked and brought up a family and tried to be a good person. And you had a trade. Singing was not a trade unless you were a cantor, and even then it wasn't exactly a trade. He felt you could be a good person without all the rigmarole of religion, and only out of respect to the memory of his own parents did he attend synagogue on the High Holidays. Mom *bensched* the candles on Friday night simply out of superstition, and every Sabbath of her life the white cloth and the candles were placed on the table. She wasn't going to be the one to break the ritual and possibly bring the wrath of God down on her household. It was easier to continue, and the neighbors would have been shocked otherwise. Didn't she sing at weddings and *bar mitzvahs?* And, after all, she *was* Jewish.

Now that I had arrived on the scene—better late than never—followed shortly by my brother Gidalia, Momma began applying the pressure that was to create a permanent strain on the family. There was always something just beyond our reach—and she was going to get it. But her good and unimaginative husband could extend himself just so far, and then the nagging and the arguments would begin and the Polish profanities would fly from my sweet father's lips. He would be driven, at the end of a hard day's work, from gentle fatigue to a screaming rage. "I should never have married so young!" was the announcement Poppa made every few days. I knew that my mother, who never let go of the reins, drove him to these tantrums, and I resented her; but without her energy and drive, we all would have lived and died on South Second Street.

Poverty may be romantic to those who have never known it firsthand. *La Bohème* is glamorous only if Rudolfo and Mimi are attractive and in particularly good voice. If it's snowing outside that immense skylight that looks out over the roofs of gay Paree, so much the better.

But South Second Street was not a Paris slum designed by Guy Pène du Bois. It was a filthy, roach- and baby-infested, chalk-marked block that got the sun for a few minutes at high noon and for the rest of the day lay in shadows as if under a cloud. It was ugly, gray, and foul, and across its face in colored chalk was a scrawled message to its inhabitants: "Drop dead!"

In winter it was damp, freezing, and cheerless, except for that moment after a blizzard when the freshly shoveled piles of snow made great white hills that lined the street and became fortresses to play on. But they were soon stained yellow and brown by little boys and dogs. If the weather held, they became filthy, disease-ridden battlefields that sent many a boy to the hospital. Kids would be found half-dead and blue where they had fallen through the snow and been left for hours. Our flat had no heat, and I would be so frozen in the morning that I couldn't relieve myself.

The spring thaw would make the gutter a flooded sewer, our own little road-company Venice. When summer arrived, the street would steam with smells and heat that drove everybody to the roofs or fire escapes. I can see the hairy bellies of the men and the sagging breasts of the new mothers hanging over the rusted iron balconies. There wasn't much privacy on South Second Street. The whole libretto was played out without shame. Birth and death—with everything in between—were played out in a great big circus; my family was part of it, balancing on a clothesline—without a net, a daredevil act, believe me. The death-defying immigrants! Watch them! Don't take your eyes off them! Any moment may be their last!

I can still hear the screaming sirens and mothers and kids. The ambulance was a frequent visitor on our street, for it seemed that every few days a small child would fall from a window or fire escape, suffocate in a dumbwaiter, or be run over while the Momma was cooking, washing, or tending another of her brood. The jam of humanity was such that the loss was barely noticed by anybody but the mother herself—who was too busy to mourn but aged ten years overnight. No one on South Second Street looked young, not even the kids.

During a heat wave, everyone hung from the tenement windows like limp, wrinkled wash or sat on the stoops like garbage until four in the morning or climbed to the dirty roof for that last breath of air.

Through all this, my mother tried to keep me at her side. If it had been possible, I would have been breast-fed straight through high school. Momma trusted no storekeeper, no restaurant,

nobody. My brother Gidalia was something else. Gilbert, as he
was soon to be called, was always outgoing. I was a different
story. From the beginning I was saved from experiencing any
fun that was available on the block. My mother, without a
doctor's diploma, was the greatest diagnostician in the business
and decided I was a cardiac case. I was forbidden to play
dangerous games in the dangerous street with the dangerous
boys. I wasn't allowed to play in the dangerous school, and
later, through some collusion, she produced a doctor's note to
exempt me from the dangerous gymnasium. Her head would
shake tragically as she spoke of my "leaking valve" and my blood
pressure.

Living on the sixth floor of a walk-up, *schlepping* groceries and
a baby carriage, my mother kept in training. If you didn't die
of a heart attack before you were twenty-one in that house,
you could live forever. Up and down, up and down, and God
forbid she forget the string beans or beets for pickling. But *I* never
had to make these trips—not me. Moishe was a cardiac case.
"He's got a murmur, the kid! *Oi!* High-strung like a violin." For
me, Momma would lower bread-and-jelly, fruit, or a dime for the
store on a string from the window. Lifting a fork to my mouth
was the only exercise she allowed me, and when I wanted to
play in the street she would shanghai me to the docks.

After negotiating with the captain of a tugboat under the
Williamsburg Bridge, she would take me for a ride in the
"fresh salt air," dragging Gidalia on a short lead so that he
would not fall overboard.

"Look at the color in the sailor's cheeks, singer mine. That's
from living such a healthy life. Breath in, *meine kind*. In! Out!
In! Out! Gidalia, if you fall in the water and drown, I'll break
every bone in the body! Moishe, darling, take a deep breath . . .
deeper. That's it. Let it out, Moishe. *Let it out, already!*"

My kid brother, unlike me, always got his own way. He had
perfected the convulsion to a high art. When he wanted something, he could hold his breath longer than an Olympic swimmer.
He would lie on the floor kicking his feet and turning navy blue.
For a second-act curtain, he would become stiff and his eyes
would roll up to the top of his head. He didn't fool me for a

moment, but it worked. Even if Momma did suspect a fraud, it was awfully hard to prove—each fit could have been the real one. Gil was smart. He was the fox who kept crying wolf. He had found his way of fighting Momma. I had not.

Momma discovered I could sing the moment I let out my first cry. To my mother, my delivery was a debut. All through my first years, I almost died of embarrassment every time she asked me to entertain the aunts and uncles. Invariably, I refused, and when she made it clear that she was going to have her way—and she always did—I sang, but only after I had turned all the lights out or gone into the bathroom and closed the door. When everyone laughed, Momma would say, "It's all right. First things first. He'll start on radio. That's bad? Nobody'll see him, but he'll sing. Music is in his blood from me and my own Poppa." Then she forced piano lessons on me through a teacher who was a friend of hers. I practiced on a thirdhand upright she got somewhere. I was so afraid that the kids outside would find out that—hot as it was—I would close every window so no one could hear me practicing. I literally sweated through my scales. I got up to Clementi for two hands and that was the end of the piano.

Momma was convinced that music was in my blood, but she wasn't convinced that my blood was very good. So I had to drink beef blood.

With all our money problems, I cannot say we ever starved. Through the miracle of Momma's organization, there was always a broth on the stove or bread in the oven, always marrowbones and the luxury of beef blood. In good time and bad, there was always enough to eat. In fact, with my lack of exercise and her constant feeding, I was puffing up like a spongecake. It wasn't bad enough that I spoke only Yiddish. Now I was quite accurately called "Fatso" by the kids on the block.

My first relief from my Yiddishe Momma was Public School 19. It was a dirty, dingy, overcrowded school, but I was on my own from nine to three. To my classmates, I was a complete freak—a human knish. I was ridiculed unmercifully, and it might have been in this setting, as I first learned to speak English, that I began to stutter. Of course, it could also have been on the

Fourth of July, when after stealing two dollars from my mother's drawer in the kitchen, Gidalia and I were caught by my father. Poppa gave me the beating of my life and then locked me out of the house, naked for everyone to jeer at. Luckily for him, my brother was considered too young for such character building. I cried and scratched at the door, pleading to be let back in.

Momma was petrified. "Abe! He'll catch pneumonia!"

But this one time, Poppa was boss. "Better yet, maybe he'll catch honesty."

Poppa's idea of discipline didn't stop me from loving him, nor did the punishment stop me from joining the other kids in ransacking the food boxes that sat outside the windows and on fire escapes in the days before refrigerators. Ice for the icebox cost money, and winter itself was employed to keep the food fresh. But we kids were fresher; when I could escape my mother's watchful eye or when she was out singing at a wedding, I'd tag along with the gang to steal fruit and milk and potatoes, which we put on long sticks and cooked over a fire in an empty lot. The tenement basement and the empty lot—those were the shifting scenes of my childhood.

I never saw that famous tree that grows in Brooklyn. I saw no green except cabbage, until the day we visited my mother's cousin Guzik in Massachusetts. Guzik was a shoemaker who had settled his little family in a small house on the outskirts of Worcester. My brother and I went wild at the sight of the trees and grass and frightened our country cousins.

A tree was such a novelty to us that we were first stunned by its bigness and then overjoyed by its beauty. We chased around it, banged ourselves against it, climbed it, made love to it. That day in Worcester was an important one in my life. It was the first time I had ever seen beauty, the first time I'd ever seen a living thing reach up to the sky, green against the blue, tall and straight and dignified. Imagine. Just a tree—but my first.

We actually saw cherries growing on trees that day and picked them in such a state of excitement that we threw them at each other instead of eating them. Who ever knew where cherries came from? From Finkel's store!

In my day there were no parks or playgrounds in our neighborhood—no place to play even if your mother would let you. In the hot months, P.S. 19, with its handball courts and playing area, was closed; we kids would have to climb over the high chicken-wire fence that senselessly separated us from a place to play.

We had to do something, of course. We were considered social outcasts if we didn't steal pennies off the newsstands and flatten them into the size of nickels on the trolley tracks. Then when we sneaked into the Congress movie theater, we would use them to get Suchard chocolates from the boxes on the backs of the seats. Any corset drying on a clothesline lost its stays— we used them for swabbing out the peanut machines in the subway. There we sneaked in under the turnstile, or if the entrance was an unattended revolving door, three or four of us would squeeze in for one nickel. We also swiped bamboo shoe trees and smoked ourselves green in the gills in some basement.

Whenever I could escape my jailer, I did. And most of the time it was to play baseball. At first we played in the streets, with hydrants and fat old ladies peeling vegetables as our bases, and then in vacant lots surrounded by torn election posters of smiling candidates long since defeated. Barely readable were their promises of parks and playgrounds—but no matter their party, there was no ice cream and cake for the kids, and no place to play but the sandlots. And how I loved baseball!

But it's hard to be sentimental about the old neighborhood, because I remember too many ugly things—like the Black Hand, the scourge of P.S. 19. For three years I didn't go to the school toilet because of the awful story that a boy was found dead there with a disembodied hand at his throat. The legend was so powerful that no child was allowed to go to the bathroom without a teacher. I wouldn't go at all. Even the police, mystified by the sworn testimony of children and faculty, suggested extreme caution, although their eyes glazed with skepticism whenever the Hand was mentioned.

They never took the Hand into custody, but the superstitious immigrant parents—volatile Italians, dramatic Jews, and mystic Irish, peasants all—were only too ready to believe any old wives' tale. My own mother used to pull my earlobes every time someone looked at me cross-eyed. This was supposed to dispel the curse cast by the evil eye. It's a wonder that I have my ears left. She would pull on them like a milkmaid and then, uncertain that the Devil was gone, would spit in the air around me. If Satan didn't get you, Momma's head cold would.

Williamsburg was tough on Easter Sunday, but there is no way of conveying what Halloween was like.

I will never forget one Halloween. I couldn't have been more than ten. After school, I played in the shadow of the Williamsburg Bridge. The cobblestoned street at its entrance was the spot where the Republic Theatre stood, and it was also the scene of absolute horror. I found myself walking across the bridge with a few of the kids I palled around with when I could escape Momma's eye. We had decided to stand over the water and drop stones and yell at the boats and barges that passed beneath us. We also wanted to see the Woolworth Building, which was the tallest in the whole world, and the rest of Manhattan's skyscrapers, so we walked to the middle of the bridge.

It was beautiful there, and I can still feel the bite of that autumn wind on my cheeks as I caught sight of what looked like a carpet unfolding toward us from the Manhattan side. It was all so fast and terrible. A gang from the Lower East Side had spotted us. We stood paralyzed with fear as the mob rolled toward us brandishing long stockings filled with stones and flour, pieces of rubber hose, the pockets of their jackets filled with rocks.

They were bigger than we were, and I remember their hats— old fedoras with the brims cut off and scalloped or turreted like a medieval crown and covered with campaign buttons of all kinds and colors—made them look like kings of the gutter. The attack was silent at first because they all wore high-laced sneakers with big solid circles on the ankles.

Somebody yelled, "Cheese it! They'll kill us! Run!" and our frozen tableau splintered into fragments, melting, receding, flowing to the Brooklyn side of the bridge, with this mob of cutthroats now screaming after us.

My heart grew big in my chest as I tried to keep up with the hysterical retreat, but my mother had fed me too well. I was fat and slow and further overweighted with bulky sweaters under my jacket and overcoat. The woolen scarf my mother had knit was strangling me. My buddies were screaming blue streaks ahead of me, disappearing, being squeezed by the parallel lines of the bridge, while the profane threats of the enemy were directly behind me. It could have been a loose shoelace or just the end of my strength, but the mob was on top of me.

The police found me beaten to a pulp, left in the wake of the juggernaut, torn, bleeding, and unconscious. I came to in the station house, vaguely aware that they were trying to find my family. My stricken mother soon rushed in and took me to a nearby clinic, vowing that she would never let me out of her sight again.

When I recovered, my physical exercise was limited to digging for pickles and herring in the barrels of brine that stood in front of the butcher and grocery stores. Momma, always out for the best, would make me reach to the bottom of the barrel, so my arm always smelled. After school I was not out of her sight for a second; I had to spend my time shopping with her. Baseball was out until both Momma and I recovered from the massacre. I recovered much sooner than she.

CHAPTER TWO

I LOVED BASEBALL. It was like food and drink to me; and I often proved it by playing instead of having lunch, since that was the only time I could escape my mother's hawkeye.

Needless to say, we could never afford to go to a game. But one day Poppa learned that Boy Scouts were allowed into Ebbets Field once a week free. Gidalia and I weren't Boy Scouts—who had the dues?—but Poppa was a tailor! My adorable Poppa now got hold of some khaki cloth and, studying the outfit carefully, made us each a uniform. With long stockings and neckerchiefs, Gil and I nervously met with the gang of Scouts who gathered once a week on a street corner near the bridge to be bussed to the game. We passed muster that first day in our homemade suits, and thereafter we were recognized and accepted.

In absolute ecstasy we saw Lefty O'Doul, Babe Herman, Dazzy Vance, and Hack Wilson. The following season, in bigger suits, we were taken to Yankee Stadium to see the Great One, the Babe! The first time I was in that wonderful ball park and saw Ruth, I was so excited that I almost missed the game because of trips to and from the bathroom. On one of those golden days, I saw pitcher Elon Hogsett hit Ruth in the back with the ball, felling him. History! And my Poppa had made it possible for me to be there. Yes, he was a great tailor—but it was Momma who really cut the pattern of our lives.

Momma was studying English at night school, and she began

singing her folk songs at weddings and *bar mitzvahs.* She
was living in greater poverty and ugliness than she had ever seen
in Poland, but it was different in America. Here there was hope.
Here my parents could have a dream, along with a whole
generation of immigrants. My father woke up from the dream
early, and that was his tragedy. My mother never woke up at
all. That was hers. Her drive was unbelievable, her energy inex-
haustible, and for her brood—especially me—there was nothing
too good.

Her mother-in-law, Grandma Miller, hated Momma almost as
much as she hated her own husband. She would confide to
Poppa, "She's too fancy for you, that wife of yours. She'll land
you in the poorhouse. She wants too much." There was an ice-
berg, my Grandma Miller. She actually locked Grandpa in his
room when he wasn't working, letting him out only for important occasions. He was a shoemaker, Grandpa, and they lived in
the back of the store. I remember visiting one day and finding
Grandpa Miller lying in the corner of the room on the floor like
a sack. He was napping—like a dog. He was virtually ignored and
even had to prepare his own food. On the rare occasion when I
ate there, I remember being smacked if I left even a crumb on
the plate.

That tough, tense woman obviously hated my mother down
to her seed. Instead of thinking of me as her firstborn's child
and her own grandson, I was "that woman's kid." She was a real
charmer, Grandma Miller; and Momma returned her affections
in full. When they were forced to spend time together, the
fur really flew. And their husbands, being as passive and sweet
as they were, were helpless to stop them.

There isn't room in a family for more than one matriarch,
and I suppose that was the whole trouble. There is always
room for another weak man, but two strong women are too
much in any family. They were really not that unalike, Grandma
Miller and Momma, except that Momma had more vision and
more color.

But she was such a mass of contradictions, my mother. Protec-
tive, devoted, she never gave us a gift on a birthday. When
Christmas came and the school was decorated with wreaths and

the blackboards had drawings of Santa Claus and reindeer with cotton snow stuck to the slate and one or two kind teachers— it was all on their own—handed out red-and-white-striped candy canes and green peppermint-sticks and strings of popcorn to wind around the spruce trees that lay piled and bound in the street outside Peter Reeves' grocery, I wasn't allowed to bring them home.

We couldn't understand why we were barred from enjoying the candy and the fun. Other Jewish boys took them home and weren't struck dead.

"The others on the block, I don't care from," was her only reply. And for all those years, the happy holiday was *verboten* to us. My parents managed to live in Brooklyn as if they were still back in the old country. I suppose the terror of the pogroms, the suspicions of the gentile world, isolated them and forced them to band together with their own. Poppa's work kept him within the Jewish community, and Momma's shopping and singing were all done within the boundaries of that safe, ugly little world, so foreign to other New Yorkers, a real transplant from Middle Europe. Everybody was relative-ridden because, for better or worse, family was safer than anyone. You needed family when you first came over from the old country. The American cousin, aunt, brother, or uncle was the family celebrity in the European ghettos, and his home was first base when you left home plate.

To my family, Uncle Looey was America's doorman. Momma's older brother not only was Poppa's first contact in America— and a tailor, like Poppa—but, because of his seniority, was looked upon as the wise one of the family. A gentle, serene soul, Uncle Looey was often called upon by my mother to settle family squabbles. Invariably, he made the wrong decision.

His only qualifications for his appointment as judge were his age and his being Momma's brother. Uncle Looey would nod his head a lot and lower his eyelids in a torture of wisdom. His expression was such that you could only think that the burden of his knowledge was too much for him to bear. He was in pain from it. He would listen to our problems and then hand down his judgment. That my parents followed his advice seems incredible.

Sipping a glass of hot tea through a cube of sugar, he was marriage counselor, financial wizard, professor of philosophy, and psychoanalyst. His lack of a college degree did not disqualify him from being an authority on such matters, any more than the same lack kept my mother from being New York's leading heart specialist. But Uncle Looey meant well, and he looked like a patriarch, which was half the battle anyway. He and his wife Molly were very close to us, and no matter where we moved they always lived right near us. Their son Sidney was my best friend and only confidant.

Poppa's brother Max was a different story altogether. Shoe salesman and playboy, Uncle Max worked and played hard in the American tradition. He married late and had no children, but he was the professional man of the family, having worked his way up to be manager of a store on 125th Street in Manhattan. Max was blending into the American scene. He was a nice guy and a pleasure to have as a relative—unlike Uncle Sam, who was no blood relative but was married to Momma's sister, Tante Esther.

Tante Esther was a sweet woman and forever ailing. She was sick even when she was well, and she was the only one I ever knew who could belch at will. All you had to do was say, "Hello, Tante Esther, you look wonderful," and she would belch. Her husband Sam—the boor, the obnoxious one—resembled the late actor Victor McLaglen. He was a carpenter and a highmuck-a-muck in his union. Aggressive and insensitive in the extreme, he bullied everyone he came in contact with, starting and ending with Tante Esther.

The minute he'd see me he'd yell, "Fatso!" and imitate my stutter, embarrassing me into muteness. "W-w-well, l-l-look who's h-h-here. M-M-Moishe P-P-Pipick, why d-d-don't you r-r-recite s-s-something?" I hated him. I hated him. I used to dream that he was in terrible trouble and asking me to yell for help. The world would pass us by as I stuttered "H-h-h . . . ," never finishing the word. It was my passive way of killing Uncle Sam.

My family tree might not have had any golden apples on it,

but it didn't have any nuts either. Uncle Abe Bernstein was just eccentric. As the richest of the family, Uncle Abe could afford to be different. He was the first one in our family to have a radio, which no one but Abe himself was allowed to listen to. He had a Persian rug, which no one was allowed to walk on, in his living room, which no one was allowed to live in. Uncle Abe had an automobile, which he treasured more than he did his son Morris; and no one was allowed to ride in it but Abe himself and his immediate family. Uncle Abe also owned a wife named Molly, who was top-heavy and rarely seen, although I don't think these facts are necessarily related.

Uncle Abe would drop in on us for a visit and a little schnapps, and he acted like a great landowner visiting his serfs. Momma was just as responsible for this impression as he was. He was *her* cousin, nobody else's, and we children called him "Uncle" out of respect for his station, his age, and, no doubt, his bankbook.

It was at funerals and *bar mitzvahs* and weddings that Abe's wife Molly and their son Morris would join him for a trip in the La Salle automobile. Uncle Abe also loved to show off the car at hospitals and synagogues. His greatest diversion was sitting in the car with his family and watching the world go by, his hands at the wheel, his elbow and eye out the window, the ignition off, the gasoline safe in the tank. Often, he, Molly, and Morris would drive to the Lower East Side, where they would buy hot rolls for eight cents and then eat them, parked on Second Avenue—the cheapest picnic known to man.

Once, on a terribly hot day, Uncle Abe took us all out for a drive to the country in his precious car. When Gidalia got carsick and vomited all over the upholstery, Uncle Abe almost had a stroke.

Aunt Molly, always a quiet one, stared out of the window like a catatonic; Cousin Morris conspicuously held his nose; Uncle Abe held the wheel so tightly that his knuckles turned white. I think he was imagining Gil's neck in his hands. There was no way of breaking the silence; and the longer we waited, the worse it got. At our destination, Uncle Abe dumped us at a remote subway station.

The incident was absolutely a tragedy to my uncle and almost caused an open break in the family.

Besides Guzik, the shoemaker, Momma had a country cousin named Meyer Cohen. The Cohens also had moved to the hills instead of the slums when they came to America, eventually making a hotel of their old house in the Catskills, building it wing by wing as they became more successful. The Cohens looked heartier than the rest of the family.

I must have been about ten or eleven when Momma decided to take us to their place, the Sheldrake. It was to be for a few weeks in the heat of the summer. We had never been away for more than two days before.

The Cohens informed Momma that for eight dollars a week, including food, we could stay there. Poppa insisted we couldn't afford it. Grandma Miller was so scandalized that she went around saying that my mother was destroying her son. "To the country, imagine! She thinks Abe is a millionaire. Mark my word, she'll land him in the poorhouse, that one."

With his mother needling him, Poppa too became outraged that Momma could throw away the money. It wasn't that Poppa was cheap or stingy like Uncle Abe. He really didn't have it to spend. The smallest unexpected outlay of cash would throw him off balance. There was never that extra coin that could be thrown away on pleasure. If and when he took my brother and me to see a "colboy" picture (my favorite cowboy being Hoot Gibson), it meant that he didn't smoke that day or gave up lunch. That must have been why, after we would return home from the movies and Gil and I would run around the apartment acting out the picture for Momma, Poppa's excitement would fade and he'd say, "Ah! Who needed it?" We needed it and so did he.

He was always counting pennies, and when he had to spend them it was physically painful to him, like losing part of himself. Even when it was absolutely necessary to buy me a new suit and when, after many preliminaries, one was purchased wholesale, there was never an occasion important enough for me to wear it.

"Are we rich that you get dressed up just to tear the knees and wear out the elbows? Don't they know that it costs my sweat to buy that suit and it's gotta last?"

I never wore out a suit. I always grew out of them before I could enjoy them, and then Gil would inherit the clothes and the problem. Gil was getting to look just like a miniature version of me.

Momma had obviously made up her mind about the country and its benefits, and she *noodged* Poppa till he almost went crazy. "I'm going to listen to *your mother*, who never saw that *you* got fresh air and grew taller than a boy?" she would say.

"Don't start with my mother. I've had enough."

"Our sons will grow tall, Abe. Eight dollars a week. We can do it. I'll go to the sage tomorrow."

My mother, like all women of her generation and class, didn't make a move as revolutionary as taking her children so many miles away over mountains and boundary lines without the sanction of the sage, or *tzaddik.* If the sage said it was all right, Poppa could be handled.

Uncle Looey was, with all due respect, an amateur; this was too important a job for him. Uprooting the children was a giant step, and so Momma packed up Gil and me and *schlepped* us on the subway to the Lower East Side of Manhattan to visit the prophet. This was a common practice among immigrant families. The rabbi, by virtue of his position, was considered the wise man—the very word *rabbi* meaning "master," "teacher." All rabbis, therefore, were wise, but some were gifted with more than wisdom. Some chosen men could foresee the deeds of men and look far into the future and, for a price, tell what they saw. These oracles could tell a family whether it was wise to bring Cousin Hattie over from the old country. And who else but one of these prophets could know whether Goldberg and Feinstein should really go into partnership? Friendship was one thing, millinery another. The prophet's word was law, his decision final.

So now we went to the dark, dismal hallway to keep our appointment with Destiny. I can still smell the whiff of snuff that greeted us as we opened the door of the prophet's room. He was a wisp of a man, a walking corpse—waxen, sunken-

cheeked—his long white beard yellow with nicotine, his eyes
glazed. Far from looking wise, he struck me as looking particularly simple; but that, he surely was not. He blessed us with
that bony hand upraised. Momma and he sat down, and she told
him of our plans.

Was she falling into the Fates' trap and feeding her young
to wild animals who would jump from behind trees and eat us
up? Or would we grow tall and strong from the fresh mountain
air? To give the rabbi a push in the right direction, Momma
would always do a little selling.

"Rabbi, it's my own flesh and blood we're going to in the
country—good people. Would they feed us poison? Would they
let anything hurt us? Is it a jungle or *Finster Afrika?* Is it Siberia
I'm asking to take my family?"

The old man had sat listening, bored to death. But now that
he had heard what he wanted, he grew rigid and began to moan.
He was going into his trance. His croaking voice sounded like
the wind howling far away, and his eyes had completely disappeared up into their sockets. He was even more impressive
than my brother Gidalia—and far more frightening because he
was so old. He was obviously communing with God's sister-in-
law now, and his arms and legs jerked like a puppy's in sleep.

When he came to, he informed Momma that she should go
ahead with her plans, that no misfortune would befall us. He saw
golden skies ahead and a happy summer for the whole *mishpucheh*, and then he saw the coins that Momma gladly paid
him for prophesying the right future. As he took the money, he
showed the vaguest suggestion of a smile. What a fraud he was,
Old Man Mose! But his word was Law, and there could be no
haggling in the home once the prophet had made his decision.
It must have been worth the few coins to have a divine ally and
an absolute voice.

The only thing about a trip to the sage that I loved was the
malted—and maybe a pickle—that Momma would treat us to
after the vision. In victory, my mother was always expansive.
She did love in her own way.

Now that the prophet had settled things, Momma forged
ahead. We were off to the country. The hotel sent—through a

company on Pitkin Avenue—an old Cadillac to pick up all the people who were going.

Every time we went to the Cohens' place in that old car, we broke down and had to get out and push or change the tires. But that first time, we were huffing and puffing our way up a hill when the old war-horse turned over, with children and six *yentas* screaming from the windows. A couple of farmers helped us right the car. No real damage was done, but the oracle's reputation hung in the balance.

The poor Cohens didn't make any money on us that summer and doubtless had known they wouldn't. It was the biggest bargain my mother ever managed for us. As if we weren't eating enough, she had us drinking tumblers of heavy cream instead of milk with our meals—after all, it was the same price.

Even Poppa had to admit that it was worth the expense. He joined us on Sundays and really unwound in the fresh mountain air. When he got back home, he filled the neighbors' ears. "We should all live and be well—so help me God, we slept with blankets on Saturday night."

Momma sang her repertoire of folk ballads for the other guests and was such a sensation that she got all sorts of privileges.

We did the Cohens a great big favor and returned over the next few years. If it hadn't been for these relatives, my brother might not have started to grow like a beanstalk. The family was still a closed corporation in those days. There might have been squabbles, but you could always depend on one of your own. The Cohens took care of our summers, and Momma's Tante Lesser, my great-aunt, took care of our winters. But for her we might have lost the roof over our heads altogether.

Tante Lesser was a very large and kindly woman, built like the Bridge Plaza bus and just as dependable. When this formidable giantess was not at her job—as cook in a hospital—she moved through the borough of Brooklyn in mysterious ways helping her family and friends. She was an energetic and hearty woman who was always making a jar of broth or a basket of cakes to take to those almost-impossible-to-find people—the less fortunate.

When any of her relatives was at sea, Tante Lesser was the North Star that guided him back on a safe course. She always managed something. Sometimes Tante Lesser would visit with us from Flatbush and stay over. She slept like a reawakening volcano. Her snore could be heard for blocks. But in the morning, Tante Lesser rose like the sun and radiated energy and warmth all day. She was a tonic, and I loved it when she came to see us.

One morning, shortly after one of these visits, I woke up to find the bedroom completely upset. Drawers were pulled out, shirts, socks, and underwear were strewn on the floor. Our whole apartment had been ransacked. Closer inspection revealed large footprints on the window ledge and a broken flowerpot on the fire escape with a piece of torn coating material obviously left by the crook.

"Thief! Thief!" Momma yelled out of the window. "We've been robbed!"

The idea that a stranger with such enormous feet had been in my room during the night terrified me. When the police left, I begged my mother not to make me spend another night in the room until the mystery had been cleared up.

She pooh-poohed my fears with an impatient shrug as she sat making a list of our losses with my bewildered father. "The coat with the torn sheepskin lining, Uncle Hooner's pure-silk tallith with the fringe and the buckles from Momma's wedding, and the mink tails from the muff when I came over from the old country, and the brass goblet for Seder. . . ." Momma kept wetting the pencil with her tongue.

"But, how?" Poppa asked. "Why us, like we're rich?"

"Please, Momma. P-p-please, d-d-don't m-m-make m-m-me s-s-sleep there t-t-tonight."

"Stop it, Moishe," Momma said, brushing me aside. "You're acting like a baby. You think he's a *schmendrik* who'll come back to get caught?"

It was impossible to believe that my mother, who protected me from my best friends in the neighborhood, was willing to throw me to the boogeyman. But there was a logical explanation: the robbery was a hoax, a performance staged by Tante Lesser so that we could collect on the fire-and-theft insurance that Uncle Looey had made us take out years before. We were penniless and our credit at the stores was gone. There was no other way according to Tante Lesser. She believed that to survive was the first consideration, and my mother shared this view. The two women kept this secret from my father and the rest of the family for years.

My father's rage would have been biblical, but women like Tante Lesser and my mother lived under such pressures that they had neither the patience nor the inclination to moralize in the face of starvation. If you told them that it was like stealing, that they were breaking a commandment, they would shrug. They also had the immigrant's distrust and awe of giant industry. Con Edison, Bell Telephone, and the Metropolitan Life Insurance Company were immense, impersonal governments and you couldn't hurt them.

"They can't afford it?" was the typical justification.

"What stealing? Who's the poor millionaire company we did such a terrible thing? That corporation with offices all over the world, yet? *Billions* they have, not millions, and didn't we pay in all these years like clockwork? Fifty-six dollars in premiums we gave them. So isn't it our money if you think about it? Is it better that we were thrown out into the street? And who's going to say, 'Oh, look, there's some honest people—let's give them a place to live'? Don't be a fool! Nobody lost anything. They make it up on the others."

I'm only glad my father didn't know. He never knew that the great deception brought us the sum of eleven dollars and sixty cents. Momma went along on the theory that what he didn't know didn't hurt him. Let him dream. It was up to her to act.

CHAPTER THREE

THE ONLY THING Abe Miller was able to assure his Lotza—and it was something in his world—was a place to lie when she was dead. Not everybody has a reservation for eternity. Pop managed this miracle by belonging to the Pultisker Progressive Society on Second Avenue. He and Momma paid dues and on occasion went to an affair there, but the main reason for joining was the burial plot that came with the membership.

As the members of the Pultisker Progressive Society danced the hora to Charlie Needleman's Symphonic Five and Momma sang her folk songs, the merry group could look at one another in the sure and certain knowledge that they would all lie down together when they were tired; this was a group that would never break up, no matter the squabbles, despite the feuds. Once in a while the children were allowed to attend a special function, and I would shudder as I watched all the potential corpses laughing and dancing. They were at their happiest here, my parents, with their own kind of people, knowing that, no matter how hard it was to make ends meet in this life, they would meet their end with dignity and would not have to be buried in potter's field.

One of their friends and a fellow member, Chaim Shapiro, was a worrier and a born economist. Very poor, he actually starved himself to pay his dues to the Pultisker Progressive

Society; but he had pondered over the situation, pro and con like a Hasidic scholar, and determined that if he lived to be eighty, after paying dues for fifty years, it wasn't such a bargain to be given a grave. Conversely, if he dropped dead soon, preferably the next day, then his membership would be a good deal. I always felt, after that, that Chaim's whole energy from then on was directed toward a heart attack. He seemed never to eat, and when he danced the hora he jumped up and down so hard that it was obvious he was looking for real value for his money.

Although Pop did show some pride when Momma sang at these affairs or at someone's house—he certainly appreciated music and loved listening to classical records—he always scoffed at my mother's talk of a career. On occasion, Momma would make three dollars for singing at a wedding. "It doesn't hurt to bring home a few dollars, Abe. We could use it, you know," she would add pointedly.

"Yeah! And if you didn't spend five for the fixing of the hair and the paint for the face, we could see a profit instead of a loss. Music is no trade. You spend five and earn three. So your job cost me two dollars."

"The next time I'll make *five* dollars, my big provider."

"The next time you'll buy shoes also. It will always cost, and you'll never get it through your head that I'm not a rich man. Music is no trade."

It was true that, for all her talk, Momma never really contributed financially with her singing. Eventually she sang her songs on WEVD, a radio station near the top of the dial, but it was always a sustaining program that paid her nothing or one that paid very little; again her carfare and preparations cost more than she earned. But she was giving pleasure to people and felt that her life was not being wasted.

From the first time I yelled "Momma" from the courtyard on South Second Street, Momma was sure of *my* future and called me "singer mine."

No matter how hard I tried to hide it, to make believe that I hated it, to avoid any mention of my voice, I did love to sing. If Momma had just gone about her business, I might have come around to it early; but she pressured and pushed and pulled until, in my shyness, I refused to sing for anybody.

My soprano voice, which Momma talked about like a press agent, had become well known in the neighborhood, but her preoccupation with it drove me to silence. Nobody will ever know how much of my hesitancy was fear and how much rebellion. My resentment of my mother was equaled only by my need for her; my irritations were exceeded only by my gratifications. It was my first experience in loving and hating the same person, and I was ridden with guilt; my stuttering was only one indication of my torture.

The only thing that is absolutely clear is that I refused to sing, to the distress of both Momma and Poppa. My father liked music, if not as a trade, certainly as a pastime. His boys were really all he had, and he wanted to be proud of us and show us off. That was why now I could have killed Gil altogether.

Poppa had brought home a harmonica from somewhere, and Gil—completely out of left field—put his big mouth around it and began playing "East Side, West Side." He had never played a mouth organ before, but he could play it by ear. It was his claim to fame. He quickly increased his repertoire and played the damned thing constantly. When someone came to the house and we kids were asked to perform, my refusal to sing was doubly aggravating to Poppa. Now I was even more of a *schlemiel*, because Gil—Williamsburg's answer to Borah Minnevitch—would jump up and start things off with that damned imitation of a choo-choo train. After this fabulous opening, I was expected to sing. Gil had me coming and going with his new-found talent. The kid was killing it for me, especially since my performances were given offstage, from the bathroom.

So I bent Gil's harmonica out of shape. Poppa replaced it. I broke the new one in two with a hammer, and another appeared in the house. It was a mystery where the money for all these harmonicas came from.

Poor Gil! Little Gidalia. We did a lot of fighting in those days—usually over something as important as who got the larger pickle. We became so intense that we'd throw the pickles instead of eating them, destroying the spoils in the battle in the doing. But the reason for the fights was more serious. Gil was difficult because Momma gave me so much attention, and I stuttered because I wanted to be a wild Indian without her attentions. It's a wonder we allowed each other to grow up.

But we survived each other as we survived the sacrifices we had to make. And no matter what we sacrificed, we were still always behind in the rent, still without something. One hot summer day my mother hocked her wedding ring to buy Gil and me bathing suits so that we could cool ourselves at the open hydrant in the street. I banged around the house in a fury of frustration. Gil was too young to understand, and there was no one else I could talk to about it, not even my cousin Sidney. I didn't want anyone else to know how poor we were.

It was hard to keep it a secret, because things became so bad for a while that we had to take a boarder into our already crowded apartment. Momma had moved us all down the block to a smaller building, and we now had an extra room. Our new flat was on the ground floor, so I no longer had to walk up six flights even once a day. Momma thought it was an improvement, but we couldn't manage the small raise in rent and had to take in this boarder.

Although Poppa and the uncles and aunts—and certainly I— didn't see anything wrong in remaining on South Second Street, Momma now found an apartment in a new building on Prospect Place. For the new tenants, the real estate people called this part of Brownsville Crown Heights. There was hot water at all times, and steam heat, and all the plumbing sparkled. There was no reason to believe that Poppa would suddenly come into a fortune, but my mother couldn't get this new place out of her mind. Poppa's seasonal slump was over for a while; with a few sacrifices here and there, she was sure that we could manage it.

Poppa, characteristically enough, saw no reason for the change. "What's the matter where we're living now? We don't have the extra room? And on the ground floor also?"

Momma girded herself for the battle. "But we don't have steam heat."

"And who does have steam heat besides your cousin, Abe Bernstein the millionaire?"

"I don't care who else has."

Once again they were at an impasse that demanded the detached observer, the arbiter—Uncle Looey. Uncle Looey would solve my parents' problem. The white Sabbath cloth was put on the table, strong tea was brewed, the sugar bowl was placed before him.

Uncle Looey listened to the pros and cons and sighed deeply. "In the old country, who ever heard of steam heat? An impossibility! Who ever heard of heat without fire? Can you get wet without water? Who would have dreamt that heat could come from steam in pipes from a corner of the room?"

My parents waited patiently.

"And, you know, we survived without it."

"Aha!" my father yelled, because Uncle Looey was siding with him. "And our fathers before us."

"But this is America," Uncle Looey continued, "the land of miracles. And if God helped man put hot water in pipes and gave it a name even—a radiator—who says it is wrong to want it?"

"Aha!" my mother yelled. "The beginning is to want something. The end is to get it."

"Sometimes, Lotza," Poppa said, "a person wants so much they get it in the end."

"That's so much? To want my children to wake up in a room that's warm? The Feldmans from October fifteenth are warm like toast. So warm they have to open a window in January."

"So we can leave ours closed. The Feldmans she talks about. Phony-baloneys! They're a recommendation?"

Uncle Looey sipped his tea noisily. "Did you ask *me* to decide? Abe! Lotza!"

Momma had a special look that she gave her brother at these moments.

"I think," Looey announced, "that it could be a move in the right direction."

"With due respect, Looey," Poppa interrupted, "you said that we should move here from down the block, and a stranger had to come to live with us—not a relative, even—a stranger. It's more money again in Brownsville."

"Maybe you want to go to the prophet?" Uncle Looey drew back in pain.

"Looey, Abe didn't mean . . ."

"Looey, that isn't what I meant. Only, I'll land in the poorhouse if I keep spending money. A little extra I've made by working my fingers to the bone. If my work drops off, who's going to pay the rent? The Feldmans? Next she'll want Second Avenue."

"It could be a move in the *wrong* direction," Uncle Looey reconsidered.

"Aha!" shouted Poppa.

But Momma changed her tactics. "Every time you walk in the street it could be the wrong direction. You can get hit by a taxicab. You got to take chances in this world. Didn't we come to this country? Who knew what it would be? We heard such things. Gold in the streets. *Oi! Mrs.* Gold is in the streets. But we came and we're still alive, and if we move to Brownsville we'll be alive also, only with steam heat and clean new floors. The air is better there, the ground is higher . . ."

"It could be a move in the right direction."

"I'm glad you advised us, Looey. Abe! You'll see. You won't be sorry. Looey is right. God bless him."

And so we moved to Brownsville, and nobody was really sorry. Although it was hard to keep up with the bills, we managed. Not even Pop would have gone back to a cold-water flat; he accepted the new luxury as a matter of course, as if Momma had had nothing to do with it. But she had. My mother always seemed to be working at something—working out a blueprint that only she could read.

I never had a birthday party—Momma wasn't given to that kind of thing—but the years passed anyway and I was twelve years old and ready for my indoctrination into Jewish manhood. In order to prepare for my *bar mitzvah,* I had to spend four afternoons a week in the dirty old house of a dirty old man in his shiny green-black gabardine suit. I dreaded those horrible indoor afternoons in Brownsville. I would leave my baseball glove in the hall and walk into his dingy little dining room, and we would sit at the table, where he would eat herring while he turned the pages of my book with his dirty hands. The book reeked of him; and every day, while I learned Hebrew, I yearned to fly from his presence. I hated most of these teachers. Their orthodoxy seemed to make them cold, mean, and unfeeling. There was no joy of life in them, no affection. They would walk the streets of the ghetto—the original deacons—blind to beauty, deaf to laughter, suspicious of any sensuality. Their chastity seemed obscene, because all their natural needs were apparently satisfied orally. They were either muttering prayers or eating.

These men in their long black frock coats and large-brimmed velvet hats, their beards often blond or red wispy things framing their pasty faces, their earlocks—*payis*—bobbing up and down, walked grimly through the streets, looking neither right nor left, on some kind of divine business. Suddenly one would veer off to chase a boy who had been trying to avoid his Hebrew lessons. These soft-looking bookworms were, strangely enough, fleet of foot; they always caught their boy and would drag him off by the ear to a dark flat and fill him with the word of God.

Having been brought up without religion, just with ritual, my approaching *bar mitzvah* was a big bore to me. Studying English was hard enough for me; Hebrew was impossible. And the idea that I was going to be the center of all attention made me dread the ceremony. My *bar mitzvah* was the dark cloud that covered my whole twelfth year, and there was no way of avoiding it except suicide or conversion to the Catholic Church.

Rich or poor, religious or not, a *bar mitzvah* is the day of days to a Jewish family, the social event of the season and of a lifetime. There is no arguing about money for a *bar mitzvah*—any more than there would be about a needed operation. And so a tiny orthodox temple on Avenue B across the bridge in Manhattan was chosen; and to this *shull*, which should have held only about thirty people, my parents invited a hundred, mostly members of the family and the Pultisker Progressive Society. The place almost burst. It was filled to the rafters, the women upstairs, the men on the ground floor. It seemed to me that only in *shull* was the fiction of man's superiority in evidence.

Dressed in a navy-blue suit—with my first long pants—a gray fedora with a brim so wide that it could have protected me from a cloudburst, and a long, striped silk prayer shawl, I was led up to the altar—the sacrificial lamb. I was quaking with fear and was not in the least relieved when I saw the ancient rabbi who stood there waiting for me. He was so old that he made our Rivington Street prophet seem like a student at P.S. 19. He was so ancient that all that was left of him were the things that I had heard grew even after death. With his long, wispy hair and beard and his yellow fingernails, he looked like Fu Manchu. But for his colorless eyes there was nothing of substance except the velvet and silk of his robes and tallith. His skin was so thin that I could see the veins all over his head. He was nothing but essence. He could have walked through a brick wall or a closed door. He was a wraith that smelled of death and halitosis.

The Torah was carried out of the ark with great ceremony. Its cover of red velvet embroidered with gold thread was removed so that the scroll could be laid out before me. Everyone waited for me to begin. I wanted to die. There was silence in the synagogue as I fought my way through my portion. The old rabbi used a silver pointer in the shape of a pointing hand to mark my place, and with every mistake he would suck in his foul breath in shock and hatred and jab the pages as his eyes burned into me. He was a series of remembered reflexes. Shy and unsure of myself even at home, I now stuttered in Hebrew, not knowing what I was saying; my only prayer to God was that I would somehow get through this ordeal. I was in a constant blush, hot and wet with terror. But there was worse to follow.

Everyone who could crowded into automobiles to make the trip back to Williamsburg, where Grandma Miller was giving the reception in her basement. There was much confusion in the street as cousins shouted to one another and uncles and aunts scurried around trying to get a lift. Uncle Abe took nobody in his precious La Salle, and some of the relatives finally had to go by bus. As each person arrived at Grandma Miller's, a present was shoved into my hands and something traditional said about the day and God's blessing. No one cared about me. They were all trying to impress Momma and Poppa. No one looked at me when the gift was given, because it was not so much a ritual as a symbolic ticket to the festivities. They wouldn't eat this well again until the next *bar mitzvah* or wedding.

Some of the more prosperous members of the family gave me gold pieces set in little velvet-lined boxes, but most of them gave me Waterman fountain pens. I begged Momma not to, but she forced me to make a speech thanking the family and that dirty old teacher for the triumphant day I was supposedly having. I had to stand in the middle of the room and stutter my gratitude in English while my sniveling cousins were eating all the cakes off the table.

There seemed to be no end to my suffering that awful day. Because Grandma's apartment was so small, the reception was given in two shifts; a lot of relatives and friends were walking around the block or standing outside—just like waiting for the first show at Radio City Music Hall to let out. When I was told that I had to make the same speech to a brand-new audience, I locked myself in the bathroom and was sick; but I had to come out because Tante somebody had to get in. The whole ghastly nightmare was repeated while Gidalia was roughing up some cousin in the kitchen. Poor Grandpa was actually allowed to attend the festivities. If only I hadn't been.

But not only good things come to an end. Eventually, even my *bar mitzvah* was a thing of the past. It was ten o'clock at night when my performance was over. Pop treated us to a taxicab back to Brownsville. My pockets were filled with loot. Momma made some coffee, and we sat in the kitchen and counted the gold pieces.

One coin fell through a crack in the floor and my father became apoplectic. "What was it? A ten? A twenty? A new apartment we're not in even a year and the floor has a hole in it!" He knelt and stroked the wood in an attempt to discover the opening.

"Abe," Momma said, "calm down. Nobody's going to take it. It's in our floor."

"A floor isn't a pocket. Are you *meshugeh?*"

"Misers hide their money in a floor. It's not going anywhere. We'll find it. Abe, for God's sake!"

"*Klutz!*" my father screamed at me. "Clumsy ox! Does he do anything right? Money slips right through your fingers. *Nahr! Fool!*"

Now we were all down on our hands and knees trying to recover the money. Pop actually ripped the floor apart until he found the errant coin. Including this five-dollar gold piece, my one-night stand had grossed us three hundred and forty dollars— more money than we had ever seen at one time. In two languages I had stuttered myself into wealth. We sat staring at this fortune in gold, this glittering pile of ducats, these pieces of eight. I felt like the Count of Monte Cristo. Because of me, we would never be poor again.

On Monday morning, I was relieved of my riches as Pop took the bag of money and placed it in the Brownsville branch of the Bank of America. With this added to the money he already had in the bank, my father felt secure for the first time. He was earning his twenty-five or thirty dollars a week, and with almost a thousand dollars in the bank, the American dream had become a reality for him.

Poppa had never dared to imagine such opulence. If, God forbid, he should be sick for a couple of days, his family wouldn't starve now. He might even close both eyes for a rest one day. One son was—though just in the eyes of God—a man already. Now if only he would have the strength to keep his diabetes under control, life could be good. If he watched his diet and kept away from cakes and strudel and jellies, if he would listen to Lotza, he could be well. It would be easier to keep the diet now. When life is sweet, you don't need so much sugar.

Always, Pop worried about money, became aggravated about money, made scenes about money; but only because he had never before in his life had one extra kopeck, one extra penny. But this was a special occasion, and he took us to a Chinese restaurant with a string orchestra and egg rolls. Momma wouldn't trust the food and picked away at the chow mein, certain that it was pork. "This chicken chow mein is a chicken like Tante Lesser is a chicken," she said. But we really celebrated. Now

Poppa had savings—not a couple of dollars sewed into a *perineh*, the great feather bedcovers Momma made, but gold in the bank. The Bank of America. "As safe as the Bank of America." What a glorious feeling. This was security. And then the Bank of America failed.

The Wall Street Crash in October of 1929 was just the beginning of the Great Depression, which eventually hit the whole country and the whole world. The Crash was like a volcano—even after the lava has stopped, the tidal waves and floods caused by the eruption continue. One of these tidal waves was the failure of the Bank of America. The panic that followed is part of the nation's history and my own. Our newfound security was gone. The Crash crippled most businesses, and Poppa's was one of them. He not only had nothing in the bank but brought home far less every week.

He was bewildered. The man who had never dared to dream was in the midst of a nightmare. When the choirmaster at a local synagogue needed a boy soprano and again offered me a job, telling my mother they would give me a hundred and fifty dollars for three High Holy Days, Pop was enraged at my refusal. I worried about my family. I wanted to earn money to help; but my fear was greater than my desire, my terror at being laughed at was much stronger than my need to earn their gratitude.

CHAPTER FOUR

THE INDEPENDENT SUBWAY was being built in New York City by Samuel Rosoff, a man who, over a two-year period, through sheer goodness of soul, helped us to recoup our losses from the Bank of America scandal. This philanthropist, who had evidently not forgotten that he too had been an immigrant, saw all petitioners in his gorgeous modernistic offices in downtown Manhattan. Once he became satisfied that a claim was valid, he promised as great a return as possible. I remember him as a kind little man who, for all his wealth and position, looked like the butcher around the corner. His sympathy for us was genuine. He had not forgotten his roots.

On a cold gray day in the autumn of 1932, we and all the other families stood in front of the bank around small bonfires eating chestnuts sold by a blue-nosed old man with a safety pin holding his overcoat closed. We stood for hours that day and other days like it. And Mr. Rosoff kept his promise. Within two years, he saw to it somehow that we had recouped eighty per cent of our savings.

At fourteen, I began to attend an ugly annex of the over-crowded New Utrecht High School, which was a long elevated-train ride to an even shabbier section of Brooklyn and was renowned for its famous alumna, Hollywood's lovely Helen Twelvetrees.

I hated everything about the school. No doubt my reluctance to study, my refusal to learn anything, my terror of strangers

contributed greatly to my unhappiness. The ugly wooden building was overcrowded and dirty and graft-ridden. The principal
was said to be making himself a considerable fortune on the
lunchroom and the student activities. Until Mayor La Guardia
cleaned things up, the place was rumored to be a beehive of
corruption.

Public Schools 19 and 210 had been bad enough for me, but
at least I had known most of the kids in the neighborhood and
felt at home in my misery. But New Utrecht was the international set, and kids streamed in every morning from every
direction and by every device. I myself traveled half an hour
by train. It was an immense place, and I felt as if I would be
swallowed up alive.

Though there was no Black Hand in the washroom, the
facilities were so run down that they were unusable. The faculty
members weren't much better. With a couple of exceptions, the
instructors were our archenemies.

My French teacher had a particularly brilliant approach. "Now
look, kids, I want no baloney. In Paris, every jerk speaks French."

I had two strikes against me immediately. At no age is a
stutter endearing, but it becomes less and less acceptable as one
grows older. At fourteen, I was twice the weight I should have
been and dreaded standing in front of the class. The rooms were
so crowded that some boys sat on the steaming radiators and
others had to lean against the walls. My fear of exposure was
constant.

"Miller, stand up. You will conjugate the verb *être*—'to be.' "

I would rise slowly; without looking up from my desk, I knew
that all the kids were nudging each other in happy expectation.
Even if I had known how to conjugate *être*, I wouldn't have
remembered at that point.

"I said conjugate *être*, Miller. Are you deaf as well as dumb?"
He got his first big laugh.

"Okay, present indicative—or I'll change your future for you."

A chuckle rippled through the classroom. I prayed for an
earthquake or fire that would destroy us all before another
second passed.

"Oh, come on, Miller. What's the big deal? If you're worried about your stammer, don't be."

Don't be! Obviously all I had to do was not be worried. It was so easy. There is nothing like just getting hold of yourself—if you can do it. I couldn't—not in that dingy classroom with a hundred eyes on me.

"Je-Je-Je—ssss-s-s-sssss . . ."

It didn't matter that I didn't know my homework. I couldn't get past the first couple of consonants anyway. And the class, beside itself with hysterics, was so appreciative of my perform-ance that I would have been drowned out.

My teacher quieted the kids with arms upraised. He then looked at me hard. "You know, Miller, it occurs to me that this can be a shrewd device to hide your ignorance. I'll know on the written exam—that is, unless your hand shakes too."

He was building to his finale. The class was in an uproar.

"Your hand doesn't shake, does it, Miller?"

"N-N-N . . ."

"Oh, n-n-never m-m-mind, M-M-Miller."

This was his big finish. As time went on, I began cutting his class to avoid being straight man. He was typical of the faculty.

But there was a Mrs. Marinello, our music teacher, who began my lifelong love affair with the Italian language and Italians. She was an attractive, warm woman who was sympathetic to my shyness and miraculously aware that behind my crippling stutter there was a voice. She tried to encourage my singing, but I purposely sang off pitch when she auditioned me for the glee club. I wanted to please Mrs. Marinello, but I was helpless.

I avoided school whenever possible. With the twenty-five cents a day for lunch and the dime carfare for the elevated train, I had enough to go to the Star Burlesque House when I cut classes—if, with the rest of the kids, I shared plain bread spread with mustard and sneaked under the turnstiles.

The Star Burlesque was where I saw funny Rags Ragland and sad, middle-aged women, naked and powdered, with American flags and whirlers on their nipples; where I saw Dutch comics, and grinding, bumping strippers—and, one unbelievable after-

noon, my dear Poppa sitting there. We guys had gone to see
Georgia Southern; and when I saw my father, I almost dropped
dead right there in the seat directly behind him. Quickly moving
to the other side of the house, I managed to avoid a meeting,
although our mutual guilt would have canceled out any trouble.
It's a cinch Momma would never have found out. Somehow I
loved him even more for this unsuspected new dimension. Our
conversation at supper that night was a scream.

"*Oi!* Lotza, what a full day I had! The work didn't stop. It's
good to relax. And you, Moishe! You bum. I'll bet you ran to a ball
game instead of being in school. Not a serious bone in his
body."

How romantic he had become to me, my Poppa. It was
probably the one time in his life he did the unexpected and
satisfied some simmering urge; but to me, Poppa had become a
man with a double life. I had fantasies about his changing from
the harassed and sweet little tailor to Warren William or William
Powell or some other sophisticated man-about-town the minute
he arrived in Manhattan every day. There was more than meets
the eye, I decided. My Poppa!

I was growing up, and not only my life but my voice was
changing. Baseball was taking up my spare time, but Momma
had other plans. My name might have been Moishe, then Merrill,
then Robert, but to Lotza Miller it was still always "singer
mine." She'd been biding her time all these years, but now
she was ready for action.

When I still refused to sing with the synagogue choir, she was
stunned. "You don't understand, Moishe. You *can't* fight me.
God gave you a voice and you gotta use it."

"I wanna play ball."

"You walk on your feet, you sit on your *tuchis,* and you'll sing
with that voice. I hear you in the bathroom in the morning. You're
going to sing."

"I'll *talk* with my voice, Momma, like I walk with my feet.
I walk. I don't dance."

"You're still a *pisher.*"

"I'll *pish,* but I won't sing."

"And I'll crack you in a minute. Don't be fresh with me."

We were having supper. Poppa put down his fork. For a change and for his own reasons, he sided with his wife. " 'Go to America,' they said. 'Raise children.' *Banditten!* Wild animals. Indians with no respect. The *shamus* told me the *shull* offered him even more to sing for the High Holy Days."

"It's true, and someday he'll make his fortune."

"God gave him a voice!" Poppa roared on. "You'd think he'd be grateful and sing for God in the *shull* and at the same time bring home a few dollars. But no! Why should he? His father is a rich man, a Rockefeller. His father, Abe Miller, can pay for *everything!*"

"Someday your son will make his fortune."

"He'll never make a penny *singing*—singing is not a trade."

"Caruso died on relief?"

Gil took some more potato pancakes and opened his mouth.

"I'd be glad to play the harmonica in *shull*," he volunteered.

"Shut up, Gidalia. All right, Abe. Enough. Let's enjoy the supper. Someday, Moishe will sing and the world will listen."

"Singing," Poppa said, "is for the birds."

"All *right*, already, Abe!"

But Poppa was wound up. "You buy him a new suit of clothes and what does he do?"

"So, what does he do?"

"He wears it! Like they grow on trees. You're not a baby any more. More than a hundred fifty dollars for the High Holy Days and big mouth who's so fresh with his mother won't open it to God! There's your singer, your Cantor Rosenblatt, your Caruso!" He turned to me. "Maybe they'll let you stand in the toilet."

"P-P-Poppa . . ."

"I said all right, Abe. I got a plan."

"Your plans always cost. Never mind!"

"Why do you all fight me when I know? And you're not supposed to have so much salt, Abe. It turns to sugar in the system."

My poor mother.

When I was by myself or at home with just the family, every melody I heard echoed through my head until I would begin to hum and then to sing. I had always loved singing, and my

stutter disappeared when I sang. It was also true that singing
made me happy. But more than anything else, I wanted to be
accepted by my friends and not considered a sissy. It was
tough enough to avoid this stigma with all the restrictions forced
on me by my loving mother. Everything seemed to be taboo.
If, added to all this, I were to sing duets with my mother—who
had now graduated from Polish folk songs to Jeanette Mac-
Donald's complete repertoire—I would be sunk forever.

Momma interrupted my thoughts. "Moishe, singer mine, you're
going to start singing and studying." She had a look that was very
familiar. She got what she wanted when that look was in her eye.
Tradesmen knew it, my father knew it, Gil knew it—and so did I.

In a last-minute try, I cried, "I'll study m-m-music on one
c-c-condition."

My mother looked at me suspiciously, but there was a glint
in her eye. "So, Mr. *Chutzpah*, what's this condition, like you're
in a position?"

I knew that my answer would change things forever, and I
was gratified that Momma was cornering me. She was acting
and so was I. "I'll s-s-study like you want, Momma, but I want
to s-s-sing like Bing Crosby."

My father sprayed his coffee all over the table. "Pink Cruspy
from Cremo Cigars—a crooner, bu-bu-bu-bu? He stutters also?"

"Sh, Abe! Pink Cruspy is a very popular singer and typical
Amerikanish, and isn't our Moishe—I mean our *Morris*—born
here, a real Yankee Doodle? Cruspy, huh? A Rosenblatt he's
not. A Caruso he's not. But it's not such a bad sound when you
get used."

My mother wasn't acting true to type—at least not apparently.
I had expected her to hit the roof at such heresy. Every record
we had in the house was a Victor Red Seal. Singing to her was,
at the very least, semiclassical. I couldn't believe my ears.

I decided to clear the air once and for all. "If I'm going to
s-s-sing at all, I want to b-b-be a c-c-crooner." I exaggerated
the sound as I crooned, " 'When the *blue* of the *night* meets the
gold of the *day,* someone waits for *me-e-e-e!*' "

But Lotza Miller was far cleverer than her son Moishe.

"Very nice, darling!" She turned to my father. "We can't be

old-fashioned, Abe. If he wants to sing like Pink Cruspy, that's a beginning." Now she looked at me in triumph. "So, singer mine, we'll start with Pink Cruspy!"

My defeat was, of course, my victory. Since my birth, my mother and I had had an unwritten contract. Now it was really official. But only the codicil made the contract possible. She could preserve my voice if I could save face on the block. If I was allowed to play ball with my friends, I'd play ball with her. It was a fair exchange. It was a bargain, and Momma cleared the table for the rice pudding.

She was looking very pleased with herself, and strangely enough I wasn't unhappy. It was fascinating to imagine what she would do and how she would go about it. There was never any question that despite my rebellion, my embarrassment at her mollycoddling, and my fury at her humorless and constant vigil over my every breath, my mother was my fortress. I felt safe only with her. That my fears were created by her didn't matter. That she was both fortress and prison was far too complicated for me to grasp. Best friend and worst enemy, it is clear that she was everything to me.

There was something inevitable about Momma. You might be unhappy or angry about what she was doing, but you were helpless to stop her. It was like shaking your fist at the storm that called off the ball game. You could curse at the sky, but it would stop raining only when it was good and ready. Momma moved like the elements, and you were helpless in her path. Out of her way! She was going to do what it was written that she do.

It was actually impossible for me to love my mother as I did my father or any other mortal. You have awe and admiration and respect and anger and terror and gratitude for the super-human, not love. You may worship God and say that you love Him, but it is not the same kind of love that you have for your child or your wife or your friend. If Wagner had known my mother, he would have written another *Ring*.

Very early in life I developed a healthy respect for women and what they could do. Grandma Miller wielded her power like Genghis Khan; Tante Lesser ran her precinct like the Great McGinty, benevolently but without much attention to the rules; and, in spite of Poppa's loyal and loud opposition, I knew that it was Momma who was boss in our house. Perhaps that's why I felt a tenderness for Poppa that I could never feel for her.

Momma's first move was to take me to the William Fox Theatre Building, where the many tiny studios were supposedly incubators for the future stars of stage, screen, and radio. For a dollar and half a lesson—and a reminder from Momma that in bad times that sum could feed our family for two days on a good soupbone and *kasha*—I was taught "popular interpretation." My mother was keeping her word and, for the moment, holding her tongue.

Popular interpretation was, as far as I was concerned, a complete theft of all Bing Crosby's arrangements and tricks. Without shame, I stole, with the teacher's help, the crooner's complete style—down to the casual whistle that substituted for the lyric in the second chorus. It was grand larceny. Crosby was a real troubadour to me—a *trovatore*—my idol. I worshiped him with a devotion I could never display in synagogue. There I stood—a fat little boy lowering his eyelids romantically and crooning "I Surrender Dear" and "Just One More Chance" as if I understood the romantic sentiments. The imitation was good enough to land me on a local radio station, WFOX, three times a week, singing all of Crosby's hits. Well, it filled the time spot, and I suppose the hard of hearing might have thought they were listening to Crosby. That bright young star's quick rise to fame seemed meteoric. Nothing was further from the truth. Crosby is a fixed star if ever there was one, and at fourteen I hitched my wagon to it.

Momma now added Friml and Romberg to her growing repertoire and was singing on the same station. We would return home from the Fox Building in the evening as it was turning dark with a sense of accomplishment and an illusion of success and collaboration. Momma would arrive in her kitchen on a wave of happiness. She and her son were on radio and all was right with the world. We might have been Frank Crummit and Julia Sanderson for all her pride in that tiny band of space, WFOX.

In an attempt to keep my musical activities secret from the gang, I used the name Merrill Miller, though I suspect that the management of the station would have balked at introducing their young crooner as Moishe *anyone*.

But I was growing older and discovered that when I went on a summer's evening to Coney Island with my buddies, they were grateful when I played the ukulele and sang my Crosby songs. I attracted girls as if I were a bronzed lifeguard. My "popular interpretations," my Crosby songs created real mass hypnosis. The girls flocked to us under the boardwalk, succumbing to the sensual sounds. I was like a male Siren; but I was still wet behind the ears, and while the older fellows now went off in twosomes with the girls—the Communist girls being the best, according to the guys, because, along with Stalin, they believed in free love—I was left alone. My job done, I would have a two-cents-plain and a knish that weighed a pound and, with my ukulele under my arm, would waddle off to the subway.

Those broadcasts on WFOX continued for my mother and me for about eighteen months, and I wasn't unhappy doing them. But school was unbearable, and after my sophomore year, dreading each day with a fresh urgency, the authorities agreed that I would never win academic honors and suggested that I go to a trade school.

Poppa found this turn of events to his liking. In a trade school you had to learn a trade! My broadcasts, which were nonpaying, only proved his lifelong contention that music was not a trade. The idea that I would at last begin to learn one was most welcome to him. After all, his wife and son would arrive home from the studio, flushed with triumph, and then eat food bought with the money he was earning as a tailor.

P.S. 19 and New Utrecht's annex were Eton and Oxford compared with the trade school, a blackboard jungle. Every misfit and malcontent who was still too young to be unleashed on society filled its hallowed halls, all of them hating it as much as I. You took your life into your hands just attending classes there.

I emerged from the crucible of aptitude tests a potential cabinetmaker. Furious that I was thrown into the same category as my *bulvahn* Uncle Sam, especially since he was one of the heads of his union and I might need his influence someday, my future seemed bleak. The blueprint was drawn, the die cast.

I can still smell the balsa wood and the sandpaper they gave me the first day, still hear the handsaw and see the pale-yellow dust flying. The decision had been handed down: cabinetmaking was my talent. But I couldn't make anything without shedding blood. I couldn't even make a pair of bookends that matched. They would get smaller and smaller—until under my expert planing—they would shrink to tiny formless things that couldn't support a book of matches. Cabinetmaking? My only contribution to carpentry would have been to fill all the delicatessens of the world with sawdust.

But at home the Board of Education's edict was greeted characteristically.

"*Gott sei danken!*" Poppa said. "He'll have a trade now. Furniture isn't important? You gotta sit down like you gotta eat and keep warm. Enough of this music *chazarai!*"

"It's not enough, and it's not *chazarai!* My Moishe's going to walk around with a hammer and a saw, yet, like Sam the *bulvahn?*"

"Sam may be a *bulvahn*, but he's a good provider. And the union is a good union. He'll never starve."

"There's worse than to starve."

"Ah! You don't have an appetite? You've given up eating?"

"I give up nothing."

Each of my parents was again committed to a side, and the scales were even once more. Uncle Looey was chosen to tip the balance.

Over his *tchai* and sugar, after he had heard the latest bulletins, the problem was presented to him. Should Moishe learn the trade of carpentry at the school? Or was a whole new avenue leading to music to be explored? Uncle Looey had heard me on WFOX. Cousin Sidney thought I was great, but neither he nor his father was a music critic.

Uncle Looey assumed his role of Chief Justice. I never understood why his fingers didn't burn from holding the glass of steaming tea. He was finishing his third.

He began badly for Momma. "*Oi*, Lotza! Poppa, God rest his soul, would drop dead from Moishe singing jazz like that."

"Poppa would understand with that ear and that voice."

"I heard him myself on the radio. Bu-bu-bu-bu. I thought he lost his stutter when he sang, he should live and be well."

"That's the style, Looey—like Pink Cruspy."

"The style? Pink Cruspy can't talk also?"

"It's the style. He can talk, but it's the style."

"Moishe and his stutter is in style? Forgive me, mine boy— the whole world is so *moishe kapoy* it will be the style also may- be to drag a foot? If we wait long enough, I'll be in style also."

"Looey!"

"Forgive me, Lotza. I am trying to understand this new style. The boy has a beautiful voice, and why not? Wasn't our Poppa a voice that made you cry? But to put all his eggs in is another basket."

"Aha!" said Poppa.

"But Moses, our great leader, saved the people and gave us our law, and Aaron, his brother, had to speak for him. 'Why?' you ask." Uncle Looey sipped his tea noisily and then smacked his lips. "Because Moses also stuttered—and still he became a success."

"Aha!" said Momma.

"But, God forgive me, Lotza, not as a singer."

"Aha!" shouted Poppa.

"Looey, he doesn't stutter when he sings."

"Bu-bu-bu-bu!" Uncle Looey reminded her.

"But that's the style."

The carrousel went round and round, and then Uncle Looey grunted with unmistakable finality. "You have asked me, Lotza, to weigh the facts and make a decision. There is no doubt Moishe's voice is a gift from God, and he gets it from our own dear Poppa. But Poppa had a trade also. Like me, he was a *schneider*, and like Abe, the boy's father, also. So why shouldn't Moishe sing for his pleasure and the pleasure of the family and for God and still have a trade? He doesn't want tailoring. The school says he's a carpenter—it's not so terrible. Esther's *bulvahn* Sam doesn't provide for her with everything she needs? He won't

bury her and himself like royalty in mahogany from the union
—with brass, yet?"

Uncle Looey was also a member of the Pultisker Progressive
Society and was as impressed as everyone else with mortuary
real estate. Since a respectable death rather than a good life
was the greatest goal, Uncle Looey now sided with my father.
"The boy becomes the _mensch,_ Lotza. _Umberschrien,_ God bless
him, he's a big boy for fifteen. He'll learn a trade, have a family,
and he'll live in honor and die—God forbid—in the knowledge
that there's a plot of ground for him and his."

I was fifteen and already disposed of—buried alive. It was
all so neat and orderly.

Poppa breathed easily. "Your brother Looey has a head on
his shoulders."

"And your son has a silver voice in his throat," Momma ob-
served, in furious defiance of the decision.

"Enough of this craziness you fill the boy's head with!" Poppa
shouted in a temper. "The two of you singing on the radio for
nothing and costing carfare and extra food and a _bissel_ this and
a _bissel_ that. Enough! I'll hear no more. That's no life, with bums
and phonies—even if the boy could do it—and your own brother
has spoken and decided. Enough! Stop _hocking mir a tchainik._"

Momma grabbed Uncle Looey's napkin and stuffed it in the
napkin ring aggressively. "While he's making _coffins_ with a
hammer and nails, _I'm_ going to polish the silver."

I continued at trade school, manufacturing excelsior by the
ton, while my mother searched for a singing teacher for me. She
lauded Uncle Looey's wisdom only when he agreed with her.
As the years passed, she felt more and more that her brother
was not the Solomon she had once imagined. Her defiance of
his decision didn't bother her at all. "I'm going to be arrested
because I think my brother is wrong and want the best for my
son?" I don't remember ever hearing a simple declarative
sentence in my family. Everybody spoke in questions and answered in questions. The real question was: where was I head-
ing?

I was in a quandary. Carpentry was obviously out, and my
mother held her heart when I talked of professional baseball. I

was now at the height of my flirtation with the game and was actually playing semipro games. Some of the confidence I needed was gained on the sandlots of Brooklyn, and I'm sure that had I continued I would have made—despite my small hands—a damned good pitcher.

Baseball was the weak link in the chain my mother had around my neck. She couldn't have stopped me from playing by forbidding it, any more than she could really have stopped me from singing by forcing me to. I was beginning to see that. But one day she arrived on the field at one of our church-sponsored games like some kind of divine umpire. When I saw her stalking along the diamond, I ran all the way from the bullpen to the subway.

There was no escaping my mother—and no escaping my obvious destiny. What she had always known, I was beginning to accept. Somehow I was going to be a singer. The radio experience was a taste that I liked. The friends I had made on Coney Island, I liked. I still balked and beefed, true to my act, but all judgments were suspended as things came to a head at home.

While my mother persisted in her search for a Svengali, Poppa created his own magic by pulling the rug out from under her feet. With a wise nod of approval from Uncle Looey, Poppa took me out of trade school and put me into a trade.

His brother Max was then the manager of an A. S. Beck shoe store on 125th Street in Harlem. Now I would learn the shoe business and follow in his footsteps. But with the same dexterity that had made me a master carpenter and artisan, I now fumbled my way through reams of wrapping paper and miles of string, spending hours trying to wrap one item for shipping. Poor Uncle Max didn't object to the waste as much as he did to the wait his customers had to endure as, under the pressure of a patron's disgusted gaze, I became all thumbs.

It wasn't long before I switched jobs and uncles and I went to work for Uncle Abe on Thirty-ninth Street.

CHAPTER FIVE

WHEN I WAS sixteen years old—at the depths of the Great Depression—Thirty-ninth Street and Seventh Avenue in New York City was the center of the universe to Gatti-Casazza, Lawrence Tibbett, Lucrezia Bori, Lily Pons, Giovanni Martinelli—and Abe Bernstein. All these names dazzled me, and I actually knew Abe Bernstein, since he was the relative of my mother's whose precious La Salle was ruined when Gil got carsick.

Though he was a second cousin once removed, he was of an age and station that demanded a title of respect. He would have preferred Sahib, but he settled for Uncle Abe.

Uncle Abe was the one glimmer of hope in our poverty-stricken family, the one pillar of society, the one rich man; and through his interest in me, I was now—according to him—a young man of expectations. Through his influence and blood loyalty, I was not without promise. Uncle Abe would not fail my mother.

Uncle Abe was a dapper, stocky, and cocky little man who had earned his big belly and wore over it a watch and watch chain that proclaimed, like the old poster, that he sold strictly for cash and *not* for credit. I can still hear the rhythm of his speech and see those piercing black eyes. Abe Bernstein's words had all his weight and all his gravity.

When he decided to rescue me from the obscurity of a

Brooklyn slum, he nodded his head wisely and held fast to my mother's arm. "Lotza! I know what you want for your boy Moishe—I'm not a father? But I want to tell you that in this great English language there is a word: *availability*. And this availability I am giving, whence he should use the opportunity to be available, can be beautiful if he isn't a loafer but respects and is conscious of the availability, which he can be tops in the field with God's help—and, for your information, mine also. For in this great U.S.A. of ours, where my own son Morris, *umber-schrien*, is already on the way to the top of the ladder of success, and 'Why?' you ask? Because he saw the truth, and at the end of a workday his availability isn't all shot."

He now turned to me gravely. "Moishe! Stick to your cousin Morris and he will make a man of you. Remember these words well today that I have made available to you."

It wasn't easy, but I have tried to capture the brevity, depth, and beauty of expression that was uniquely Abe Bernstein. He had learned the word *availability* from a salesman from Chicago, and it was his word of the week. He had no idea what he was saying when he started one of these endless speeches, but my mother always listened intently and nodded as if she were agreeing with him. Momma always understood him. It was then I learned that when money talks, even the deaf hear poetry.

Uncle Abe might not have had an ear, but his eye was worth a million. Before returning to Brooklyn in the evening, he would go up to Fifty-seventh Street and stand in front of Milgrim's or Henri Bendel and admire the dresses in the window. He couldn't sketch, but his eye could retain the designs—the way a sick retina holds the image of a naked light bulb—until the next morning, when he returned to his factory and relayed the information to his tailors. The samples were then cut and sent to a jobber who knocked them off an assembly line in the tens of thousands.

Uncle Abe was a big wheel, and I was lucky enough to be a cog. In this complex of creativity and high finance, I was to be the link between the rapidly cut sample and the mass-produced copies. I pushed a dress cart full of "Frocks by Bernstein" up Seventh Avenue.

For all of Uncle Abe's eloquence about his generosity, he was not an easy boss. I was a slave, and the slightest complaint brought the quick reminder that I was the luckiest boy in the world that in this Great Depression—with Mrs. William Randolph Hearst giving milk away in Columbus Circle and men with families selling apples on the street and bank presidents living in Central Park's shantytown and some of them lying dead in the gutters of Wall Street—*I* had a job. Not only was I working, but the job could lead (if I availed myself of the availability) to the next best thing to being a doctor—the dream of my father, the provider of my mother, adored by women, envied by men, respected by gentile buyers from Texas, with an expense account and alligator shoes—a dress salesman!

These last words were said in a hoarse whisper, as if the gods, on hearing of such great fortune, might in a fit of jealousy put the evil eye on me. When Uncle Abe first mentioned this goal to my family, it was almost too much to comprehend. To everybody but my mother, the words *dress salesman* struck awe and were repeated throughout the room, barely audibly, like some ancient incantation. Only in America! One of my aunts was said to have fainted. If so, it wasn't from awe but from envy: she too had a son.

Well, he could gladly have had my job. You didn't become a dress salesman overnight unless you were Uncle Abe's son and therefore heir apparent to the throne. Cousin Morris was already wearing white-on-white shirts, eating pollyseeds all day long and dropping the shells all over the floor. No! You started at the bottom for eight dollars a week, swept up after Morris, and pushed a dress rack past the Metropolitan Opera House.

Every day I would pass it and read the threesheets announcing Elisabeth Rethberg as Butterfly, Lawrence Tibbett as Emperor Jones, Lauritz Melchior as Tannhäuser. Ezio Pinza was the great Don Giovanni, his foot arrogantly resting on the prompter's box; Lily Pons was the tiny Lakmé; and Edward Johnson, still a tenor, was the romantic Peter Ibbetson—a role that Gary Cooper had played in a movie, without music, of course.

Every evening I would stare at these posters and then go home to Brooklyn, where my parents fought constantly—about money, which they never had enough of, and about me, who was becoming too much for them. Home was a prison, and Uncle Abe's was a work farm. I wanted to escape from this narrow world, which was bounded on the north by Milgrim's and on the south by Moscowitz & Lupowitz. But I beat my path daily from the factory to the jobbers and then home to Brownsville and then back to Uncle Abe's, forever forced to be grateful that I could continue this honor another day. I just kept pushing that damned dress rack up Seventh Avenue and east on Fortieth Street.

One day, as I passed the back of the Metropolitan, I saw that sets were being moved in. With some difficulty, I managed to get the filled rack up on the sidewalk and near the entrance, where I heard music and voices floating out of the large portal. The sounds were irresistible and drew me nearer. Wheeling the dress rack up to the entrance, I pretended the "Frocks by Bernstein" were costumes and lumbered in with the moving men.

It was dark, and my heart almost stopped when I heard that baritone voice. I had seen Lawrence Tibbett in *Rogue Song* and, with Grace Moore, in *New Moon* at the Republic Theatre in Brownsville, and I recognized his voice immediately. He was an idol of mine. The soprano who joined him didn't sound like Moore; and, forgetting my dress rack, my eyes becoming accustomed to the dark, I stole further into the theater and hid behind a flat marked *Das Rheingold*. It was the first time that I inhaled the dank, glorious air that is the life's breath of the stagestruck.

Some camp chairs and a work light that blurred the view behind it were all I could make out at first. Shifting my weight and eclipsing the light with the back of my hand, I now saw the breathtaking interior of the Opera House, the largest auditorium I had ever seen; its many tiers looked to me like layers of a birthday cake. There were some mumbling and sudden laughter, and then I heard the strains of Verdi's *La Traviata,* which I knew from my mother's records.

In a moment I was treated to a duet between Violetta and Germont and I could now make out Mr. Tibbett, wearing a sweater and singing not with Grace Moore but with the marvelous Lucrezia Bori, who had her hat on. Creeping closer, I be-

came tangled in some netting that would one night become part
of a sylvan glen or the Nibelungs' backyard or something. I
stood very still and listened to my heart and the rehearsal. The
singing was beautiful; and when it stopped abruptly in the middle of a phrase, I was certain, in the dead silence, that my
presence had been detected. I held my breath in terror. But
then there was a ripple of laughter and the music began again.
I exhaled in relief.

Looking up into the flies, I saw sandbags and ropes and all
the paraphernalia of the backstage heaven ruled by the "God
of the machine." For me, a little heathen, this was the beginning
of my conversion. Shy as I was, I felt that this was a world with
no boundaries, a world I could live and grow in. Hiding in the
shadows behind that piece of Wagnerian scenery, listening to
Tibbett's and Bori's ringing voices and their good-natured
laughter, hearing the tuning up of the musicians in the pit, seeing the hundreds of different curtains and hangings in the flies
that could change life into anything you wanted it to be, smelling
the past, sniffing the future, I almost believed in myself.

When I was discovered by some assistant stage manager and
removed from the sacred premises and led to the street, it wasn't
the sudden change that made the sunshine harsh, the colors
of the samples garish, and the din of Seventh Avenue deafening.
I couldn't articulate it then, but I somehow knew that inside
there was form and that here in the street there was only chaos.
Inside the theater a beautiful world was in the making; outside
it was a jungle. I will never forget the shock of reality when I
saw daylight and the sinking feeling when I saw that damned
dress rack.

Completely confused, it came over me that this newly discovered world was the very one my mother wanted for me—and
I had been fighting her. In frustration, I grabbed the rack,
pushed it back into the gutter, and aimed it uptown. I turned
at the corner and nicked someone in the ankle.

"*Klutz!*" a fat little man yelled. "Do you own the streets?"

"I'm s-s-sorry," I stuttered.

"I'll give you s-s-sorry. Such a hurry like the customers are
begging! So! Not such a bad garment. How much?"

"They're j-j-just s-s-samples, s-s-sir."

"I don't know samples? What'll they retail for?"

"Ten ninety-five."

"You work for Abe Bernstein?"

"Yes, s-s-sir."

"When I see a Milgrim dress for ten ninety-five, it's gotta be Abe Bernstein. You work for a *goniff*, and if I have even a scratch on the ankle tonight, I'll take him to court. Now go, rush to your grave like all the kids today with your carioca and your hotcha!"

When I returned to "Frocks by Bernstein," Uncle Abe was waiting. "Ah! Look who's here. *Schmendrik*, who I pay a fortune to promenade through the streets of New York. How do you expect to predominate if you promenade without predomination that you should be back here immediately, for predominant above all else is the tempo of the times when the jobber calls and asks, 'Where is my new line?' Here. Sweep up the floor and earn the fortune I'm offering only because blood is thicker and more predominant than water. Remember these words always!"

I swept up Cousin Morris' pollyseed shells and thought of that dark, expectant theater. Momma was right. She was always right. There was something about that stage I had just been on, something about that theater out front.

I had never seen an opera, and now it enraged me that Uncle Abe paid me so little that I couldn't afford even to stand at the Met. Eight dollars a week, and I was lucky to be bringing home that much. He was the stingiest man alive. In my poverty I was spending more on lunch than he did.

When he discovered that, he was amazed. "You gotta spend forty cents on an egg cream and two sandwiches when you can have a little Jell-O—with colored stripes, yet—some coffee, and a roll from home, and all this for fifteen cents?"

My time in Uncle Abe's employ was one of the low points in my life. But it was through him that I had set foot on the stage of the Metropolitan Opera House for the first time.

Momma was still biding her time. She often got singing assignments from some cantor in Manhattan Beach who on occasion sang with the Salmaggi Opera Company; he now suggested a singing teacher for me. On his recommendation, she took me to the man, a stocky, large-nosed person in a dirty shirt. The first lesson cost a dollar and a half, and when it was over, my voice was so hoarse that I could barely talk. The teacher informed my mother that I was going to become a tenor—with his help, a great one.

I informed my mother that I would never go to this man again, that she must not waste the money. Mother was convinced that I was trying to avoid the lessons and escape my fate, but I was genuinely concerned after the lesson. My voice was badly strained, and, despite all else, I certainly didn't want it destroyed.

Momma wasn't buying my concern about the expense. "You're a good boy, Moishe, and you know how we struggle; but if Poppa took you to the Chinese restaurant for that pork they call chicken charmain, you'd go and not say, 'It costs.' So you're going to continue lessons with Mr. Marbini."

But my instinct told me I was right. "Momma, I swear to you he's not good for me! He was twisting my voice. My throat still hurts. I can tell. He might as well choke me," I added dramatically.

My father was listening while he read the paper. "Continue!" he shouted with self-satisfaction. "The _mayvin_—she knows everything. First he stutters, and now he won't be able to talk, even. A killer she's taken him to. She will not leave the boy alone," he concluded to whatever gods were listening.

My mother ignored him and searched my eyes. "Open!" she commanded. "You swear?" she asked after looking at my throat.

"I swear."

"Open again. It hurts you, Moishe?"

"It hurts me."

She couldn't be sure how valid my objections were, but I could. It was no dodge. I was certain. But in order for her to be, Momma now invited a musical friend of hers to supper.

Nathan Siganari was a very nice gentleman who helped her rehearse before she appeared at one of her functions. She was going to sing the "Italian Street Song" at a Pultisker Progressive Society affair, and he was going to accompany her. Unaware that he was really there to audition me, I innocently joined her in a chorus of "Ah, Sweet Mystery of Life." After hearing me, he made Momma promise to take me to a man who was, in his opinion, a fine teacher; a man who worked with opera singers— a man whose office and studio were, in fact, *in* the Metropolitan Opera House Building. My mother was beside herself. To her, playing the fiddle was Fritz Kreisler, dancing was Pavlova, and singing was Caruso. She always aimed high—which was why we had by now, beyond our means, again moved—this time to Bensonhurst, with Uncle Looey following, of course.

"Moishela!" my mother announced. "Tomorrow we make an appointment during your lunch hour with Samuel Margolis of the Metropolitan Opera Building!"

CHAPTER SIX

MOMMA MET ME in front of the Metropolitan Opera House, and we ogled the threesheet of *Rigoletto* with Pons, Lauri-Volpi, De Luca, and Swarthout. As I followed her into the narrow entrance stage-left of the lobby and we approached the elevator, I watched Lotza Miller's walk change. Her talk also underwent a complete transformation. Special circumstances demanded special speech, and my mother now put on a languid, insufferable air that would have put even England's old Queen Mary and her hat in their place. The pacing was very slow and very deliberate.

"Uh! We would be wanting _vehry_ much, uh, Music Master and Professor Samuel Marrrrgolis—who is expecting, I believe on the third floor, mine son, a singer, and his mother, also a singer! If you please."

The elevator man was already past the floor when Momma finished her prologue. "Yes, ma'am," he answered with respect as he reversed his course. On every floor we heard singers exercising. Momma was in her element; her eyes were shining.

The elevator at last stopped at the third floor, and Momma swept out, thanking the elevator man with outrageous eloquence.

We soon found ourselves in a little office that opened onto a larger room with a piano and a whole wall filled with photographs of singers who had all written across their necks and chests what proved to be messages to Mr. Margolis. They were a strange group of friends, I thought, everyone made up and in costume for Halloween. Faust and Rigoletto, Otello and the mad Lucia were hardly the usual sights to a kid who didn't know the opera, the characters, or anything.

I liked Mr. Margolis on sight. He was kind and distinguished looking and, according to Momma, knew the difference between a nice voice and a good one. He wasn't looking for customers, Momma made it clear; and even if he liked me, she had no idea how we could pay him. These considerations she swept away. For Lotza, one bridge at a time.

That first day I sang scales for Mr. Margolis, one after another, and he made a few minor suggestions as I vocalized. Then I sang "One Night of Love," the title song from Grace Moore's sensationally successful movie.

Mr. Margolis nodded occasionally, and at last he spoke. "He can be a tenor or a baritone. We'll let nature take its course, Mrs. Miller."

My mother was sitting with her hands folded peasant-style on her lap. She now released them and grabbed the neckline of her dress. "*We?* Am I hearing right? Do you *mean*, Mr. Margolis, that you'll *teach* him?"

"Yes, Mrs. Miller, I'll teach him. He has the gift."

"*Gott sei danken*," Momma cried, ready to move on to the next problem. "Can a mother tell you what this means? Mr. Margolis, the gift he's got—but money? That's another question."

She cupped her mouth in her hand and shook her head in the time-honored reflex of her ancestors. You'd have sworn the problem had at that very moment first occurred to her. "How am I going to pay you, Mr. Margolis?"

"Eventually, Mrs. Miller, eventually. I have faith in the boy. When he becomes a star, he'll pay me."

"God bless you. You won't be sorry," Momma said, and she stood up in triumph. "You'll never regret. He'll never stop working."

It was the most prophetic statement my mother ever made.

Unlike that first teacher, Mr. Margolis gave me exercises that immediately freed my voice. Any doubts about my instinctive rejection of his predecessor evaporated. I knew that Mr. Mar-

golis would be good for me. Four times a week, I would go
straight from work to the Metropolitan Building to have my
lesson. It settled into a permanent routine, and I rarely broke
it. No matter what other problems I had, I always showed at
Mr. Margolis' before I went home to Brooklyn.

I was still miserable with Uncle Abe and with Cousin Morris
and his white-on-white shirts and all those shells I had to
sweep up. When Uncle Max left the Harlem shop, got himself
a partner, and opened his own shoe store—the Paradise Bootery,
right across the street from the Strand Theatre on Broadway—
and asked me to come back as a shoe salesman and learn the
business from the ground up, I jumped at the chance.

Then there was trouble in Paradise, and I got the boot. The
partner—to my people, a necessary evil, the thorn on the rose of
commerce, and always an object of loathing—now acted out his
traditional role by running off with all the money and ruining
poor Uncle Max, putting him out of business altogether. Max
Miller was a salesman again, and I was one of the unemployed.

I never stopped studying with Mr. Margolis, but everything
else was terrible. Under pressure at home, I went from one
awful job to another in quick succession. First I worked in a
seltzer-bottle factory on Avenue B on the Lower East Side. It
was a dungeon, but again I was told how grateful I should be,
since only family influence had enabled me to work in the
middle of the Depression. I did assembly-line work: throughout
the day, I blasted sand on some black goo, tattooing the names
of various seltzer firms on the bottles. I especially remember
the name Good Health. Good Health Seltzer was slowly killing
me. The sand was getting into my lungs and creating a chronic
cough. The perfect job for a boy who was taking singing
lessons!

Mr. Margolis would ask whether I had been watching construction work. "Your voice sounds as if you've been inhaling
gravel or sand."

I did not tell Mr. Margolis about the job. The salary was immense. Eighteen dollars a week was not to be coughed away
when families we knew were on relief. My salary almost equaled

the amount Poppa brought home, which should have made me proud but only made me grateful I wasn't dying in vain.

While I hacked away, another family conclave was called at which Uncle Looey presided. Momma was worried about me. Although Good Health Seltzer was good for digestion, she was concerned about what it would do to my voice. Uncle Looey, to her distress, decreed that in such times, with people starving, a boy couldn't give up such a good position and that "maybe if he tries not to breathe too deep or wears a little something over the nose and mouth, maybe," everything would be all right.

But it was another relative who saved me from silicosis. Uncle Max's sister-in-law, Hattie, got me a job with the Ideal Toy Company on West Seventeenth Street in Manhattan. There I stuffed animals with excelsior all day long. I turned rabbits inside out for eight hours every day in a loft without one solitary window. Evidently, I was doomed to choke to death. Every day on my lunch hour, I would lose the little breath left in me as I rushed uptown to Mr. Margolis. For months this horror went on.

The only people who can afford to be poor at all are the young and strong. It's a wonder that so many of us survived. How many of us have laughed over those years, glamorized them beyond belief—as if unhappiness could ever have been happy? I'll never forget arriving at Mr. Margolis' in the Met Building in that rotting leather jacket I was forced to wear. If anyone shared the elevator with me, I blushed all the way up with embarrassment. Poverty has never been good for a talent, though there are those who believe it is. Life itself is enough of a character builder without being poor besides. I thank God that my children have never had to know it.

The temptation is to keep your children from knowing the heartache you've known. If they're knocked around a little bit, perhaps they're better immunized to the Fates, who don't always share a parent's concern for their future. But the time for that is when they're their strongest, not when they're little, not when they're helpless. If I vacillate like my Uncle Looey, it's because it's hard to know where to stop with kids. You don't want to spoil them rotten because you had nothing, and you don't want to begrudge them one thing that can enrich their lives. There isn't much point in having achieved anything if you can't make things easier for your family.

Fortunately, I can avoid these decisions without danger. My wife knows instinctively what do do. She knows when to give and when not to give, when to hold them close and when to let them fly or fall. I don't know how she knows, but she does.

It is true that my mother knew I was going to be a singer before I ever dreamt it. But I remember exactly how our ambitions became one, and the exact moment.

My jobs were so short-lived and so numerous that I don't remember whether I was working for Good Health Seltzer, Ideal Toy, or a ladies'-belts factory. But no matter where I worked, I never missed a singing lesson. Although I still wouldn't sing for anybody but my buddies out on Coney Island or in Lincoln Terrace Park, my time with Mr. Margolis had improved my voice. It was growing stronger, clearer, easier.

One day Momma met me at the studio. She was unbelievable. It wasn't enough that Mr. Margolis was teaching me without a fee, she now wanted something else.

"Mr. Margolis—mine boy, is doing all right?"

"I'm quite pleased, Mrs. Miller, with his progress. I am starting to give him some Stradella."

"Stra . . ."

"He's an Italian composer who wrote long before Verdi or even Mozart. Seventeenth century. Alessandro Stradella! His work is very florid, very colorful, exciting."

"It can stretch the voice, take it new places?"

"That's right, Mrs. Miller," my teacher said in awe.

"Moishe's lucky to have you, Mr. Margolis. I mean *Morris*, my singer of the Italian seventeenth century. I feel nothing but good from this."

She now grabbed my earlobes and pulled them. "So nothing will _beshrie_ mine boy," she explained.

"I understand, Mrs. Miller."

"The boy has never heard opera—the whole thing. Isn't it good for him to hear an opera?"

"Very good."

She pointed at his wall, filled with the autographed pictures of singer friends and pupils. "Mr. Margolis! Through a friend, maybe Mr. Martinelli up there, you can get us free tickets some night—or the cheapest? Only, even the cheapest we can't afford so good. We can sit anywhere, who cares?"

I was embarrassed. Mr. Margolis was doing so much already. "Momma, Mr. Margolis is too busy t-t-to . . ."

"I talked to you? Is your name changed again? First Moishe, then Morris, now Margolis?"

My teacher laughed. "I will try. It's a good idea, Mrs. Miller."

"Thank you. You see, it wasn't such a calamity my asking. Mr. Martinelli is singing a lot this week. I was reading the program."

My mother was all *chutzpah*—the ultimate in nerve. Nothing ever bothered her, no obstacle ever made her hesitate. Why should the great Martinelli give us tickets? I was mortified by her request, but not so much that I refused to go a few nights later when Mr. Margolis managed to get three tickets to *Il Trovatore*. I never saw Momma so excited.

A year or so earlier I had regaled her with my backstage adventure, an excited description of that immense auditorium and the layers of lights that rose and disappeared beyond my line of vision as I hid behind a *Rheingold* flat. There was no doubt that I had conveyed some of the excitement I had felt that day. "It's like a big mouth, Momma, smiling—wide and beautiful with lots of teeth."

Three nights after Momma had wangled the invitation, Mr. Margolis led us to the upper plate, the Family Circle, the highest point of the Opera House—so near the ceiling that I found myself reminded of Lon Chaney's *The Phantom of the Opera*, the climax of which was the crashing of the great chandelier. I read the names bordering the proscenium: Gluck, Beethoven, Mozart, Verdi, Wagner, and Gounod. We were in the first row on the side, and I gingerly peeked over the rail; we were precariously perched on the edge of the peanut gallery. The sweep of the theater was dazzling in all its red-and-gold glory.

Mr. Margolis pointed out the Diamond Horseshoe—the rotogravure's name for the Parterre Boxes—as the place where the "society people" sat. He told us that some of these families had held the same boxes for generations. Above that glamorous tier were the Grand Tier Boxes, also filled with elegant men and women—the white of the stiff shirts creating accents in the blur of color, along with any red that was worn by the beautifully dressed women. The white and red stood out, hitting the eye. The Dress Circle, two levels below us, was also crowded; its patrons too looked prosperous. I wondered how there could be so many rich people in one theater. My eye followed the line of the balcony just below us until it disappeared beneath me. Unless I leaned forward on the rail, which kept me from falling into the orchestra, I could see only the opposite side of the theater. It seemed an odd arrangement. Obviously it didn't matter that the poor couldn't see. Well, opera was meant to be heard anyway.

I sat with my chin resting on my hands, my eyes drinking in the wonder of that theater. Not Loew's Pitkin, not the Congress, not even the Star Burlesque had ever given me the slightest hint that a public place could look like this. Mr. Margolis lent us his opera glasses, and my mother and I shared them to scan the audience. I had never before seen people look so beautiful except in movies. Down the aisles of the orchestra, which still had its stalls, were streaming more and more ladies with fur wraps and gentlemen with black coats. I was inside a tremendous paint box and the colors were running. It was a crazy thought, but I was that exhilarated.

When I heard a smattering of applause, I turned to Mr. Margolis and saw him pointing toward the orchestra pit, where the lighted stands created a marvelous sight from that great height. Moving through the gully was a tiny figure that scurried and dodged the bright obstacles until it reached dead center and then turned to face the audience, which now applauded loudly.

"That's Papi," Mr. Margolis said. "Gennaro Papi, the conductor."

He began to clap his hands also, so Momma and I joined in the ovation. The buzzing grew fainter as the theater darkened; only the borders of the tiers remained lit. I was surprised, at that great distance, to hear distinctly Signor Papi tap his baton on the stand before him, and then there was absolute quiet. *How can so many people be so quiet?* I thought as the hush became almost ominous, like the moment before an earthquake. Little did I know just what a tremor was in store for me.

The curtain parted on the entrance to the Count di Luna's palace. Mr. Margolis had told us the story of *Il Trovatore*—an almost impossible task—and now I watched in fascination as the confusing tale unfolded. The music hypnotized me. Signor Martinelli's Manrico and Elisabeth Rethberg's Leonora were revelations to me—so beautiful to hear—and the gypsy Azucena, sung by Kathryn Meisle, was both terrifying and marvelous. Her firelit incantation scenes held me, as well as her gang of gypsies, under her spell.

But it was Richard Bonelli as Count di Luna who altered my life forever. I was impressed beyond belief—stunned by him. He wasn't just singing, making melody; his soaring voice was expressing not only the character he was playing but my own unformed feelings and thoughts. He sang for *me*, and I seemed to be singing through him. That night Richard Bonelli changed me from a confused, stagestruck kid to a true opera student. Why wasn't it the great Martinelli? He was superb. But it was Bonelli whose ringing voice echoed in my ears.

The elevator was so crowded that we quietly spiraled down the stairs, leaving the theater in a daze. After we thanked Mr. Margolis and said good night, Momma and I started for the subway. But I couldn't leave, so we turned the corner of Fortieth Street to Broadway and stood in the main lobby watching the elegant audience depart in their limousines or wander off to hail their taxicabs. When the last of them had trickled out, we walked outside and looked at the posters announcing future programs, praying that we could repeat our luck through Mr. Margolis.

Some of the threesheets had bands with *Sold Out* across them: Lotte Lehmann as Tosca; Rosa Ponselle as Carmen; Grace Moore and Nino Martini in *La Bohème;* Kirsten Flagstad, the new sensation of the opera world, and Lauritz Melchior in *Tristan und Isolde;* Rose Bampton and John Charles Thomas in *Aïda;* and Helen Jepson, Martinelli, and Bonelli in *I Pagliacci.* A gala

farewell to Lucrezia Bori was announced; she was retiring at the
zenith of her power.

I was dizzy with excitement, floating on a wave of happiness
that made no sense when I remembered that I had to be at the
factory the next morning at eight-thirty.

We circled the block to make sure that we wouldn't miss
anything, then we descended into hell again and caught our
subway home. We sat rereading our programs as the train jogged
along to Brooklyn. I looked up from my program at my mother's
strong and beautiful profile.

When I spoke, there wasn't a trace of a stutter in my voice.
"I want that, Momma. *That's* what I want," I repeated, to make
certain all the facts were in.

My mother never even looked up from her program. "That's
good, Moishe. I'm glad."

She seemed to have no idea of the revolution that had taken
place inside me. It never occurred to me that she had prepared
the way for that revolution and was not in the least surprised
now that all her plots had begun to thicken. As far as she was
concerned, I had just picked up the option on that contract she
and I had had all my life.

"I'm glad, Moishe," she now repeated. "So tell me—why?
What makes you so sure now?"

What could I say? I was filled to brimming. A completely
new feeling carried me away. "I just know I can sing louder
than Bonelli," I said.

CHAPTER SEVEN

I WAS EIGHTEEN YEARS OLD and for the first time in my life knew exactly where I wanted to go and how to get there. There were two things I could do well, and I knew it. Along with playing baseball, I could sing; and, strangely, listening to a real artist that night only made me more sure of myself.

Greatness in any of the arts is awesome, but so is heaven on a million-starred night. There are some who feel insignificant when confronted with such grandeur. But not me. I feel bigger—as if I must be pretty good to be part of such a thing. So with art. I think that when a man achieves any great height he pulls everybody along with him. If Bonelli could do to me what he did, perhaps I could do it to somebody else someday. Anyway, it was certainly worth a try.

My lessons with Mr. Margolis took on an immediacy now. My trust in him was so complete that all he had to do was say, "I hope you don't smoke cigarettes," and I answered, "Of course not," the most honest lie imaginable—since on leaving his studio that day, I threw away an almost full pack of cigarettes, never again to touch one. Somehow Mr. Margolis made me respect my voice, made me realize that the biggest fool in the world is the man who throws away his gift.

When I had no singing lesson, I would spend my lunch hour at the public library reading about Caruso. Me—indoors, reading! It *was* a revolution. I read everything about him I could get my

[75]

hands on. Since he was the most famous singer of the century and the acknowledged master of *bel canto*, it seemed that his life story might reveal the secret of his genius. Over and over I played his records, listening not only to those gorgeous notes but to the spaces between them, the breath that prompted them. It is true that he was a tenor and that my voice now was obviously, like Bonelli's, going to be baritone, but that was unimportant. Caruso was the greatest singer within memory, and even with my limited studies I could recognize this.

How could I ever have imagined that a career in classical singing would make me ridiculous or contemptible? Six levels of the Metropolitan Opera House had cheered Bonelli and yelled "Bravo!" And those people were important, educated—pillars of society. The boxes were owned by influential people in industry and politics and the arts. They all loved Bonelli. Tibbett was also a great favorite and even a movie star. As for Caruso! Caruso was by now a saint, he was so revered. What the hell did I care what the kids on the block thought! Who were *they?* There was a whole world outside of Bensonhurst, beyond Brooklyn, right over the bridge and uptown, and I was lucky enough to have had a peek at it.

Poppa still had his own ideas concerning my future. The jobs I had were all detestable and short-lived. He was sure I would be a loafer. Forever fearful that I would never learn a trade and earn my keep, he got me a job at his own place—one of the last sweatshops in New York City. Poppa was a sewing-machine operator for a cloak-and-suit factory on Eighth Avenue, and I worked with him one whole summer. We left Brooklyn every morning at 7 A.M. and arrived home every evening at 7 P.M. Never healthy, now constantly plagued by diabetes and stomach trouble, living on medicines, Poppa was now for the first time revealed to me in his own setting.

The factory had almost a hundred machines, one crowded next to the other in rows, with a twenty-watt bulb set above each operator barely giving any light at all. The first time I saw my father take his place, his back bent over to get nearer to that damned little light, his steel-rimmed glasses on the tip of his nose, his eyes squinting, his fingers skimming nervously over his work, I was both sickened and awed. There was only one window in the entire loft, and that was the one in the toilet. It was a sight, that great big room with those hobgoblins crouched over their work.

Poppa and the rest of the men got paid by the piece, their job being to sew what had already been designed and cut. He would sew a garment together and then throw it into a large box; the box would later be emptied and the garments counted. The more garments, at twenty-five cents a piece, the more money he could bring home. All the men sat like buzzing bees all day; but my Poppa was really Saturday's child. He never stopped sewing. Not until the day was over. Sweat would pour down his cheeks, down his forehead into his eyes. In fury, he would wipe his glasses on his shirt and keep sewing straight through lunch hour, interrupting the flow of work only to push a homemade onion-and-egg sandwich into his mouth. He seemed to be working against some kind of curse: when he ran out of pieces, he would scream for more, caught up in a kind of delirium. He was insatiable for work—and it was horrible to watch. Seeing him at home, listening to his complaints against my mother and the smallest of her expenditures, I had thought him unreasonable. Here, watching his race against time, I came to understand his thrift and preoccupation with money. It was difficult to believe that he had such energy—and shocking to discover that he actually loved his job.

I do not believe that my father ever left that room—even to go to the toilet—in all the years he worked there. The boss would walk through once in a while and whisper something to the foreman and Poppa would grow a third hand as the garments went flying into that great box. Certainly, he was the best worker they had. Though I had joined the ILGWU and paid dues in order to stamp buttonholes all day long, the lack of air drove me wild, and I would escape to the toilet air shaft.

Seeing my father at his machine broke my heart, but instead of working harder, for some mysterious reason—perhaps to spite his bosses—I goofed off completely. I was considered a bum who spent his time reading the newspaper in the bathroom; but with the help of the pinochle-playing union delegate, I lasted until the fall, when I reached another crossroad.

One of my cronies who stood in front of the candy store devouring charlotte russes, one of the beneficiaries of my singing, banjo-playing evenings under the boardwalk, was a guy named Cal, whose father was in the wholesale-grocery business and fairly well-to-do. The old man was giving a big wedding for a niece, and Cal invited me. Not only could I be a guest at this ritzy party, but his father, in search of entertainment, was willing —on Cal's recommendation—to pay me ten dollars to sing a few songs.

My salary at the sweatshop was twelve dollars for a long, asphyxiating week. Ten dollars to go to a party and sing a few songs! A combination of things prompted me to say yes this time: Bonelli that night at the Met, my father every day at the sweatshop, Mr. Margolis, and the confidence I had developed in my small repertoire. I now sang the "Donkey Serenade," "At the Balalaika," and "Chloe." That was my program. Now that I knew what my father went through to support us, I made up my mind to earn money the best way I knew how.

The affair was the first of a hundred I sang at. The engagement was a success and led to another wedding, then to an anniversary, then to a *bar mitzvah*—and suddenly I was no longer shy about singing publicly. Momma watched my progress with a smile, and Poppa could hardly be displeased with the money I was bringing home.

Mr. Margolis had added an eighteenth- and a nineteenth-century Italian composer to my increasing repertoire; like Stradella, they were good for my voice: Giovanni Pergolesi, who composed exquisite sacred music and several operas, and Umberto Giordano, who wrote *Andrea Chénier*. I've never stopped singing Pergolesi's "Nina cara mia bene."

Mr. Margolis' wife, Mary, taught me my first aria at this time, the "Largo al factotum" from *The Barber of Seville*, known more popularly by the name of the character who sings it—Figaro. I sometimes think that if Rossini had never written this opera, I'd still be in Bensonhurst imitating Bing Crosby. Never was there such a wedding as this marriage of Figaro and me. It became my trademark. The musical line, the sassiness of the character, the infectious, explosive patter of the rascally barber—the *recitativo secco*—is such a remarkable virtuoso piece, such a showcase for a display of vocal fireworks and coloratura technique, that I felt it was written for me. For a kid who stuttered, the almost impossible flow of rapid Italian dialogue eventually proved to be a cure for both my impediment and my shyness—which, after all, were fruit of the same tree.

Every day I gained more confidence in myself and in the future, The world didn't look half as dreary as it had just a short time before, and I attributed all the good things I was discovering to Mr. Margolis and the happiness I felt while singing—and earning money at it. Although I had been bitten by the opera bug that night in the Family Circle—and remain infected for the rest of my life—I had to eat.

Singing jobs came fairly frequently now. The "Donkey Serenade," with its "Senorita-donkey-sita-not-as-fleet-as-a-mosquita-but-so-sweet-like-my-chiquita-you're-the-one-for-me," always earned me applause and pats on the back in these hired halls. This pleased me no end, but I never missed a lesson with Mr. Margolis, who had moved from the Metropolitan Opera Building to Fifty-seventh Street near Carnegie Hall.

I had just finished a lesson one day at his new studio, when I bumped into a casual acquaintance. He told me that an audition for a summer job in the country was being given down the block at Steinway Hall. "If you rush you can make it. Some of those voices really stink!"

I raced to the studio, picked up some music, and ran to Steinway Hall. David Bines, artistic director for Scaroon Manor in the Adirondacks, was sitting there in his shirt sleeves and listening to singers with a bored look.

My heart pounded as I waited in line. Finally, I handed my music to the pianist. The whole room seemed to go around as my panic returned; but when the introduction was over and I began singing "At the Balalaika," I settled down.

Dave Bines' expression told me nothing as he wrote on a pad. "Do you know anything else, kid?" he asked casually.

"Yes s-s-sir. 'Donkey Serenade,' 'Chloe' and 'The Barber of Seville.'"

"You mean that thing, the 'Figaro,' that Tibbett does?"

"That's r-r-right, s-s-sir."

"Do you stutter, Miller?"

"Not when I'm s-s-singing, s-s-sir."

"Oh," he said absently. Then he looked directely at me and smiled. "It would make a helluva 'Figaro' if you did, wouldn't it?"

"Yes, sir."

"Okay, let's hear it."

"I don't have the m-m-music with m-m-me."

"Come back with it tomorrow, same time, same place, and we'll see, Miller. Next?"

I returned the next afternoon, sang "Figaro" and got the job. Two hundred and fifty dollars for twelve weeks in the green, beautiful country, high up in the mountains, plus room and board. Memories of my cousins' hotel and pitchers of cream and all the food you could eat filled my mind. I had the job! It was the first real competition I'd ever been in, and winning made me soar. I flew home to show the family my first contract.

Momma bit her lip at the news that I would be gone for three months, but she could hardly be displeased that her faith had been justified.

Poppa presided at the table, where we all sat eating grapes and examining the document. He wouldn't let it out of his hands and kept muttering from its text. ". . . do engage Merrill Miller as singer . . . twelve weeks from June twenty-fifth . . . sum of two hundred fifty dollars . . . inclusive of lodging . . ."

Over and over he repeated the lines, nodding his head. He seemed to be praying, *dahvening*. Poppa was very proud. "Moishe," he said, breaking his meditation. "You'll need a tuxedo with a white jacket, yet, with such hoity-toity. It's all right. It's an investment. Moe on Division Street on Sunday we'll go and we'll get."

"Thanks, Poppa."

"Gee whiz! You gonna be up in the mountains *all* summer?" my brother asked. "Do they have a lake?"

"Three months can be a lifetime," said my mother.

"He'll bring home two hundred and fifty dollars *clear*," said Poppa, ending the discussion.

By Sunday evening I had a pair of tuxedo pants with bell bottoms, a white jacket with Tony Canzoneri shoulder pads, and a matching bow tie, cummerbund, and feather carnation in deep maroon. With cuff links and studs by Swank, I felt I could have been on the cover of *Esquire*.

"Are your shoes supposed to be brown?" Gil asked.

My heart sank. There was no more money to spend, the only dress shoes I had were tan.

"Oh, no!" I yelled. "I'll look like a bum! I could die."

"You won't die, Moishe," Momma said. "But the shoes will. What's such a _megillah_, when every day people are dyeing one color to another? They'll look like Fred Astaire patent leather when I'm finished."

Scaroon Manor was owned by the Freebergs who also ran an excellent restaurant in Manhattan. It was there, in front of the Dubonnet on Forty-fifth Street right off Fifth Avenue, that I was to meet other members of the staff who were being driven up to Schroon Lake.

Manhattan at 6 A.M. is a breathtaker. As I turned north on Fifth Avenue, the city looked washed and flushed with the sunrise—ready for anything. The tall buildings seemed to be the outstretched arms of the island, yawning its last, waking to the excitement of the new day.

It's really the dawn of a new day for me, I thought, almost breaking into a run as I turned east on Forty-fifth. A job singing in the country, an escape from Brooklyn and my parents! My heart leaped again as I realized that I was in what *Variety* called "Show Biz," that I would actually be able to bring money home!

Mr. Margolis and I would take up where we left off in September; he was pleased with my progress, *very* pleased, he said.

I couldn't have missed my new colleagues if I tried; they were the only people on the street. They seemed bathed in a pink baby spot outside the restaurant, talking and laughing.

My God, they're complete strangers to me. I'm leaving home

*and going miles away among strangers. I'll be alone for the first
time.*

"Hi! Are you Miller? My name is West. West Moreland. I'm
your roommate, I think."

"Hi!"

"This is Florence Wyman and . . ."

Soon I was part of a chummy little circle with West, the tenor
from Texas; Florence, the vocalist; and six—count them—six chorus girls. Everybody's bags were on the curb, and I placed my
leatherette valise next to theirs. It was filled with my entire wardrobe: a tuxedo, a pair of sneakers, slacks, a sweater, a few shirts
and socks, and that was it. But my future couldn't have looked
rosier. It was in the bag.

My colleagues were warm and friendly and already beefing.

"Do they really think us *and* the bags can get into two cars?"

"Have you worked for them before? I never sat down last
summer."

"The money isn't bad—*if* they pay you. I ended up waiting table
at an enemy camp to work my way home."

But no one was really unhappy or even doubtful about the
summer. This cynical attitude was the supposedly "professional"
one, an immediate notice to the world that nothing would ever
catch "these babies" asleep. The idea that *I* might be stuck in
Lake George someplace both frightened and excited me. I was on
my own at last, and this was show business. Merrill Miller was
ready for anything.

It was a beautiful place, Scaroon Manor, and even my accommodations weren't bad. Behind the main building, near the
kitchen, there was a group of bungalows on stilts, and these
quarters were divided between the men and the women of the
staff. West and I were assigned to share a room; we unpacked and
immediately went to rehearsal.

The Fourth of July weekend was supposed to mark the season's
gala opening, but we gave indoor shows for the early guests from
the middle of June on. The formal extravaganzas were given outdoors in a big amphitheater. David Bines was an ambitious director, and for Red Skelton's guest appearance, which would open

the season, he was in the process of installing a revolving stage. Charlie Siegal, one of the electricians and stagehands who were building the stage, became a friend of mine, along with the Freebergs' nephew Rudy.

David Bines' wife, Cookie, was in charge of the girls and was our choreographer. Their shows were really ambitious. There were big production numbers like "I Love a Parade," with everybody in uniforms and waving flags of all nations but ending, of course, with a blaze of Old Glory, and "A Pretty Girl Is Like a Melody," which West sang while the chorus marched around the stage in elaborate costumes like Ziegfeld show girls. The changing of costumes backstage was new to me, and the nonchalance with which these kids ran around naked really upset me. My mother's warnings had seemed so pointless back in Bensonhurst.

"You're a good boy, Moishe. Don't get mixed up with any tramps —they're all *kourvahs* at those places in the mountains. They're filled with girls—cheap like onions. Pooh! Watch out. A girl like that can destroy the voice!"

Momma was under the impression that sex was the nation's number one killer.

"Who ever heard of a Jewish chorus girl?" she philosophized. "They're *shiksas* in the chorus. Pretty, who denies? But listen to your mother, Moishe—stick to your own kind."

"You mean Jewish boys, Momma?"

"You're not so big I can't smack you. It's not to laugh."

"I'm sorry. I was fooling."

"You're always fooling. Life's not a joke, mine big man of experience who's never been off the block! A fish out of water chokes and lands on a *milchedik* plate with parsley and a little lemon. Stick to your own," she warned, quickly adding, "but not too close. Who knows what type of *Jewish* girl goes up to the mountains by herself? A working girl, a secretary, maybe. You can trust them?"

"Confidential secretaries, Momma. Who can you trust more?"

"A mother you trust more! That's who! *Family!* The rest means *nothing.* You think I don't know what goes on? You think it's like the old country? There only a bum was a bum, and you recognized. A *bumikeh* you knew right away by her clothes, by her paint on the face. Here they fool you. For your information, they're all the same. Just do your work like a good boy and watch the step."

Her whole performance had been as unnecessary as it was transparent. I was still as bashful as the Disney dwarf and as pure as Snow White. I still got tongue-tied and knock-kneed if I looked at a girl—of any profession or any religion, saint or sinner. These chorus kids were dancers, and their casual attitude, their lack of modesty, embarrassed me.

The backstage flurry of naked bodies making quick changes shocked me into paralysis. Standing openmouthed, I didn't know where to look when they suddenly tore off their costumes, flailing their arms and legs. My popping eyes didn't know where to rest —but they learned. Every day I became less timid, and soon I adjusted to the permissive new environment. After all, my voice had attracted the girls for my buddies. Lots of malted had flowed under the boardwalk since then, and my buddies could go to hell. If the girls swooned over the romantic "At the Balalaika," they could fall in my direction for a change.

My mother's advice wasn't as academic as I had thought. The worm turned, and my timidity was displaced by cockiness: Scaroon Manor became my oyster, and there was even a girl named Pearl. Poor Momma would have had a conniption. I noted with a great deal of satisfaction that my voice remained unimpaired. It might very easily have improved at Scaroon Manor.

Scaroon Manor was a marvelous place. I danced and acted and helped with the scenery; I learned my trade there. The stage may have been outdoors and it may have starred burlesque comedians and musical-comedy players, but I learned how to feel at home in front of an audience. These weren't weddings. Performances on weekends were given for an audience of a thousand people. This wasn't some rustic little hideaway. There were seven hundred guests and three hundred people who paid admission to see the great weekend entertainments headed by stars from Broadway and Hollywood. Names like Eddie Cantor and Sophie Tucker drew them in, and the excellent productions brought them back for more.

Our first show starred Red Skelton. He was engaged for two

weeks, and I appeared in both shows with him as dancer and singer and eventually as his straight man. He had a very funny routine with donuts, and before our first performance, despite my three squares a day and midnight raids, I was so hungry that I ate his props. His expression, when he checked the table and discovered I had eaten them, was something that should have been recorded on film. After closing his eyes in utter disbelief, he examined me with a disgust that must have been difficult for a man as sweet as he. Fortunately, the kitchen was able to replenish the plate before the curtain went up.

I also worked as straight man for the Three Stooges and one night took a flying leap that tore the one sport jacket I owned. But my singing was going great. The first time I sang "Figaro" —which Eddie, the pianist, arranged for me—it was so successful that no matter the setting, the theme of the show, or the mood of the evening, I had to sing it every weekend. It became a ritual every Saturday night, like a bath. The audiences would yell, " 'Figaro!' 'Figaro!' " and I'd oblige. The barber was becoming my signature. My friend Charlie, the electrician, was as big a fan as I ever had up there. Every week, Charlie swore that I would sing at the Metropolitan someday. He was as sure of it as my mother, who came up to visit me.

I was now spending all my spare time with a dark and beautiful girl from Newark named Lola. In one of the fastest switches in history, I now fancied myself a lady-killer, and I couldn't understand Lola's reluctance to be killed. She was a doctor's daughter and very aloof. It was impossible to "score" with her; respect combined with attraction created a new sensation for me. Lola loved music and books and pictures, and I didn't know what she was talking about half the time. She was a cultivated young woman and always seemed cool and shiny, even in the middle of a blazing set of tennis. Lola always made me feel as if we were doing *The Princess and the Bellboy.*

When Momma came up to visit and the management put her up with one of the "*bumikehs*," she cased the joint; through her own radar, she sensed something. "So you met someone, Moishe? A nice girl, I hope. It's the dark one with the blue-and-white scarf? She's not a little ritzy, maybe?"

How in God's name she knew the wheat from the chaff, I'll never know; I had introduced her to *everyone* in the dining room that lunch hour.

"Not ritzy, Momma. Just too classy for me."

"Classy? What's classy? She's a schoolteacher?"

"She's just a lovely girl. She's still at school—at college. Her father's a doctor."

"A chiropodist?" Momma asked spitefully.

"A famous brain surgeon," I lied, already furious. "He's operated on many famous people—Queen Marie of Rumania and Georgie Jessel!"

"They were both crazy?"

"You don't operate when somebody's crazy!"

"You've learned so much about medicine with a doctor's girl? Maybe you should meet a baritone's daughter."

I was so enraged that I was sorry I had arranged her visit. I had more confidence here in this strange place than I had ever had at home. And the experience was mine, mine alone. Suddenly my mother was there, dominating the situation again. With her penetrating eye, she had already detected the one person who was upsetting me. She was already disapproving of someone I wasn't sure about. Just as her insistence that I sing when I really wanted to had driven me from it, in the same way she was now pushing me into Lola's arms.

I showed Momma around the whole place, and when I was free from work we spent time together. I walked with her along the lake shore; I took her to Saratoga for the races and the mineral water. She met all my friends, and I made every attempt to include her. But if—God forbid—someone asked me to play tennis or swim or hike or talk, Momma would materialize to stare at me in shock.

She also wanted very much to sing in the show and told me so. She had come to the country prepared with a whole Jessica Dragonette medley. But I was not the producer or the casting director, and I really didn't have the nerve to ask Dave. She did hang around backstage, though, which pleased her, and she met Eddie Cantor, which made it all worthwhile.

The morning of the day she was leaving, I was out on the lake

risking my life in a boat with Lola. Momma stood on the shore
like a lighthouse, its beacon aimed straight at us. No matter where
I rowed, her eye followed us like the path of a light on water.
Forced to row back, although she wasn't to leave until after
lunch, I was met with recriminations. How could I avoid her the
day she was leaving? I might never see her again as long as I
lived! And was I crazy to go out in a boat?

At last Momma left and returned to Brooklyn. The management
promptly subtracted forty dollars from my salary for her week's
vacation. I threatened to quit, and the Freebergs returned half
of it.

There was really no cause for complaint. They were wonderful
to me at the Manor, and the next year I was asked back and raised
to four hundred and fifty dollars for the summer.

After another year with Mr. Margolis, my voice was even
stronger, and Dave Bines got me a job singing on the SS. *Rotter-
dam*, a Dutch ship that was cruising the Bahamas for thirteen
glorious and golden days. In the middle of winter, I could lie in
the sun and swim outdoors!

As I stood at the stern of that immaculate ship and inhaled
deeply, it was impossible not to think of my mother, Gil, and the
weather-beaten tugboat captain floating like jetsam under the
Williamsburg Bridge, breathing in the stench of the garbage that
floated alongside us on the bottle-green opaque surface of the
choppy East River.

"Breathe in deep, singer mine! Look at the color in the sailor's
cheeks. Take a deep breath, *meine kind!* In! Out! In! Out!"

Her voice echoed through my head and was as clear as the rush
of water in the wake of the ship. Alone on the deck, with just sky
and water meeting in a circle all around me, with not another soul
in sight, it looked like the day of creation, and a surge of energy
made me sing into the wind like a madman. I sang the way a
small child starts to turn somersaults—for no apparent reason—just
because he's alive and young. My life was beginning to look as
golden as the day.

I returned home from the cruise brimming with well-being and
confidence. There was nothing I couldn't do. My shyness had
blossomed into arrogance.

Charlie Siegal got a job as an electrician at the Metropolitan Opera House, and he would sneak me up to the flies. There I would sit, my legs dangling a mile above the stage. My heart was in my mouth, but a plot was hatching in my head. All I could see was the tops of my idols' heads and their shoulders, but I could hear them: Flagstad and Melchior, Moore and Traubel, Kipnis and Albanese, Pinza and Milanov. I knew what I had to do.

Armed with dreams of glory, my arrangement of the "Largo al factotum," and all the cheek of a summer entertainer, I knew I could not fail. I decided to keep it a secret from Mr. Margolis and Momma—to surprise them with my triumph.

Professional to my fingertips, accustomed to winning competitions, I now entered the Metropolitan Opera Auditions of the Air. Easily qualifying for entrance by singing for Wilfred Pelletier in a small studio on the sixth floor of NBC, I smugly went on to the preliminaries—singing "Figaro."

Through records I had discovered Titta Ruffo. I worshiped him even above Bonelli and Tibbett. The great Ruffo had become my god—all the more secure in my adoration because he was beyond falling from grace; his genius was permanently engraved in the minds of opera buffs I knew and on my Red Seal Victors. His "Figaro" was electrifying in its power, vivacity, and glee. His apparent control of that wildly glorious voice drove me to imitation. I would give to the aria the same marvelously contagious fun that Titta Ruffo did on the record.

My performance was an outrage, and, of course, I never got to the semifinals. Totally unprepared, I showed not one bit of musicianship or discipline. Wit became slapstick; I threw my gift in their faces like a custard pie. Worst of all, I was again proven an amateur. Somewhere in the middle of my arrogant rendition, I heard what was happening, but it was impossible to dam the torrent. This wasn't the social hall of a country club where five minutes after my aria I would take a pratfall with the Three Stooges. This was an audition for the Metropolitan Opera House. I suddenly realized what I had done and wanted to cry.

It was my own fault, my own confusion. I'd never lost the urge to be Bing Crosby even as I dreamed of bringing Ruffo's thundering baritone back to the Met.

What nerve! I thought on the subway home to Brooklyn. *Even a comic refines his technique and polishes his act. What a perfectionist Skelton is. That's why he's an artist and you are nothing! As for Ruffo, he wouldn't have sung in the bathtub without more rehearsal. Who the hell do you think you are?*

With all the people interested in my career—Mr. and Mrs. Margolis, my mother—no one was able to keep me in line and properly direct all that energy I was expending. In the tryout for the big league, I had confidently strutted out onto the field and struck out. *Who the hell do you think you are?* Merrill Miller was still a snotnose, and that was the long and short of it.

CHAPTER EIGHT

QUITE APPROPRIATELY, I now auditioned for *Major Bowes' Amateur Hour* on radio and was paid ten dollars to sing "Figaro." I won the competition that night, and became a favorite of the old Major, whose gravelly voice was one of the most famous on the air and whose dewlaps gave him the benign, sad look of a St. Bernard.

I joined one of the Major Bowes Traveling Units and was sent on a three-week tour that took me to Fort Worth, San Antonio, Buffalo, and then a big finish in New York at the Roxy. This theater was still a showplace as a first-run movie palace with first-class live presentations. Comedian Jack Carter and ventriloquist Paul Winchell were on the bill with me. By the time this short tour—for which I was paid a hundred and seventy-five dollars a week—was over, I had relinquished my amateur standing forever.

Fanchon and Marco, producers who sent vaudeville units out from coast to coast, had their offices in the Roxy Theatre Building; and on the last day of my run, Sammy Rausch, their booking agent, came to my dressing room.

Sammy was a no-nonsense guy. "Miller, we need a 'Star-Spangled Banner.' We'll pay you a century note for one chorus. How about it?"

A hundred dollars for one stanza seemed most generous. The army had made me 4-F because of severe allergies, and I was glad to do *something*. "Fine. Where do I sing—at a bond rally?"

"Into a mike, kid. Easy as pie."

I recorded the national anthem—one chorus, it is true—and it was played in every single theater throughout the country. Since it was wartime, all the circuits added the two-minute patriotic reminder. It was certainly odd to hear myself everywhere I went. *Into a mike! Easy as pie.* True.

Sammy was so pleased that he signed me to a six-month contract, and within a few days I got a call for "something big." I ran all the way to the Roxy and those plush offices, and I was offered—and accepted—a week headlining in Philadelphia with Pinky Lee and the Roxyettes in a little red-white-and-blue production called *Hats Off to MacArthur*. They told me it was an important tribute to our recent hero of the Pacific. Rehearsals were to begin at 9:30 A.M. a week from that day.

Leaving Brooklyn at five in the morning, I arrived at the theater in Philadelphia and examined some of the signs that were stacked outside the lobby. A wide photograph of the line of Roxyettes, all dressed like Uncle Sam without pants, was leaning against a picture of me that was blown up and titled "Merrill Miller, the Star-Spangled Baritone." I saw a poster of Pinky Lee, but my eye was caught by something else that was leaning against the wall of the lobby. It was a life-size cutout of a naked girl with bright red hair that she could sit on, and she was doing just that. Her eyes were colored blue, and her skin was creamy white, which color combination, I gathered, was excuse enough to keep her state of undress from being treasonable. *It must be left over from last week,* I naïvely thought as the workmen started to put her name up in lights. Zonia Duval, stripper *extraordinaire,* was the real star of *Hats Off to MacArthur*. It should have been called *Everything Off for MacArthur*.

The theater was a fleabag, and when I went backstage, the cop barked, "Dressing room forty-four. Rehearsals in ten minutes." Forty-four was a filthy little room on the fourth floor. After I hung up my coat and hat on a nail in the room and left my valise, I took my music and went down to the stage. There I met the boys in the pit—six of the unhappiest musicians imaginable. The Roxyettes straggled in, and then I met Pinky Lee, who asked whether I would shill for him during his act. It was necessary that someone yell, "Be a Russian dancer! Do a Frenchman! What about Sweden?"

Miss Duval was nowhere to be seen at rehearsal; but that night when we opened, the audience was breathless for her. I looked out at the audience applauding for the lady. They hardly seemed like a patriotic group—they looked exactly like the audience at the Star Burlesque. There were servicemen, it was true, but looking very much at ease, and the rest of the orchestra was coatless and breathless. I soon saw why.

Every light on stage went on; there was a crash of music, and Zonia Duval, even larger than her life-size cutout, stepped out through a paper ring. Needless to say, she stopped the show with her uninhibited act. I was so stunned by her heroic proportions that I didn't hear my cue when she was finished, and I got tangled in her natural props as we collided in the wings. When I did get out onstage, it didn't matter, because they were still yelling for their favorite all through my "Figaro." It was obvious that I didn't have what it took to follow Zonia Duval, so I cut quickly to "Donkey Serenade," knowing that these guys would never have let me get through "Chloe" alive. I was learning my trade the hard way.

I had professional photographs taken; and it was as a professional entertainer, billed as Merrill Miller—"Songs as you like them"—that I got myself a live-wire club-date agent named, unbelievably enough, Mike Hammer. His cubbyhole office was in the Palace Theatre Building, and it was just large enough for a telephone and Mike, who was pretty small. He got me five or six jobs every weekend at five to ten dollars apiece, which was damned good money in those days. I averaged fifty to sixty dollars for the two days but had to move fast.

With Eddie's arrangements of "Balalaika," "Donkey Serenade," and "Figaro" tucked under my arm, I would do a banquet at the Hotel Astor on Forty-fifth Street, rush into the subway, sing at a wedding at the St. George in Brooklyn Heights, and then go back underground for the long trip to Flatbush and the swanky Château d'Or for an Italian wedding. Weddings, *bar mitzvahs*, birthdays, anniversaries! They were happy occasions for all of us, as long as I didn't think about the Met. Just before I left each job,

I was paid in cash; and on Monday mornings, I would meet Mike in front of the Palace, where the old vaudevillians hung out, and pay him his commissions.

Gil, by this time, was working at the Brooklyn Navy Yard. He bought a broken-down Ford, and now I paid him to drive me from one date to another. We had little time to eat at these functions, but we would stuff our pockets with food from the banquet table and eat on the way to the next engagement. On weekends, that Ford was piled high with smoked turkey, onion rolls, corned beef, coleslaw, pot roast, and hundreds of *schnecken,* Danish pastry, and cookies. Although I was no longer fat, I still ate for ten people and carried off what I wouldn't finish on the premises.

At this time I accepted my first synagogue engagement—in Bensonhurst. I sang my first solos for Yom Kippur and Rosh Hashanah, to Poppa's never-ending pleasure. The synagogue paid me three hundred dollars.

Oscar Julius, the choir leader, wrote and arranged these solos. He was a real taskmaster. It was he who taught me solfeggio, the art of sight-reading. To my busy schedule of club dates and lessons with Mr. Margolis, I now added a few sessions a week with Oscar in Bensonhurst. He was my third coach, since Mary Margolis, my teacher's wife, had taken great interest in my future and was helping me to build a repertoire. This petite Englishwoman had taught me the "Largo al factotum" and then the "Toreador Song" from *Carmen.* At this time, she was patiently engaged in teaching me the complete role of Germont in *La Traviata,* singing the Violetta so that I could learn my role properly.

At the time, I didn't realize what an exciting period that was for me. Moishe Miller was in the crucible; Robert Merrill was being molded. There was really nothing else on my mind but the drive forward, and I can never be grateful enough to the Margolises and Oscar Julius. When my energy was at its zenith, they were wise counselors who didn't allow me to neglect my studies.

The choir sang not only in Brooklyn but in synagogues throughout the area, and we often had to sleep out of town, our leader being given an allowance for our accommodations. The money was certainly not sufficient to put us up at the Ritz, but I remember one engagement when all twenty of us landed in a filthy Turkish bath and were given slabs to sleep on—like the morgue —and I half expected an identification tag to be pinned on my big toe and a sheet to be pulled over my head. It was so depressing that I got up during the night like a zombie and walked around town until I found a boardinghouse with a clean bed for one dollar. The choir thought it had lost its baritone, but I met them at the appointed synagogue, where the cantor was furious because I had so many solos. It was my first trouble with a tenor!

Poppa was amazed that my voice was not only paying the rent now but filling the cupboard as well. I wasn't exactly bringing home the bacon—but, all things considered, that was all right with the family too. Anyway, Mike Hammer was seeing to it that I sang for my supper and midnight snacks as well.

On Mondays when I went to his cubbyhole to pay him, I would have to fight my way through a mob on the sidewalk. Every midday, when the actors awoke, they would storm the gates of the Palace. Many a dethroned song-and-dance monarch held court outside as he waited for the royal edict to be posted that would announce the revival of vaudeville, the return of the old regime, and the subsequent revolution that would return him to glory. Some of these men were once headliners, some were still famous, and they would block pedestrian traffic in front of the Palace while they traded tales of woes and practical jokes and rumors of possible bookings.

It was there that I met the actor's *agent provocateur*, Prince among paupers, King of the Catskills: redheaded Charlie Rapp. My last twelve-week summer at Scaroon Manor had brought me four hundred and fifty dollars. Charlie Rapp now got me six hundred for only eight weeks at the Young's Gap Hotel. I was impressed.

Charlie Rapp was the live wire of the borscht circuit, but he almost blew my job with a short. Some agents don't work enough for their clients; Charlie worked too hard. With his flushed face and red hair, he always seemed to be ablaze.

The Young's Gap Hotel in Parksville, New York, was masterminded by "Ma" Holder, a dark, thickset woman with pince-nez glasses. She looked like an older version of my mother, and it seemed quite natural when I skipped off to avoid her watchful eye. We did three shows a week at the hotel, on Tuesday, Saturday, and Sunday; so on the other days, Charlie booked me, without Ma's knowledge, into other hotels nearby. It was moonlighting at its ugliest, but I really made money. Each extra performance I played brought in fifteen dollars a crack, and soon Charlie and I became drunk with power. It wasn't enough that we were getting away with murder; my agent now decided I could be at two places at the same time. Only the twin cantors could have competed with me that summer.

Charlie became smug with our success and our deception. He was beside himself, where I should have been. "Merrill, you are now going to see a real magic act. I'm going to double you!"

"Double me?"

"Kiddo, you are going to be in two places at the same time."

"You've blown your top, Charlie. It had to come, with all our running around."

Sacha, the accordion player who accompanied me on my furtive trips across the mountains, was a fat Russian with a green-black tuxedo that was never pressed once all summer. He was six feet three, with Slavic eyes and a sound philosophy. "Merrill, listen to me. I am a musician, but not for free. If you don't get paid good, you don't enjoy singing. Even my accordion won't stretch without money. If you can get paid in two places, you can sing twice as good, and that goes for my playing. What's the plan, Charlie?"

"It's as simple as ABC," Charlie insisted. "You open the show, Merrill, take your bow, and then disappear backstage. You're in the john or taking a breath of air or playing a hand of rummy or anything else Ma thinks. You can play a date across the mountain and be back in time for the finale. The MC says he'll cooperate. We're not breaking any law."

"Something tells me it's an unwritten one."

"The Eleventh Commandment is the most important one, Merrill."

"At last count there were ten."

"Uh-uh! Eleven!"

"All right—what is it?"

"Thou shalt not be found out."

"Amen."

Every Saturday and Sunday, with our smuggled music, the unholy three would speed to a rival hotel in our getaway car, do a couple of songs and sometimes a fast encore, and then race back for the photo finish. It was a miracle that we got away with it as long as we did. That summer, I brought home a thousand dollars and dazzled Poppa altogether.

After the shows at Parksville, the entertainers, like the waiters, had to mingle with the female guests. It was part of the job to dance with the single girls.

Ma Holder would give us our orders at her Thursday conferences in the social hall. Her husband never opened his mouth all summer; she ran the conclaves as if they were at Geneva or Versailles. Armed with notes on yellow lined paper, Ma would hand down edicts. "Merrill, Goldstein's daughter, *nebich*, is no beauty; but her room faces the sun and costs like she was Greeta Garba. You'll dance with her Saturday night till she falls exhausted."

I always got the ugly ones. "What happens, Ma, when *I'm* exhausted?"

"You are not a comedian, Merrill, but a singer. Joe, you got the Karp girl. And also the Horowitz niece—she's here on trial, and if she has a good time this weekend, she may stay all summer.

"Which one is Horowitz's niece?" the victim asked.

"The kinky blond with the fisheyes and the bad sunburn."

He moaned.

"Never mind. A little Noxema and a lot of attention. . . . You, Merrill, also have the Rottenberg girl with the eyes close together."

Always the beauties? That's the way it was written. Even without the moonlighting, I was kept hopping.

With all these extracurricular activities, it was easy to stay thin despite my intake of food. Ma set a good table. A hundred of them. That was one thing about these hotels, the food was always good and plentiful. I should say "almost always," because the next summer of my salad days I worked at the President Hotel at Swan Lake.

"My mother had a beautiful soprano voice. She was a woman born to sing and to die dissatisfied with her lot. But she never stopped trying, never stopped battling the Fates."

Dressed in a navy-blue suit —with my first long pants— just before the *bar mitzvah*. Gil, Momma, and Poppa arrayed behind me, ready for the festivities.

"Merrill Miller—Songs As You Like Them!"

"The winning tenor, Thomas Hayward, and I were presented by
Edward Johnson, handsome in striped trousers, morning coat, and
winged collar."

"If Wagner had known my mother, he would have written another *Ring*."

"I was doing so well that I was able to buy a house on Long Island and moved my parents and myself in after we burned all our old Brooklyn furniture."

"This is a great cast, and it's going to be a great picture." On the
set (with Moe Gale) of "the biggest bomb."

"I got two good tickets to the opening and took Claudette Colbert. We dined at Sherry's.... Claudette touched my hand gently, as if she had read my mind. 'You'll be back here, Bob. You'll see.'"

"I loved the kind of mass adulation I could get in the popular field. I still loved 'Show Biz.'"

"The front pages were filled with us. 'Baritone Robert Merrill and soprano Roberta Peters, the two young, rising stars of the Metropolitan Opera....Always in close harmony, the handsome couple plan a permanent duet.'"

"Now here I was about to appear with the stylish and beautiful Gladys Swarthout looking like a bum." (This photo was taken *before* I donned my costume!)

"The President's Margaret and I sang many duets, with Mr. Truman accompanying us or simply turning the pages if José Iturbi was at the piano. 'Thank you for being so sweet to my baby,' the President would say after I would sing with the delightful Margaret."

"Eisenhower! He made it possible for me—little Moishe Miller—to be driven up the Rhine in style—by an ex-Nazi. Life was really astonishing."

The President was owned by two gentlemen named Leschnick and Padolnick. Padolnick I met the first day I arrived and never saw again. He was evidently locked in the kitchen for eight solid weeks, making sure that no one ever got enough to eat. He counted out the peas. Three green peas on a solid white ground was the Padolnick coat of arms. The President Hotel was the perfect place to lose weight without trying. And while Padolnick slimmed you down, Leschnick oiled you up. He was the official greeter, the Grover Whalen of Swan Lake. He was very short, with his hair parted in the middle; he wore plus fours and black-and-white shoes, and he sounded exactly like Donald Duckstein. Completely ignorant of show business, Leschnick was, of course, the producer of the shows, the impresario.

Leschnick hired five musicians and turned them into a ten-piece orchestra by making them all double in brass. There were a pink and eager little pop singer and Johnny Howard, the MC, and a female impersonator who had one hundred beautiful costumes and was adored by all the women. He, in turn—which frightened me half to death—adored me for my deep voice. I was still just getting acquainted with the "Song of Songs," and any variation on the theme petrified me. Nonetheless, he and the rest of the staff were an excellent supporting cast for the guest stars.

Poor Leschnick! Charlie Rapp booked headliners in for the Swan Lake weekends, and when one of the stars arrived, our local Hurok regarded him suspiciously. "Who are you? Such a *lunga lukshen.*"

"I'm Hal Le Roy, Mr. Leschnick," the star answered with some amazement.

"Haller Roy! And what do you do, Haller?"

"I'm a dancer," Hal said, sure that he was being ribbed.

"A dancer? Where's your potnah?"

"Partner? I have no partner. I do a single."

"Who ever hoid a dancer vidout a potnah? Dis I never hoid."

Leschnick was used to tango acts named Lopez and Pepe, or Rosita and Gomez. They were always Spanish and did the rhumba; the girl always wore her black hair slickly painted to her head, with a bun; and the boy had Cuban heels, no hips, and black pants that buttoned under his chin. Those were dancers!

What was this skinny boy with the curly hair? Leschnick was furious at the "deception," but Charlie settled things, and, of course, the customers loved Le Roy. His success really surprised our producer. Leschnick and Padolnick! Klaw and Erlanger they weren't.

"Merrill, sing—you know, sing that song when you give the shaves all the time." "Figaro" again. It had become my middle name. By this time, every orchestra on peak or valley of the Catskills could fake an accompaniment.

It had started when some big sport at some club date yelled, "Twenty-five dollars if you'll do 'Figaro-Figaro-Figaro' for me!" I had quite understandably come to adore money. A quick word to the leader and we'd faked it. It was simple. Vamp in C, a chord in C major at my finish, and a round of applause. Rossini would have revolved in his grave.

My mother had taken a *kuchelehn* near the President Hotel for the rest of the family, and Gil used to drive Poppa up on Saturdays. *Kuchelehns* were small bungalows with cooking facilities that mushroomed around many borscht-belt hotels. They were inexpensive, and the *kuchelehners* arrived like migratory workers, with stoves and mattresses and extra bedding on the tops of cars, and settled like Okies in these shabby, hastily improvised communities.

The *kuchelehners,* of course, had none of the privileges of the hotel guests: they would hang around at a distance like tenant farmers surrounding a manor house; they would sit in the sun on camp chairs set on the one inch of soil surrounding their shacks. All the poor old people who would otherwise have spent the hot July and August days in front of their tenements on the Bronx or Brooklyn sidewalks, sitting in a line and commenting on their neighbors and the passersby, now spent a few weeks, if they were lucky enough to have sisters-in-law send them, in their *kuchelehns* dressed the same way—who had special summer clothes?—and doing the same thing, but the air was fresher and there were some pine trees.

Momma became friendly with a Turetzky family, who had the *kuchelehn* directly across the dirt path from hers, and Gil became interested in one of the daughters, a sweet and pretty girl named

Julia. Since she worked in the city, Gil and Poppa would bring her up with them on Saturdays so that she wouldn't have to take the train.

There were plenty of *kuchelehns*, so the people who lived in them had one another; but they were considered second-class citizens and looked down on by the *yentas* who rocked on the porch and were paying good money for their three meals a day, the hotel's facilities, and, most of all, the entertainment. When these fortunate ones saw strange faces at the social hall and realized that the *kuchelehn* mob was attending the shows, there was an uproar, and the hotel was forced to take action.

Leschnick and Padolnick were not to be made fools of; they had policemen guard against the invasion of the *kuchelehners*. Tickets to the shows were given out in the dining room to the bona fide guests of the hotel, and then their arms were stamped with a magic ink that could be detected only by a special light. This wise and dignified device was one of many desperate measures taken against the enemy.

In order to negotiate the trip from the *kuchelehn* to the hotel's social hall in the country darkness, the women needed flashlights. Without a flashlight, it was impossible to get around at all. The husbands who worked in New York and came up for Sundays would have valises filled with batteries; they were like gold to the *kuchelehn* housewife. However, the S.S. men, if they detected a telltale bulge in the purse or pocket, frisked the audience and, on finding a flashlight, immediately knew the owner was an interloper who had claimed that her brand had been erased through rubbing elbows with the high society. The crashers were then thrown out, but they were not so mortified that they would not gird themselves for another try the next week.

Momma, though a *kuchelehner,* was spared all this intrigue. At the President, I was secure enough to ask whether she could be in the show. Lillian Miller with her Polish songs was a sensation and a privileged character. Mother could even bring guests from her compound because she was such a success. The women would march in proudly, brandishing their searchlights, and outstare the entrenched, who would pull in their necks and knit furiously as they waited for the show to begin.

I moonlighted at the President too, using a window backstage for both exit and reentrance during the show. Again it worked beautifully—until the last week of the summer. I was climbing back through the window and had one knee on the sill, the other leg dangling, when I looked up straight into the smiling eyes of Leschnick.

"Vell! Good evening, mine boy. And vere haf you been flyink like Peter Pen?"

"I was just getting a breath of fresh air, Mr. Leschnick. It's so smoky inside."

"Vid your foot hanging? Maybe the air is fresher at my competitor?"

"What do you mean, Mr. Leschnick?" I asked, still balancing on the one knee, since he was barring my entry.

"Liar!" he screamed. "*Goniff!* Do you think Leschnick is a dope? So you're like the rest, never satisfied! I feed you, give you a roof over your head, and you're picking up ten dollars here and ten dollars there. *Mahmzer!* You should have five ungrateful sons. Now get inside for the finale or I'll make it yours. Go!"

He was really very kind.

I think I played every one of the hotels: the Nevele, Tamiment, the Laurel Country Club. They all blend into one another now and make a kind of crazy blur. I always had a room near the kitchen or behind a barn and would sleep late and grab myself some coffee and a Danish en route to the tennis court or a game of baseball with the guests. There was always an ugly girl whose father wanted a singer for a son-in-law and had the money to push my career or to have me set up in supermarkets or jewelry; always "Donkey Serenade," "Balalaika," and "Figaro"; always lots of work and play. I remember meeting and working with crazy Danny Kaye and rooming with Phil Foster one summer at, I believe, the Laurel.

And I'll never forget the Sunday nights at Ben Slutsky's Nevele. Ben Slutsky liked his Sunday nights serious; he brought culture to the Catskills every Sabbath. Regina Resnick was there too, and she seemed never to get out of her kimono or put down her fan. She was forever doing Madame Butterfly—that was *her* Figaro. Regina was always a great gal, and after our solo we sang our

Victor Herbert duet that always ended with "Sweethearts" and
the satisfied clucks of the old ladies. Those Sunday nights at the
Nevele! They prepared you for anything.

Those summers may sound like hard work, but my winters
made them look like paid vacations. For a kid who had been
too shy to open his mouth, I had gotten to the point where I
would now sing for anyone who would pay. It was essential that
I never again hear an argument about money at home. Having
tasted the applause of a knowing and large audience, and earned
my keep by doing it, I became a musical version of my father in
that sweatshop—begging for more piecework. My drive was
boundless—and, my mother's medical knowledge notwithstand-
ing, mine was obviously an iron constitution.

There was no singing job I wouldn't take, and several agents
saw to it that I never stopped. Charlie handled only the big
hotels, so I now had traffic with the cockroaches who infested
the Palace Theatre Building. These creatures would book their
own mothers in a stag show to make a buck, and what they would
do for their own flesh and blood they did for me.

"Say, kid, I caught you up at the Nevele. Great! How would
you like to play a smoker? Monday night, ten dollars; for fifteen
dollars, three songs—and all the grub you can eat after?"

All the fifteen-dollar jobs would add up, but not, it turned out,
to the sum paid out. Phil Silvers and I were often booked together. We would be paid separately, of course, so one wouldn't
know what the other was getting. The expression on the agent's
face implied a conspiracy between us that must not be revealed
to the other performer. For *you* and you *alone*, because he loved
the way you parted your hair, he was paying this much. I wondered why I was so lovable, and so did Phil, until we discovered
that our great admirer was a thief.

It all became clear one day when a club owner met me and
said, "You were great, kid, and worth every penny of the thirty-
five I paid you!" And the agent had even taken his percentage of
the fifteen and handed me thirteen dollars and fifty cents while
he kept the difference! Sometimes the *vahntz*—that bedbug—
would receive a hundred dollars for a few acts and then pay us
each behind the steps, playing one against the others so we

wouldn't add up our salaries to find the total was only forty or
fifty. These men were unbelievable, and against this exploitation
I had cards printed—"Merrill Miller, Bensonhurst 0640, Baritone
Available," etc.—and I got many of my own jobs.

There was one agent, though, whom I remember well. He was
a skinny little fellow with a waxed mustache and a freshly ironed
dirty collar and dickey-front shirt. A wet, half-chewed cigar dan-
gled from his shiny red lips.

He sidled up to me on Forty-seventh Street like a good-natured
streetwalker. "Hiya, kid. You gotta real pair a pipes. I heard you
sing. How about I represent you?"

I looked at him suspiciously. "Where's your office, Mac?"

His smile was engaging. He pointed to the pavement. "Right
here." He now pointed to his head. "It's what's here that counts,
right?"

"Right," I agreed.

"I've got a proposition, Miller. Let me take you to lunch."

Such largess was rare, and I figured he must be fairly legitimate, so I accepted his invitation to Chock Full O'Nuts. This
almost dapper little man ordered two coffees and removed a
paper bag from his overcoat. He unwrapped two large liverwurst
sandwiches on white bread, with mustard, and a pickle, which he
divided in half, squirting us both.

He spread the food on the counter, ignoring the disbelief on
the faces of the girls behind the counter. "Eat hearty, kid. I think
I gotta good deal for you. The Martinique is holding auditions
tomorrow for a singer—somebody with class, you know? Carlos
Ramirez just closed there, and I think I can pull this off. You're
the guy for the job. You're perfect. How about we give it a try?"

It sounded too good to be true: the Martinique was the Met of
nightclubs. If I couldn't have one world, maybe I could have the
other. I met my new agent in front of the Martinique on Fifty-
seventh Street the next day, then we went downstairs into the
club. The tables and chairs were stacked and there were a lot of
chorus kids sitting around in shorts. Busby Berkeley was rehearsing a dance step with a couple of kids; and Dario, the owner, sat
at a table going over notes, having coffee. After we were introduced, he asked me to audition, and clearing my throat and hand-

ing my arrangement over to the pianist, I broke into "Figaro." When I was finished, Dario yelled, "Bravo!" and my whole future hung in the balance. Then Busby Berkeley whispered something to Dario. The hushed conversation ended with my being thanked and dismissed. Dick Haymes got the job and I was brokenhearted.

When I complained to Mr. Margolis the next day at my lesson, he tried to comfort me. "But, Merrill, have you forgotten? You were meant for opera."

Little did he know that the opera world didn't want me. Now neither did the smart cafés. I was getting it from both directions.

CHAPTER NINE

IN RECOIL, I retreated to my own background. More summer jobs in the Catskills were in the offing. Then I also accepted a job singing weekends at a Jewish theater on Second Avenue. The impresario, who had heard me at some banquet, was instituting a vaudeville policy because the legitimate theater was on its last legs there. With stars like Moishe Oishe and Yetta Zwerling, he had sketches, comedy acts, chorus girls, and guest stars. With my mother's help, I translated my repertoire— you should have heard the "Toreador Song" and "Figaro" in Yiddish. Those weekends were a thrill to my family, who came every Saturday night.

Alexander Alshenetsky, the conductor, was quite young and dapper and a good musician, but he had embarked on a career that was more serious than that of a Japanese Kamikaze pilot. The Yiddish theater was filled with Jewish "ham," and every day was Judgment Day. Everyone was tragic, especially the comics, and temperament ran high. The self-absorption and the _tsimmis_ that was made over the smallest detail were incredible. They were all terribly funny, terribly talented, and quite wonderful—but every night was the end of the world. I lived through one whole season of those lost weekends with actors so actorish that Barrymore would have seemed like a TV repairman beside them. They were the biggest frogs in the smallest pond, and I seemed doomed to croak louder than any of them.

Then one Thanksgiving I went off to the Palace of the borscht circuit, Jenny Grossinger's. One evening a manager heard me sing the inevitable "Figaro" and asked me to his table.

His face was so kind, his look so penetrating that I felt he had known me for years and was already my best friend. "What are you doing here, Merrill? You're an artist."

No one had ever said that to me before. "I love to sing, sir, but I also love to eat."

"I love listening to you, and I love to eat too."

He handed me his card. "Come to my office when you get back to town. I've got a feeling about you."

There was something different about Moe Gale, and I felt it immediately: he was both an agent *and* a gentleman. I believed in him. When I returned to New York, I went to see him, and he welcomed me like his best client.

What a guy he was! In one day he had me auditioning with Mr. Margolis for H. Leopold Spitalny for the *NBC Concert Orchestra* program, and one week later I was singing "Figaro," "Songs My Mother Taught Me," and "Gypsy Love Song" on a national hookup—from coast to coast. This Mr. Gale was a man of action.

The initial broadcast went well, and I was immediately signed as a sustaining contract artist at ninety dollars a week, appearing on three fifteen-minute programs called *Serenade to America*. NBC, it seemed, had open time and a great orchestra that had to be put to work. It was a far cry from WFOX in Brooklyn. Singing with this orchestra, I had about the most exalted accompaniment possible. And Mr. Spitalny, whose brother Phil was noted for his all-girl orchestra, was one of the most important men in musical radio. He was orchestra contractor, which meant that even Toscanini himself, as maestro of the NBC Symphony, had to fire and hire through Spitalny as well as the musicians' union.

Spitalny was extremely short, with a long nose and even longer ears; he looked more bird than man and even waddled. His accent sounded exactly like that of radio's Mad Russian. He was also a man of infinite talent and energy, though he is best remembered for his eloquence. Even my Uncle Abe was a Winston Churchill beside this master of the English Language.

He was good to me from the outset, and on the first day he announced, "If you don't understand my directions, mark an X around it." Clarence Menser, an NBC vice-president, didn't think I was commercial enough, but Leo, bless him, and Samuel Chotzinoff, the network's music consultant who had okayed my original audition, insisted that I be kept on, and so I sang my four songs a program plus the theme, "Ma Belle," for many, many months.

Leo always knew what he wanted and trusted his own judgment. One day when he sent a messenger to the music library and the man returned with the wrong titles, Leo shouted, "The next time I send a jerk, I'll go myself!" And when the orchestra did not satisfy him at one rehearsal, he screamed, "I hov taught you everyting I know, and you know *notting!*" Then, topping himself, he added, "I vant only dee rhythm section. Now dee strings section. Now dee brass section. Aha! Dot's vot I taught! Tomorrow ve vill hov a special sexual rehearrrsal!"

Once, at a rehearsal, he spied a musician's chair—empty. He hated lateness and, in a tantrum, pointed to the seat and yelled, "And who, I vont to know, eez sitting in dot empty chair?" He had so much to do and so little time that he was always under tremendous pressure. On one program I began to sing "On the Road to Mandalay" and was amazed to hear the men under his direction playing the "Bolero." I yielded. But on another occasion, Mischa Mischakov, the concertmaster—now with the Detroit Symphony—pulled the men out and let *me* continue "One Night of Love" after they had already begun the "Poet and Peasant Overture."

Every St. Patrick's Day I did a special broadcast and sang "When Irish Eyes Are Smiling," which pleased everybody but Leo. "Merrill, you don't get dee Irish accent. Vot's dee motter? Eet should be 'Veed dee leelt of Irish loffter, you con hear dee ayngel's seeng.' "

What an angel *he* was. When his brother visited the studio one day, Leo shouted, "Pheel, how do you fil?" He was unbelievable; and I will always be grateful to him because I got my first commercial program through his faith and kindness.

It was a summer-replacement show, in which the composer Sigmund Romberg—whose *Student Prince, Desert Song,* and *Blossom Time* were standards—conducted his own music: *An Evening with Romberg.* They had been looking for a male singer, and good old Leo came through and arranged my audition for Romberg. Rommy not only paid me—through Pall Mall Cigarettes—seven hundred dollars a week, some jump from ninety, but became a special friend.

Rommy was a wonderful man. Kind and humorous and relaxed, he put me at ease immediately. At our first rehearsal, he smiled and said, "I'll start with you, Merrill, and finish with you, but what goes on in between is up to you." With his sympathetic approach and his confidence in me, what went on in between turned out fine. The programs were extremely successful; those were thirteen of the greatest weeks in my life.

I was extremely lucky to have Rommy take such an interest in my future. He brought me to his penthouse, and we had lunch outside in his garden, twenty-five stories above the streets of New York. We sat on a cloud, surrounded by privet hedges and marigolds and morning glories. It was too beautiful to be real, and I actually pinched myself. Rommy introduced me to a world of gracious living: the garden furniture, the shining crystal and china, the view of New York City, the French doors that led to his grand piano—the very piano on which he had composed his famous operettas and all the melodies that my mother used to sing over WEVD!

I learned about good food and fine clothes and the often questionable manners of the celebrated and accomplished. Not able and not trying to hide my excitement, my naïveté and enthusiasms evidently charmed Rommy, whose generosity increased. I was the kid with his nose pressed against the pastry-shop window. And what pastry shop surpassed the Viennese? His world was Demel's, and he saw to it that I was treated to a different confection every week. When it was my birthday, he gave me a party that made up for all the cakeless, giftless days of my childhood.

That night I stood on the terrace looking at all the lighted buildings, breathing deeply the clean spring air, and thanked God that I had met Moe Gale, who had started me off at NBC radio. He had refused to allow me any more club dates but forced me to quadruple my operatic studies with Mr. Margolis, Mary, and other coaches. I was counting my blessings. For a while now at home, our financial problems had faded. Poppa could relax, Momma buy whatever she wanted.

Rommy had put on a transcript of one of our programs, and my own voice drifted out to the terrace. A wave of satisfaction engulfed me.

"I said you didn't have to sing at your own birthday, but you'll forgive me for breaking a promise." It was Rommy's gentle voice. "An admirer of yours wants to meet you, Merrill," he continued.

My heart almost stopped when I turned around. Grace Moore was extending her hand to me. "Happy birthday, Mr. Miller. You have a beautiful voice, and that's the best gift of all." She raised her glass to my health.

I was dizzy with happiness. Miss Moore was a great star. She glittered, she sparkled. Having seen her not only in Rommy's *New Moon* and in the glamorous *One Night of Love* but at the Met as Charpentier's Louise and as Mimi in *La Bohème*, I had been her fan for years. Now I was standing on a penthouse terrace celebrating my birthday with a world-famous composer as my host and a great and beautiful diva complimenting me. It had to be a dream, but it wasn't. The stuttering, shy little Brooklyn schnook was clinking champagne glasses with Grace Moore!

The year was 1944. So many things happened during the next twelve months that it is impossible to disentangle them. It was a crucial time for me. At a Red Cross benefit rehearsal, Mark Warnow, who conducted the *Hit Parade*, looked at me and said, "I can't stand your name, kid. It doesn't fit you. You look like a Bob to me. When I introduce you, what about, 'And now—Robert Merrill'?" Robert Merrill it became.

Mark Warnow christened me, and Grace Moore again launched me. At dress rehearsal on the Sunday before the Red Cross show, I sang "Figaro." We were all holding scripts, and when

I finished, Miss Moore threw hers to the floor in what seemed a temperatmental outburst. Everyone looked at her in astonishment, and I was sure that I had done something terrible.

"Young man," she announced, "you are going to be one of the greats at the Met!"

She was carried away, and it was lovely to hear, but I couldn't tell her that the powers that be disagreed and that I had already failed the audition. Nevertheless, it was gratifying that someone of her experience and standards believed in me.

Shortly after this, I sang my first solo at Lewisohn Stadium, with Rommy and the Philharmonic Orchestra, and again I was in a nervous sweat. But Rommy saved me. We'd had a beer before the concert, and now as he lifted his baton—and I prepared to sing or breathe my last—he changed his mind, dropped the stick, and said, "Oh, let's have another beer." After that, it was a cinch.

Erno Rappé, having heard my record of the national anthem, now engaged me for the Radio City Music Hall. For one hundred and seventy-five dollars a week, I did four shows a day and five on weekends. And I managed to work this in with my three NBC broadcasts a week.

I had to be at my first rehearsal on that mammoth stage at 8 A.M. It looked like an airplane hangar. You had to travel a mile to center stage and back, which forced every artist who appeared there, whatever his age or prestige, to run on and off like a racehorse. Backstage was a city—a self-sufficient metropolis with its own hospital and restaurants. It had everything but a post office.

We would rehearse the next production between shows, and I soon learned why the theater had its own hospital. The poor Rockettes were in perpetual motion, always rehearsing or performing. It was like a curse. I would have lost my mind, but the girls stayed in good spirits—and certainly in excellent shape. They were the real stars of the show, week after week, year after year. When they stood in a straight line—after rejoining one another at the end of some intricate bit of choreography—and the footlights and white borders lit them as they did their famous precision kicks, the audience would go wild.

My first trip to the Music Hall had been during its opening week some years before. Titta Ruffo had been announced, and Paul Richards—an old friend and fellow singing student—joined me in line so that we could hear Ruffo do the "Toreador Song." Paul and I had stood together at the Met, at the Hippodrome, at the Academy of Music; this time we waited for twenty hours and still didn't get in. We then decided to wait for the second show, but it was too late. The great Ruffo had lost his voice, was replaced, and never again sang publicly. So I was never able to hear my great idol in person. It seemed odd that I was now singing on that very stage myself.

What fantastic shows were thrown together in that Music Hall! When executives would come down to the auditorium to watch a rehearsal, Leon Leonidoff, the producer, and Erno Rappé, the conductor, would scream at each other: "Pig!" "Peasant!" But after the bosses left, shaking their heads at the travail of geniuses, Leon and Erno would embrace each other. They had played that scene just to prove that they were working hard.

Well, for a lazy guy, I was working myself into a very thin young man. Moe Gale had blown poverty away for good. And it had all been so fast! Now I did the *Prudential Life Insurance Hour* and a Chrysler program with Morton Gould. Robert Merrill was a name in radio, and doing quite well. Then RCA Victor came through.

Constance Hope, who was head of artists at Red Seal Records, called me to meet her at the Russian Tea Room, next door to Carnegie Hall. Would I be interested in doing an album of the musical comedy *Up in Central Park* with Jeannette MacDonald? They were willing to pay a hundred dollars a side. I was very interested, and I made an appointment to meet Miss MacDonald at a rehearsal hall on Fifty-seventh Street.

At the appointed hour, Robert Russell Bennett and Macklin Marrow were there, but the movie star was not. I was nervous again, in awe of meeting so great a name, a shadow I had watched at the Republic movie theater, someone impossible for the likes of me to ever know.

Miss MacDonald burst into the studio breathless. Fans had

spotted and surrounded her in the street, and she had run all the way from Sixth Avenue. I took one look at her and I too was breathless. She was a great beauty, a vision with that auburn hair, those emerald eyes, and that exquisite skin. Vivacious and sympathetic, she made me feel quite secure—even after I was told that I had to learn three solos and three duets in three days' time.

Every new job is a mountain for me to climb. I'm almost always sure that I can never do it in time, and I live in terror until the moment of delivery. On the day we recorded, Miss MacDonald stood facing the conductor and I, quite properly, stood facing her. She was a gorgeous sight in that royal-blue outfit, but I was unsure of the score and would have preferred to watch the conductor. This lovely star, who was supposedly a holy terror, sensed my insecurity and, in a move that was miraculous for a prima donna, suggested that we reverse positions so that I could see Mr. Bennett. Her back was now to the orchestra. It was one of the kindest and most unprecedented gestures I have ever seen—and from a soprano! Yes, she was prima donna in the purest sense.

Moe Gale constantly prodded me to self-improvement. Besides continuing my studies with the Margolises and Oscar Julius and taking professional engagements, I was now being coached by others as well. I was learning a few operatic roles, and I worked with a descendant of the great Bellini. This wild and adorable little Italian spoke broken English with a cutting edge. He would say, "No! No! I want it more—what can I say? Yes—potato chip!" I would know immediately what he meant because his hands would break the imaginary chip. "*Si*, Merrill! *Si*, crisp!"

Suddenly—seemingly out of nowhere—through an agent named Michael de Pace, whom Moe Gale knew, I was engaged to sing Amonasro in *Aida*, my first opera. It was in Newark, New Jersey, and paid two hundred and fifty dollars for the one performance. Produced by an independent company, the opera starred Giovanni Martinelli and a soprano named Gertrude Ribler. I was thrilled at the opportunity to appear with the great tenor, who was extremely kind to me.

The production was thrown together, and only Martinelli's flair and sense of drama made the opera go well in that auditorium. His energy made the performance exciting. Well coached for the role, I did all right vocally, but my acting wouldn't have won any awards. That I survived the evening's nerves without a breakdown or a heart attack was a triumph in itself. My family traveled to New Jersey, of course, taking up half the auditorium. To them, I was a sensation.

Signor Martinelli must have been pleased, because he asked for me again, this time to appear as Tonio to his Pagliacci, in Worcester, Massachusetts. Ethel Barrymore Colt, daughter of Ethel, was the Nedda. These out-of-town productions were never sufficiently rehearsed, if they were rehearsed at all—and when I stepped through the curtain to sing "Si puo?" I discovered that there was no space between the curtain and the pit, and I almost joined the orchestra. I grabbed the curtain just in time, and since I was dressed as a clown, the audience thought I was being funny. I almost broke my neck. Unbelievable!

Despite this, the night went well, and I had two operatic roles under my belt. Now, De Pace booked me for a performance in Hartford, Connecticut, as Escamillo to Gladys Swarthout's Carmen. Miss Swarthout was one of opera's great beauties, as well as a fine mezzo-soprano. Her brush with Hollywood had made her a glamorous international star, and I must admit that the prospect of being her leading man excited me.

I was filled with all sorts of fantasies as I went off to the Stivanello Costumers. Stivanello's had a fifty-year backlog of scenery and costumes that they supplied to pickup companies. It was a dusty, dirty barn of a place, filled to the rafters with doublets and tunics and robes of every period. I searched with one of the men for what I wanted, and at last we came up with a satin toreador costume plus hose, shoes, and hat. It was a shabby outfit, but there was no choice: the only other costume near my size was Wotan's from *Die Walküre*—hardly a suitable substitute. After I was fitted for the alterations, they promised to send the costume by evening.

Off I went to the orchestra rehearsal, my heart beating expectantly at the prospect of meeting Miss Swarthout. I was kept in suspense because she never showed up for the rehearsal; we didn't even run through the whole opera.

A half hour before the performance, I found myself, bewildered and undressed, all made up and no place to go. At last the costume arrived—in disgraceful condition. The fit was outrageous, the hat sat down over my ears, and the shoes had been forgotten completely. I looked awful, like anything but the dashing, authoritative Escamillo.

Looking at myself in the glass, I couldn't think of a thing I could do to improve myself; I was miserable. I had been making money during the last couple of years and buying a lot of clothes, and by this time I felt that I was a pretty sharp little dresser. Now here I was about to appear with the stylish and beautiful Gladys Swarthout looking like a bum. My own gum-soled brown sport shoes hastily completed my appointments.

A knock on the door interrupted my nightmare.

"Mr. Merrill, Miss Swarthout would like to see you."

Miss Swarthout could not believe what she saw standing behind her through her mirror. She wheeled around, that gorgeous woman, and her jaw hung. "No!" she shouted. "No! *This* is my *Escamillo?* Oh, God, no! It will be a scandal! Oh, no, no!"

This was our first meeting. I stood there—a Judeo-Spanish ragamuffin with a safety pin bunching the satin pants under my rotting cummerbund, newspaper stuffed in my toreador hat, and big brown sport shoes that made my legs and ankles look absurdly skinny. And *I* was supposed to inflame the heart of Carmen!

It was a joke. There has never been a tackier looking nebbish. It's a wonder that Swarthout went on, but she did. And after the chorus heralded the handsome, dashing idol of all Granada and I made my entrance, damned if she didn't look at me as if I were Tyrone Power! She showed such fascination and such passion and was in every way so considerate to me as a fellow performer that it was hard to remember her cries of "No! No! Oh, God, no!" She was truly a marvelous actress.

It is one of the miracles of the age that the performance earned us both bravos and excellent reviews. Reminiscing at her home in Florence years later, we were vastly amused; at the time, it was ghastly.

A one-night performance as Valentin in *Faust*, with Mario Berini, a tenor from California, playing the lead, completed my quartet of operatic roles. With each performance, I had gained more confidence, and Moe Gale hinted that I might now be ready to try for the Met again.

My mother, recovering from the shock of Gil's impending marriage to Julia Turetzky, agreed wholeheartedly. Hardly an impartial judge, she was down to one son, and *he* was going to fulfill her destiny or she'd know the reason why. *This* son she still owned.

We were having supper when Gil first announced his intention of marrying Julia, and my mother was hard put to find an objection. She was friendly with the Turetzky family and was fond of Julia. Extremely intelligent as well as attractive, Julia was one of New York's youngest schoolteachers. Gil had hit the jackpot, and Momma was thrown for a loss. Somehow it hadn't occurred to her that the kids were serious about each other. Gidalia getting married?

"Congratulations!" I yelled, slapping my kid brother on the back.

Poppa glowed. "Happy I am, Gidalia. Surprised, no! I could see. She's a wonderful girl."

"You love her?" Momma asked suspiciously.

"Of course, Momma. That's why I asked her to . . ."

"No speeches! I asked a simple question."

"And I'm answering. Yes!"

"And she loves you?"

Gil now glowed. "I think so."

"He *thinks* so."

"Well, it's not for me to say, Mom."

"So who should say?"

"Ask Julia."

"A stranger I should ask?"

"A stranger? Julia! Of course she loves me. We love each other—very much."

She now helped Gil to more mashed potatoes, tapping the spoon on his plate to make sure he got all there was on it.

"You're not too young, maybe?"

"No, we're not too young maybe," Gil answered.

"And when you do this thing, you'll move away?"

"Well, that's the usual thing, Momma."

My mother now looked at my father. "The usual thing. America!"

My father refused to be her conspirator. "We stayed in Poland with your parents?"

"Momma," Gil interrupted. "We'll see you. We're not going to another country or even another city."

"Hmm!" my mother answered. She was obviously trying to find something wrong with Julia, something that would prove the forthcoming marriage a dreadful mistake, something that would open her son's eyes to the coming tragedy. Her resources were boundless, and I watched fascinated and silent.

She now slapped her thigh, shook her head, and reached down to the bottom of the barrel. "I don't understand how a big boy like you, Gidalia, wants to marry a little girl like that—so tiny and short and everything."

That was the best Momma could do under the circumstances. Gil could always handle our mother far better than I could. "Julia is not a dwarf, Momma."

"A dwarf I didn't say, and never repeat that I said that. I never said a dwarf. Abe! Moishe! Did you hear me say a dwarf? 'Tiny' I said, and tiny she is."

"Good!" Gil answered. "I love her the way she is."

"You love a tiny girl—so small?"

Now I joined the act. It was impossible to stay out of it.

"Momma, you're making the girl sound like some kind of freak. I think she's very pretty. Her eyes are gorgeous."

"What is the *tsimmis?*" Poppa now added. "The girl is of normal height. A *schoene madele*. What is this nonsense about short?"

"Don't start, Abe," Momma lashed out. "You aren't tiny also? I didn't marry a man smaller than me?"

My mother was hysterical, but Poppa outshouted her. "So

why didn't you use your father's tape measure and we'd all be at peace today? Fly Gidalia! The girl is sweet like sugar. Have *mahzel.*"

"Thank you, Poppa."

Gil and his mate flew happily from the nest I was beginning to feather. It was inevitable from the beginning that Gil would escape first; I envied him. Julia was delightful, attractive, and sweet, and she obviously adored him. She roared with laughter every time he opened his mouth; though Gil has always had a fine sense of humor and a quick wit, nobody could possibly be that funny! Their romance had been plain to everyone but my mother. She had been diverted by my success in radio, and the new furniture and drapes and clothes, symbols of her rise in the world.

Yes, my brother was loved and in love, and soon he was on his own. I certainly envied him. But with broadcasts and out-of-town operas, I was having the time of my life. Add to that my teachers and coaches and there was no time to fall in love. A dozen girls take less time than one, and I was a guy who was going someplace and didn't have any time to waste. Gil's obviously ideal marriage gave me a twinge once in a while, but my trip to the top of the world had to be taken alone, with no ropes, no strings, no baggage. Anyway, I wanted to be loved not by just one person but by everybody.

Through my radio work in general and Mr. Gale specifically, I came to the attention of Marks Levine, who ran the National Concerts and Artists Corporation, the largest of such bookers in the country. He made it possible for me to win an entirely new audience. Levine had pioneered this field with Freddie Schang of Columbia Concerts, and he told me that he would launch me on a concert career modeled after those of Ezio Pinza and John Charles Thomas.

These amazing agents had gone into the hinterlands and, by themselves, had organized small towns to sell good music to their citizens—in the name of culture. The small price it cost the public was used simply to hire a hall and pay the visiting artist. Local governments were satisfied that they had brought music to their town; and as this method created an endless amount of appearances that guaranteed the artist slowly rising fees, it was an ingenious idea. A whole new audience for fine music was unearthed, and even the greatest stars became available.

During my first season, I was paying transportation for myself and my accompanist out of the two hundred dollars I received for each appearance. Fifteen such engagements grossed me three thousand dollars and priceless barnstorming experience. I was building a concert repertoire, singing groups of French and Italian songs, plus German lieder—a career in itself—not to mention the songs of Americans like MacDowell and Kern, and Negro spirituals.

I worked like a dog that season, making my first trip to the South—Birmingham to be exact—where I was introduced to the race problem, which I had always believed to be a Jewish one. There was much for me to learn. My people were lucky. This was the largest ghetto in the world, and money couldn't get you out of it.

Mr. Margolis had managed to find me an accompanist, one Freddie Maranz, who wore thick-lensed, shell-rimmed glasses and was twenty-two years old. A sensitive, retiring boy, he made me seem, by contrast, a commando in action. Poor Freddie began to suffer as soon as he got into that upper berth on the way to Birmingham, and he whined all night. In the morning, when I pulled his curtains apart to wake him, I thought he was dead: he was staring out of the window wide-eyed, his neck so stiff he couldn't turn. A dear boy, he was truly what my mother called a nebbish, doomed to be mistreated, fated always to get the short end of the stick, the south end of the chicken—and the upper berth.

A local committeeman met us at the train and transported us to a hotel, where we were given a three-and-a-half-room suite. Freddie's father had had a stationery store with gambling in the back and had saved all his money to send his son to Paris to study music. Freddie, when he was home, lived with his now widowed mother and practiced piano twenty hours a day. He was a sweet kid and a beautiful pianist, but his life had been incredibly circumscribed.

When we ordered breakfast, Freddie ordered ice cream.

"If you like ice cream so much, fine. Have it for dessert, although I never heard of it for breakfast. But what do you want first? Before it?"

"I just want ice cream, Mr. Merrill."

"I told you to call me Bob. Freddie, listen to me. It's nine o'clock in the morning. I know you didn't sleep. But it's morning. Don't you want some orange juice? Some bacon and eggs and coffee? Maybe some rolls?" I was making myself ravenous.

Freddie turned his whole body to look at me, his neck was so stiff. "No, thank you, Mr. Merrill. I just want ice cream. That's what I want. I love ice cream."

"So I gather."

He ate nothing but ice cream for the whole tour. If it was some special diet prescribed for some mysterious musical or dietary reason, he never told me.

Freddie had an old pair of tails handed down from his father that were vaguely green and most decidedly shiny. Now that I was a big shot, I had a set of tails from Hickey-Freeman, so I was feeling very superior when I fixed his collar and tie. In my own room, the night of our first performance, I appraised myself in the mirror and prepared to leave.

"Mr. Merrill? Could you come in here? I have a problem."

Among other things, Freddie had a hernia and wore a truss. He had now, somehow, just lost a screw from it.

"It's on the floor someplace, Mr. Merrill."

It was ridiculous being called Mr. Merrill, and it was ridiculous to be on my hands and knees under the bed, where I finally found the damned screw.

"Here you are, Freddie. Now, come on. We're due at the Baptist Church at eight."

"I'm in terrible pain, Mr. Merrill."

"Bob."

"What?"

"Where?"

"I said *what*."

"I said *where*."

Freddie started to whine again and then moan.

"Where is the pain, Freddie?"

"Where my hernia is. This thing may fall off. Can you screw it in, please?"

"I'll try, Freddie, if you'll *please* call me Bob."

"All right, Mr. Merrill."

Seven hundred people were extremely receptive to our offering of Schubert, Brahms, and "Figaro." We encored with Negro spirituals, which went beautifully. They loved it. Freddie was a superb pianist and a lousy accompanist, but we managed to finish together. Considering the hernia and the loose screw, it had gone well. We were now invited home by the chairman of the committee to meet the workers who had arranged the details of the concert. It was sad to see platters of tiny crustless sandwiches. There were fifty people in that house, and I lost Freddie. When I finally found him, he was sitting with a motherly woman who was feeding him ice cream. He couldn't have been happier.

Those were the early years. Today, communities have budgets that are so tremendous that they can afford the Boston Symphony and me as well. Some of these concerts are put on by local impresarios who offer a sixty-forty deal—a fee and a percentage. It has become a multimillion-dollar business from which everyone profits—from Columbia, with whom I now work exclusively, to the small-town music lover, who is exposed to the finest orchestra, instrumentalists, and singers in the world.

Everything has changed. Freddie, with his enormous capacity for ice cream and his outsized hands, became a superb harpsichordist; but I, with a series of accompanists from John Charles Thomas' trusted Carroll Hollister to the great Eugene Bossart, still roam the land, forewarning hostesses of my appetite so that I no longer have to endure tea sandwiches.

I never have anything but a little broiled fish or chicken before a concert, but afterward I adore raiding a stuffed icebox. Feasts are commonplace now, but I prefer a steak and salad in somebody's kitchen, where I won't be disturbed by all the local Pagliaccis—the usual price for these late snacks.

One night as I was sailing through a fine sirloin, my jaw froze in horror as I heard the "Prologue." It was simply awful.

That night, I unwillingly auditioned ten singers, and they were
all terrible.

On occasion, young singers do sound good, but, unlike Tibbett
or Thomas, I do not believe in telling them to come on to New
York and then never do anything about them. I always keep
my mouth shut, and when I am forced to say something to a
talented kid, I ask whether he is willing to invest six years of
his life in constant study. In that time, he could become an
excellent dentist.

Phony encouragement has broken too many hearts and purses.
I've never understood the glib advice that some of my colleagues
give to these kids. Nor for that matter do I understand some of
their parents. On one tour, a woman actually came to my hotel
room and offered herself to me if I would audition her daughter.
I was shocked and appalled by her cold-bloodedness.

As I well know, there is nothing stronger than a mother's
ambition for her child. Certainly I understood her drive, if not
the particular direction it was taking. She was such a desperate
woman, this mother; it was obscene, but it was understandable.

Returning from that first concert tour, I was a wiser young
man for my experience. With all the money and popularity I
was gaining on radio, the public's response to fine music in these
small towns was most gratifying. The growing audiences and
the adulation made me wonder. Yes, Gil may have married a
wonderful girl, but maybe that wasn't meant for me. Maybe
living without love was the price I'd have to pay for my career.
Instead of trying to win fair ladies with candy and flowers, I
now renewed my romance with the Metropolitan.

Moe Gale insisted—despite my fears—that I was ready for
another try. My failure still stuck in my craw—after all that
time. Not a month, a week, or a day had passed without the
same dull ache that had followed my rejection years before. No
one knew what I was living with—no one but Moe Gale. With
his encouragement, my hair slicked down, and my gifts, such
as they were, this time polished and gleaming, my courtship
was now dead serious. Who was I kidding? *This* was the love
of my life, and this time I was going to win my suit.

CHAPTER TEN

THE METROPOLITAN OPERA Auditions of the Air again welcomed me as a contestant, and this time I felt quite at home at NBC's Studio 8-H, where I was still broadcasting three times a week. Milton Cross, who had been a tenor and had studied with Mr. Margolis, was our announcer; and Edward Johnson, general manager of the Met, presented each one of us. There was a series of three broadcasts, during which the weeding out took place.

Just to be accepted in this competition was a stamp of approval from the highest judges in the opera world, but I had been there before. So I tried to cushion myself against the shock of another failure with the reminder that both Risë Stevens and Richard Tucker had been disqualified at different times in other semifinals but still had made the roster of the Met.

For this second try at the auditions, I sang a vital but disciplined "Figaro" and the beautiful "Nemico della patria" from *Andrea Chénier*. At the final broadcast, with just a few of us left, I sang Iago's "Credo" from *Otello*. This aria clinched it.

Momma hadn't pulled my ears and spit all over me for nothing that morning. "Laugh, singer mine; smarter men than you had their mothers pull their ears and spit at them. Everything helps, and we'll see who laughs last."

She did! We both did! I was on top of the world. It might have been voodoo, but I know that Mr. and Mrs. Margolis,

Signor Bellini, and Moe Gale backed her up. I may have sung the melody, but with this quintet as my background, it was impossible for me to fail.

Wave after wave of happiness poured over me. In my mind, like a long shot in a movie, I saw door after door opening to me, as far as the eye could see; and somewhere at the end, rays of light and some kind of formless ecstasy. There would be no end of triumphs and money, and once and for all my family would be completely secure. My labors had not been in vain. The seeds had been sown, and now I would enjoy the harvest. The Metropolitan Opera! The prize for winning this contest was not just prestige and money; this was, after all, an audition, and winning brought the greatest prize of all: a contract with the greatest opera house in the world.

The winning tenor, Thomas Hayward, and I were announced and presented to the public on a radio broadcast from the Metropolitan stage. Bigwigs of the Sherwin-Williams Paint Company, which sponsored the auditions, famous artists of the opera, important managers and agents of the international theater world, and my family, dressed to kill, sat in the audience as Edward Johnson, handsome in striped trousers, morning coat, and wing collar, announced with very rolled *r*'s, "And now, from Brrrooklyn—Mr. Robert Merrrrrrill, singing the winning arrria . . ."

I sang the first four bars from the wings and then walked out onto the Met stage for the first time. I was greeted and introduced to the public as the newest member of the opera company. There was great applause, and down front I saw my mother applauding with her hands above her head like a fighter—which she was. Poppa, still recuperating from a recent attack of diabetes, was beaming and nodding his head; and Gil and Julia were clapping wildly.

What a wonderful moment in my life that was! To be on the threshold, the beginning of everything—when nothing is impossible and everyone you love is still alive and loving you. How safe and beautiful! I was really such a lucky boy: standing there in my Howard suit with supersonic lapels, my loud tie, a white carnation in my buttonhole, with a check from Sherwin-

Williams—God bless them—for one thousand dollars and, wonder of wonders, a contract to sing at the Metropolitan Opera
House.

Tommy Hayward and I, after receiving our awards and con-
tracts and applause, now sang "Del tiempo al limitar" from
The Pearl Fishers. His tenor was beautiful; and though our
voices were blending splendidly, we began hipping each other
out of mike range! Instinctively, each of us had recognized his
natural enemy and fallen into the pattern. It was a scream!
There's one thing that no fledgling baritone has to be taught—
sensitivity to the bright, sunny tenor. In turn, the tenor has
a built-in radar that can detect a baritone's dark, moonlit approach a mile away. They become staunch allies only in their
mutual distrust of the soprano, who despises them both. The
conductor detests *all* singers, and the composer hates everyone.
This was the glorious and divine world I was happily entering
for the rest of my life. As far as I was concerned, it was a world
peopled by gods—made in man's image, to be sure, but much,
much larger than life.

After the presentations, there was a huge champagne reception
at Sherry's, the restaurant of the opera, the anteroom of
Valhalla. In my blue suit, surrounded by Momma, very formal
in black, and Poppa in a dark suit, I felt once again like a
bar mitzvah boy—only, this time, happy. I didn't need any
champagne; I was already drunk.

In the blur that followed I remember Lawrence Tibbett
congratulating me. "I've got to watch my step now, with a
baritone like you around the place."

Could I be hearing correctly? I thought.

"*Allora, mio Tonio!* So! Didn't I tell you? *Benveduto,* Roberto.
I hope we work together soon."

Signor Martinelli!

"No! No! No! Could that be my Escamillo?—I *hope.*"

I turned and stared into the beautiful and laughing face of
Gladys Swarthout Chapman. "He's the one I told you about,"
she said to her husband, who was also a baritone. "Welcome to
the Met."

And then someone touched my shoulder, and the beautiful,

dark, and sympathetic eyes of Licia Albanese searched my face.
"Welcome, Mr. Merrill. You have the beautiful voice, a born
Germont."

"Well, now, look who's here! When do we do 'Sweethearts,'
honey?"

Regina Resnik! My old partner in the Catskills. She beat me
to the Met by one season. They had been smart enough to
grab her.

She contorted her face into a mask of disbelief. "Do you
believe it, Bob? Do you believe we're both here?"

"Cio-cio-san!" I yelled. "Where's your kimono?"

"A Leonora, an Aïda, a Santuzza, but not one Butterfly! I
suppose they don't think I'm out of my cocoon yet."

Who wasn't there that day!

"How do you do, Mr. Merrill. I can swear that *we're* going
to sing together—two hometown kids like us."

Risë Stevens! My future Delila, my Carmen. My God! We
were all such kids then. We had worshiped our idols, but
they stepped down from their pedestals that day. Pinza, Melchior, Baccaloni.

When I was introduced to the great Bonelli, I almost broke
down. "It was you," I insisted. "Me who what?" Mr. Bonelli
asked.

But I became tongue-tied. It was too much. And it was
frightening too. Perhaps I was my mother's son after all, with all
her old wives' tales and ear pulling. The great Bonelli had
sung his last performance at the Metropolitan with Eleanor
Steber in *Traviata* three months before, the last of his glorious
Germonts. He was no longer at the Met; he was never to be
heard there again.

An insane thought flashed into my mind. *Can I be taking his
place? Can I possibly follow in this man's footsteps? Could I
even shine his shoes?*

People came in, milled around us, and disappeared, and my
parents were lit up like neon signs. My mother was acting the
part of a famous diva come out of retirement by popular acclaim, and my father was holding my arm with one hand and
balancing his glass with the other.

"How do you like the champagne, Poppa?"

"Good. It's very good. But seltzer, it's not."

Mr. Johnson hovered around us and was particularly kind to my family. A handsome man of great charm, Edward Johnson was the perfect liaison with the wealthy backers and board of directors who kept the opera live. He and his assistant, Frank St. Ledger, who was very active in running the Met, made an excellent combination. Edward Johnson was, that day and for the rest of our association, one of the kindest men I'd ever met. His dignity, warmth, and understanding of a singer's problems made him a most sympathetic boss. I was not alone in my admiration for him. His inheritance of Gatti-Casazza's mantle through the sudden death of the latter's assistant and successor, Herbert Witherspoon, while preparing the 1935–1936 season, was certainly a most fortunate business for us all—especially me.

The only discordant note at the Opera House that day was struck by Wilfred Pelletier, a most important man in my life. Mr. Pelletier had conducted my first audition for the Met, the one I had failed so terribly.

After I had lost, Mr. Pelletier had taken the trouble to call me to tell me why. "Young man, I heard something in your voice, and I don't hear it often. How dare you be so lazy and so sloppy? I've asked about you. You belong at the opera, not in the mountains. Why are you throwing your life away? Work hard and you'll make it. Listen to me, young man. *Work hard and you'll make it.*"

His words came back to me as the little jolly-faced maestro now congratulated my parents and took my hands in his. "So, Merrill! You've worked hard and you're here with us. That's as it should be."

While my mother and father were diverted by Mr. Johnson and some other guests, the maestro wagged his finger at me. His eyes were merry, and he recognized something in mine. "It's a great day, Merrill, and I don't want to ruin it; but better that than ruin your career. You've got the devil in you. I can see it. Be serious about your job here. Work hard! Keep studying. Don't let it slip through your fingers. Promise me."

"Do you think I'd let anything ruin this chance, sir?"

"I'll be watching you, my boy."

I signed my contract in June, and it was for one hundred and twenty-five dollars a week, for as many performances a week as the management requested. I was allowed to continue my lucrative radio and concert careers as long as they did not conflict in any way with my opera singing, which had priority above everything else. Certainly there was no argument there.

The Met recommended several coaches, and I worked hard with them, although Mr. Margolis, of course, came first. There was the whole summer in which to prepare myself for my debut, both the role and date of which had still to be decided. Then I received my repertoire! Some assistant conductor handed me a mimeographed sheet, and I read: "Merrill, Robert. Marullo in *Rigoletto*, Wagner in *Faust*, Herald in *Lohengrin*, Schaunard in *La Bohème*." There were a few others I forget, but they were just as minor. All my joy turned to despair. Checking with Tommy Hayward, I discovered that he was just as badly off. The poor guy was the Second Jew in *Salome*, Tybalt in *Roméo et Juliette*, Arturo in *Lucia di Lammermoor*, and so on. We were rookie players and couldn't be trusted with the ball.

I became anxious about my future. It is true that these roles were important to the opera and important to the story, but they weren't important to me. Once cast in these tiny parts, I was sure that I'd be stuck and never get out of them. I could hardly say, "These roles aren't satisfactory." But I neglected to study them, feeling that any preoccupation with these parts would in some way mean that I would eventually sing them. I was playing the ostrich, ignoring the day of reckoning.

In the meantime, Moe Gale managed, that summer, to get me on a program with Andre Kostelanetz, where I sang with the gorgeous Eleanor Steber; and then, plum of plums, Moe landed me the *Voice of Firestone*, which I desperately wanted. It was a beautifully produced weekly program of great prestige and high rating, with Howard Barlow as conductor. The format was permanent. First and last there were themes written by Elizabeth Firestone. The closing signature was:

And now each flower is sweeter, dear.
I know it's just because at last you're here.
We sit alone in all the world apart
And love is blooming full within my heart.

On my first broadcast, I sang "Figaro" and the "Prologue" from *Pagliacci*, and the studio audience was so receptive that I, forgetting where I was, bowed humbly, took my music—and walked off the stage. I was recalled by the furious Mr. Barlow, who was going into the theme and tearing out his hair. I rushed back to the microphone, but it was impossible to find my place without rattling all the papers and losing precious time, so I faked the words, ruining Miss Firestone's beautiful lyric. An apology was sent to the Firestone family, and I offered to burn myself at the stake. I must say they were very sweet about it; and the incident, never repeated, was forgotten.

Back at the Met, things weren't so easily solved. As I was supposed to, I reported to an assistant conductor in one of the dressing rooms. He was checking on my *Faust* and *Rigoletto* roles. Was everything all right? I nodded and sight-read from the scores he handed me. I thought I was kidding them.

For two months I asked whether there was any news about my debut. The answer was always no. Periodically, these assistant maestros would report to St. Ledger, who eventually called me into his office. "And why, Mr. Merrill, are you not prepared for Marullo and the Herald?" he said.

It was the moment of truth. Tommy Hayward was cramming up on the Second Jew in *Salome*—and I suddenly saw myself as the First Jew to have his head handed to him at the Met.

"I don't particularly like the parts," I answered maniacally, as if begging for dismissal.

"You don't?" was Mr. St. Ledger's next question. This tall, bespectacled, stern-looking man was suddenly a school principal who might expel me.

If I don't know the roles, they can't make me do them. They're not going to fire me if they really like my voice.

My *chutzpah* I inherited directly from my mother, along with the color of my eyes and my love of singing. Confidence in my voice was my new strength; my other career, in radio, in a sense, a weakness. I had managed to talk like that to St. Ledger, but it was impossible to know what would happen if my recalcitrance was brought directly to Mr. Johnson's attention. If it was, it was never brought to mine.

I only know that as time went on and as casting notices went up, each of my little roles was filled by someone else, and I breathed a sigh of relief. Then there was only Marullo left, the most loathsome part of all. And, lo and behold, *that* was filled in a couple of days. There was no part left for me; it was obvious that my cheek was so great that it was going to get slapped, good and proper.

"When are you making your debut, Bob?" everyone asked.

"I really don't know," I answered.

This little conversation was repeated until the season opened on November 26—and beyond. Tommy Hayward was Tybalt in special preview performance of *Roméo et Juliette* for the Metropolitan Guild, and he had debuted with Pinza, Munsel, and Benzell. His schedule was all set. Not a word was said to me, and my heart began to sink.

The 1945–1946 season opened with *Lohengrin,* and all New York came to hear Helen Traubel as Elsa and the debut of Swedish Torston Ralf in the title role. Kerstin Thorborg was Ortrud, and I could have been the Herald and sung that glorious night. Hugh Thompson sang the role for the most glittering audience in some years. The war was over, and the first-nighters were out in full force, led by Mrs. Cornelius Vanderbilt in her satin headache band and white fox fur; Mrs. George Washington Kavanaugh in a diamond tiara; the Astors; the Belmonts; the Hearsts; the Blisses; and in the royal box draped with the flag, the President's wife, Bess Truman, with daughter Margaret.

It is said that at the premiere of the Metropolitan Opera House in 1893—on its reopening after the fire—with Emma Eames as Marguérite and the De Reszke brothers singing Méphistophélès and Faust, the Parterre Boxes were first called the Diamond Horseshoe. That night, there were one hundred and seventy million dollars worth of diamonds worn by the boxholders. Not since those income-taxless days had there been an opening like this one, and I had missed being part of it. By all reports at the time, it was the lushest, poshest, gayest of them all. It was practically a victory celebration: the uniforms that had peppered the audience for the past four years had once again given way to white tie. Not only did this 1945 audience compete with the nineteenth century in jewels; it also had Ganna Walska in a fur dress with a naked midriff.

Evidently I had outwitted myself, once again been caught with one foot on the window ledge. But Padolnick, had been kind and let me go on. The season opened—and I hung around backstage like an idiot. And what a season it was! Pinza and Baccaloni were in *The Barber of Seville*, with Bidú Sayão as Rosina. Jussi Bjoerling, Tibbett, and Grace Moore were the trio in *Tosca*. Peerce, Milanov, and Warren sang in *Un Ballo in Maschera;* Melchior, Traubel, Alexander Kipnis, and Thorborg sang *Die Walküre;* and one performance of *La Giaconda*, incredibly, had Zinka Milanov, Risë Stevens, Ezio Pinza, Richard Tucker, and Leonard Warren—an absolute feast. Both Pinza and Lauritz Melchior, who was the spitting image of Sophie Tucker, were celebrating their twentieth season with the Met. Everything about that sixty-first season was gala, except that I had talked my way out of being part of it. And it was already December.

Loitering about the Thirty-ninth Street entrance one day, chatting with Regina Resnik, I looked up to see Mr. Johnson. He greeted me politely and asked whether I would come to his office. As I left Regina, I opened my eyes wide in mock terror. Her expression was one of a conspirator as she crossed her fingers.

I followed Mr. Johnson into the building and up to his sanctum, where he waved me into a chair. "I suppose you've been wondering what we're going to do with you."

"Yes, sir, I have. It's December already."

"Tell me, Bob, how would you like to make your debut as Germont in *Traviata?*"

My body grew slack and my mouth hung open. "Germont?" I asked, mouth still agape.

"That's right. Germont."

"Mr. Johnson, I'd *love* it! I—I—I'm thrilled."

"We've done a lot of thinking, and we feel you're up to a major role."

"I am, sir, I am. I know I can do it, Mr. Johnson."

"So do I or you wouldn't be doing it."

"Germont!" I repeated in awe.

"You'll be the youngest artist ever to sing it, you know."

"I won't fail you, Mr. Johnson. You won't be sorry."

Mr. Johnson smiled. "You may have your own radio program, Bob, and be very popular—and you wouldn't be here if your voice were not a fine one—but you know, Bob, sustaining a characterization in an opera is a far cry from tossing off an aria over the air. This is hard work, my lad."

"And I'm willing to work hard. The opera means more to me than anything else. It always has."

"I hope so. You debut a week from tonight, on December fifteenth."

A week from tonight! The phrase kept repeating itself as I sat in the BMT on my way home to Bay Parkway. Uncle Sam, the *bulvahn*, and sweet Tante Esther were at the house for supper. I hadn't seen them in ages, not since the Lewisohn Stadium concert with Rommy. Uncle Sam, who thought he was Al Jolson and was always socking out "Mammy" at our piano, was saying, "So I hear Looey's boy Sidney is going into jewelry," when I fairly burst into the apartment.

"Moishe, darling," Tante Esther greeted me. "Look at him, Lotza. He's getting to look more like Papa—*olivah sholom*—every day. Who ever thought I'd live to see him a famous opera singer?" She covered her mouth and shook her head tragically.

"Hello, Tante Esther. You look gorgeous. How are you?"

"Not good, Moishe. What am I talking?" she whined. "I haven't lived to see you there *yet*. I shouldn't *beshrie* myself. This time of the day, I run down like an old watch. It's the heart! It's not strong. It misses the beat. I tell . . ."

"Well! The big, important star!" Uncle Sam interrupted. "Your radio program is a sensation, and you're really good. Not since the Street Singer has there been such a tumult. The bobby-soxers go crazy, and who is it? It's Fatso, who's skinny now." He put one hand on his chest and extended the other. "Do you remember? 'Mmar-rta! Rrrambbl-ing rrr-ose of the wiiild-woo-ood.'"

"I remember, Uncle Sam. Hello, Poppa. Momma!"

My father was looking even smaller and paler than usual. "Hello, Moishe. Uncle Sam says that your cousin Sidney is maybe going into the jewelry business."

The smells from the kitchen were intoxicating, and I toyed with the idea of waiting until after supper before I told my news. How long could I hold in my wonderful secret? It was too bad that it was Uncle Sam and Tante Esther. I wished Gil and Julia were there, or Aunt Molly and Sidney. How long could I savor my news and not call my pal Paul Richards? If it had been possible, I would have called and had the news headlined in the *Times*. Then it occurred to me that it would certainly be an item in that paper the next day.

Germont. I wonder who the Violetta is? I never thought to ask. Oh, my God! How exciting it all is! "What's for supper, Mom?"

"*Brust deckel* and *farfel*."

"Hmm!" I cooed with pleasure. *Germont and Momma's pot roast and noodles. Life is too good.*

"It's raw out today. Have a little schnapps with your uncle. You too, Esther; it won't hurt. It stimulates."

"It makes my arms heavy, Lotza. You know that. I only look at Manischewitz sweet and I'm *shikker*."

Momma brought out some chopped onions and eggs on Ritz crackers. "Here, a little *forshpice* with the schnapps."

She looked at me fleetingly as she bustled about. "I think we're going to celebrate something. Am I right, *singer mine*?"

The woman was a sorceress. "What do you mean, Momma?"

"I mean you've been moping around the house like a sick ox —and tonight, all of a sudden, a light went on inside you!"

"Don't tell me . . . he's in love," Tante Esther ventured. "He should only find a lovely girl like Gidalia's Julia. So you found yourself a nice Jewish girl, healthy—with God's help—a strong girl!"

"Esther!" Momma handed her the hors d'ouevres.

"It won't lay on the chest, Lotza?"

"Not unless you drop it there. Enjoy, already, and shut up. I want to hear. Moishe, what's the news? They gave you a part?"

I slapped my chest and bowed to the whole family. "You are looking at the youngest singer ever to sing Germont in *Traviata*." The rest came out in a rush. "I make my debut a week from tonight! Momma! Poppa! Isn't it wonderful? Germont! You'll all come in your glad rags, all dressed up. Everybody—Mr. Margolis, Moe Gale, Tante Lesser—*everybody*. Whoopee!"

My mother clasped her hands together and held them tightly. "So!" was her only comment. But she said it as if it were really "Amen!"

"It's a good part?" Tante Esther asked.

"Only Lawrence Tibbett usually sings it, Esther," Momma proclaimed. "That's all. That's how important."

Uncle Sam pulled down the corners of his mouth in surprise. "And you almost became a carpenter, kiddo."

Poppa was glowing with pride. After I made my announcement, he stared at me in that shy, radiant way of his, and now I started toward him, tiny in that great big Morris chair. His eyes moved up to the top of his head. I thought it was a joke at first. His mouth fell open crazily, and then he toppled over, falling to the floor.

"Poppa!" I screamed. "Poppa! Quick, give me some whiskey."

Uncle Sam rushed to me with a glass and the bottle, and I forced some down my father's throat.

Momma stood over us. "Don't let it choke him. Abe! Abe! It's running down the mouth!"

She rushed to the phone and called the doctor as I carried Poppa into the bedroom and opened his shirt collar.

"It looks like a heart attack," Uncle Sam said, patting my father's hand.

"Where is that doctor?" my mother kept saying. "Where is that doctor? Esther, are you all right?"

All that was left of Tante Esther was a heap of polka-dot material where she'd been sitting. The scene had been too much for her. She was sharing all my father's symptoms.

When the doctor arrived, he diagnosed a near-fatal heart attack.

"Well, what do we do now, Doctor?" I asked. "The hospital? A specialist? We've got to save him!"

"Dr. Boaz is the greatest heart specialist around," Uncle Sam said. "I know him well."

"Get him, Uncle Sam. Please, call him now."

"Fifty dollars a visit he charges."

"Who cares what he charges! Get him!"

Dr. Boaz was home, and as a favor to Uncle Sam he came immediately. Poppa was still lying unconscious when Boaz arrived. A quick examination and the specialist called the hospital for an ambulance.

"Can you do anything, Doctor? Will he be all right?"

"I'm afraid your father hasn't long to live, Mr. Merrill. But . . . in the hospital, with proper facilities, there in an outside chance we can save him."

He felt Poppa's pulse once again, shaking his head as he lost and then found the life flowing through the little man I loved so much.

My ears strained to hear the siren. *God damn it! Why does it take so long?*

"Dr. Boaz," I heard Tante Esther call.

The doctor gave me a handful of capsules. "Give her two of these. You and your mother can take some too. It'll quiet you."

"I'm all right, Doctor. But how can we make that ambulance get here faster?"

Momma walked over in a daze with a glass of water, got the capsules, and took two to Tante Esther. "Take, Esther. You're all right. It's Abe! On a night like this it had to happen. Tonight! Just tonight!"

And then, as we heard the siren and Momma brought me my coat—so I wouldn't catch cold—my father went into a convulsion. The two orderlies who came to the apartment could barely get this one-hundred-and-five-pound man into a straitjacket.

Later, standing over the hospital bed, soothing his forehead, I was asked to leave. The fit was not over, and it was the most painful departure of my life; but as I patted him good-bye, Poppa suddenly focused his eyes on mine and thickly whispered, "I'll see you in the opera."

The next day I discovered that our family doctor and Uncle Sam's fifty-dollar-a-visit specialist had both diagnosed my father's attack incorrectly. His heart was as sound as could be; he had suffered diabetic shock. He would be all right, and he was with me—God bless him—on the greatest night of my life! Both of us had an uphill struggle, however. Once Poppa was out of danger, I went into rehearsal with Désiré Defrère, who, strangely enough, had replaced Titta Ruffo years before at that Music Hall performance Paul Richards and I had waited twenty hours to hear. Defrère was a Belgian, an ex-baritone who had sung with Caruso. Heavyset, with bright fun-loving eyes, he was now a Met director—and a tough customer. He did not believe in wearing a velvet glove over his iron fist, and he let me have it but good. Every day, I came home with fresh wounds.

Rehearsing on the roof of the Met, I made my first entrance. Self-conscious, not knowing what to do with my hands, I put them in my pocket. I froze with embarrassment when Defrère asked, "Where do you think you are, Merrill? Back in Brooklyn?"

Licia Albanese discreetly looked into her purse for something.

"You are a *gentleman*," Defrère went on. "Did you ever *see* one?"

My face was scarlet. But I didn't say a word. Despite his outburst, I felt he liked me and my voice, and I knew he could be good for me. I was putty in his hands, and Désiré Defrère actually modeled me into something resembling Alfredo's father, Germont. He was a real Pygmalion.

Albanese was patient and considerate to the point of saintliness. This beautiful artist could so easily have been put off by my inexperience and gaucherie. Instead, she encouraged and warmed me. She was certain that all would go well, which was more than I knew.

Cesare Sodero, our conductor, seemed to understand my problem. Now that I was in reality going to sing at the Met, I became aware of all my shortcomings. This was not radio, where pure vocal quality could pass for performance. This was no concert, where you stand alone, insulated, answerable only to yourself, with an orchestra to back you. This was a musical play, where I had to act *with* someone. And there were no ad libs possible.

Every word, every note was treasured and time-honored. The slightest variation or slip branded you an amateur or a vandal.

The dress rehearsal was a chilling experience. Far more nervous than ever before, feeling the fool in my wig and velour top hat, I saw everyone who meant anything at the Opera House out front—Mr. Johnson, St. Ledger, everybody. Things went well until my duet with Violetta. Then, in a state of hysteria, I missed my cue, bollixing up the whole scene. About to panic, my heart pounding, all reason flown, I felt Defrère's glance. Terror was written all over me, and Defrère could read. Our eyes locked for a split second—the whole thing took just that fraction—and then he stopped everything by walking onto the stage, signaling Sodero to halt the music.

"Wait a minute! Let's stop a minute. I want to restage something here. Madame! Mr. Merrill!"

This rough and tough director then invented some bit of nonsense in order to allow me to get hold of myself. He didn't even look straight at me again until he had rearranged our positions by a decimal. It was perfectionism to the nth degree, and only I knew what he was doing.

I caught my breath, regained my nerve, and, most of all, felt I had a valuable new friend. My gratitude knew no bounds. When he saw I was all right, he walked off, nodding to Sodero. We picked up on the cue, and the rest of the rehearsal went well; I had recovered completely. Defrère was a cigar smoker, and I bought him two dollar cigars that evening. They were the best I could find. If only it were possible to smoke gold.

From the beginning, something had told me that Deedee was a friend. He was more than that. He was a lifesaver. He had prepared me for the greatest moment of my life.

CHAPTER ELEVEN

MY FATHER kept his promise. His veins shot through with insulin, his breast-pocket handkerchief enwrapping two cubes of sugar as an added preventive against coma, my Poppa sat in the audience at the Metroplitan Opera House, resplendent in the first tuxedo he could call his own. My mother, who, according to some publicity releases, was "a retired concert soprano," sat in her black evening clothes, looking for all the world as if she believed her press clippings and might—after she had shown you her decorations from the Kaiser—reward you with a *bissel* lied. She was something, my mother; I got all my ham from her. She wore no jewelry that night, and the minks were yet to come; but she was the richest woman in the theater. Her dream had come true, and she—that is, her son—was appearing in *La Traviata* at the Metropolitan Opera House—*if you please.* Through the curtain I saw the whole *mishpucheh:* Gil and Julia, Sam and Mary Margolis, the Spitalnys, Moe and Gertrude Gale. Uncle Looey was gone, but Cousin Sidney came with Aunt Molly. Everyone was there.

Jan Peerce, our Alfredo, unfortunately took ill that night, and Richard Tucker stepped in at the last moment. What kind of omen was that? I was all nerves. I was numb. The long wait was cruel. Germont doesn't enter until the second act. Sodero, our little pince-nezed maestro, was doing well out there. Albanese and Tucker sounded great from backstage. Suppose I missed my cue again?

I read and reread my telegrams, and I laughed at the wire from my old agent Charlie Rapp: "What do you know! Down to only one job a night!" How much safer I had been back there in the mountains.

It just isn't fair to have to wait a whole act and *an intermission.*

I was pacing my dressing room when Mr. Johnson appeared. He really looked like a painting by Sargent. Tall and slender in his opera hat, his smile was an absolute bromide for me.

"John Charles Thomas always used to say, 'You're not going to the electric chair. You're just going to sing.' And that's what you love to do."

"Thank you, Mr. Johnson," I babbled. "I'll always be grateful for the chance you've given me. I hope . . . I hope . . ."

"You'll be just fine, my lad. I know quality."

"Thanks, Mr. Johnson."

He laughed gently. "And I know what you're going through. Dear me, it was twenty-three years ago. I was a nervous Avito in *L'Amore dei Tre Re,* and Bori was my first diva. This season she bids us farewell, and now I'm the general manager. You are now part of the flow, Bob. This is just a moment in time, and it's going to be a joyful one. Gatti-Casazza spoke to *me* before I went on. Perhaps, someday, you will help someone else."

"If I ever get through this," I said, smiling weakly.

"Just remember, my boy, it's not your *last* performance. *That* is the worst moment."

And then he was gone and I was walking downstairs to the wings. *It might be my last performance,* I thought.

You are never so alone as you are at the moment just before you go on. Hundreds may have helped you achieve the goal, but you are all alone in the dark as you listen for your cue.

Will my legs work? Isn't it a miracle that they move one after the other at a command from the brain? Suppose they collapse!

And then I was onstage in the kind of daze where reflexes take over completely. I remember nothing except that I was onstage and singing, but Licia Albanese wasn't there. In her place was

Violetta, a courtesan who could ruin my son's life and possibly
my daughter's chances for an excellent marriage. Licia managed
to be both dreaded stranger and considerate friend to me
throughout her beautiful performance, reaching out to me in a
sympathy that she herself, as Violetta, was begging me to give
her. What a beautiful Violetta she was, and what a sensitive
woman!

Germont is particularly challenging to a beginner. He is
physically static, given none of the movement that can so easily
pass for real dynamics. You're on your own and must stand still
and listen to Violetta—the most difficult thing to do onstage. Also,
the musical accompaniment is very light for the baritone aria—
gratifying for the veteran, petrifying to the novice. No bombast
from the pit can hide your flaws or carry you. It's a tough role
and a glorious one. Then, with Licia's help and my own sense
of survival, everything came into focus, and I became aware that
I was in the midst of the duet that could easily dissipate the
energy needed for the aria that closed the act.

Wildly, I thought of my baseball days, when I knew there were
nine innings and my arm was feeling stress in the fourth. *Take
it easy, Moishe. You got a long way to go. Don't push.* The emotional pressures were as great as the vocal. I was in competition
with myself. *This duet lasts twenty minutes. Don't give it everything, important as it is. There's the "Di provenza" coming up.
There! That went well, very well. My God, Albanese sounds
lovely!*

The duet was over, and I had come through it in one piece.
After Violetta's departure and Alfredo's shocked reading of her
note, I made my reentrance and attempted to console him with
that gorgeous aria "Di provenza il mar." The air is repeated; and
though it went beautifully the first time, the second time around
I began to tire. With most of the reprise *and* the whole cadenza
still to come, I pulled myself together, actually gritted my teeth,
and reached down to a reserve I'd never known about before.
Suddenly I was sailing on top of the notes, riding them, floating,
in complete and tireless command.

And then the house came down. As Mr. Johnson had said, it
was a moment in the flow, but a joyous one. I was now part of

the history of the Opera House. Damn it, I owned the Opera House! I owned all New York! Almost as beautiful as your first child's first cry is your first "Bravo!" And that's all I was hearing now. The cries were deafening. Every time I stepped through the gold curtain, pulled by Tucker or Albanese, the roar became louder. Licia pressed my hand, "You see. You were beautiful." I kissed her fine Italian hand as the three of us shared the calls. And then they left me alone onstage to take my solo curtain, to feel for the first time the sweetness of that moment. The approval I had been looking for all my life was now mine. This was success, arrival. The circle had come around full. The circle!

I stood there alone on the Metropolitan stage in front of the curtain deafened by the noise. Maestro Sodero was tapping his baton in applause, and beaming members of the orchestra stood clapping. The roar of the audience came over me in waves almost knocking me over. This was for Moishe the *pisher*—stuttering, frightened Moishe, who locked himself in the bathroom to avoid the searching eyes of his audience.

What can be said of such a moment? It is all love and pride and vanity—and humility too.

Listen to them, I remember thinking. *Thank God, Poppa lived to hear it. It's for me. This is how they all felt up here: Ruffo, De Luca, Tibbett, Thomas, Bonelli!*

Bonelli! I looked up to the top of the house to the Family Circle and searched the first row of the peanut gallery for a young boy who wanted more than anything else in the world to sing like the man on the stage. My eyes strained to see that kid, his eyes wet, his hands ice cold. I thought I saw him, and he was glowing with pleasure and approval. It was one of the few times in my life when I met myself and was thoroughly pleased with what I encountered.

I had wanted to be loved by everybody, and there I was, in the midst of a mass romance. From onstage, the whole theater, with the house lights up, seemed to flutter with excitement. People now stood, shouting and applauding. There was the family, shining as if they had a special light on them. Poppa was crying, and Momma, flushed and triumphant, was looking around the theater *kvelling*.

In two weeks she'll ask me to get Johnson to let her sing.

When I retired backstage, the first to reach me was Mr. Johnson. "You did it, Bob. You really did it." He embraced me.

Over his shoulder I saw Désiré Defrère. "No, Mr. Johnson!" I said, shaking my head and pointing at Deedee. "Let's not kid ourselves. *He* did it."

The rest of the opera went smoothly and quickly. There was another demonstration at the final curtain. People who had barely noticed me backstage before now were covering me with compliments and kisses. It would be dishonest to pretend that that kind of evening isn't great for the ego—and this for the kid who had always felt inferior! Oh, boy!

Nothing is ever the same as that first plunge. One can never repeat it.

The family waited for me, and we went home, all of us, and had tea and cake and talked of the past and the future, laughing and crying.

My debut was on a Saturday night, and most of the reviews weren't published until Monday. They were worth waiting for. It was generally agreed that the Metropolitan had acquired an important new member. Although everyone was wonderful to me, I remember, with some immodesty, one of the major critics speaking of my voice as "rich and so rotund that it makes you forget that the Met is too large to allow most singers to be heard at their best." That really pleased me. The reviewers were generous with their praise for my singing. The most important reviewer of all, Olin Downes, of *The New York Times,* heralded the "*bel canto* singing of the new, young baritone."

These glorious reviews went to my head, but there was another side to the story. If I thought that Deedee Defrère was my Pygmalion, many of the same critics felt that young Merrill was a statue. The consensus was that, while gifted and musically authoritative at all times, with a presence as Germont that had dignity and poise, I was somewhat less than a great actor. "But that will come in time, with more experience and maturity. He has all the qualifications of a real find."

All in all, my press was better than I had dared hope, and it was rather difficult to keep my balance. *Traviata* was my real beginning and my good-luck opera. That same season, I recorded the second act for Victor Red Seal, and it won the award as best classical record of the year. Already starring on my own program on NBC, called the *Robert Merrill Show,* I was signed as star and master of ceremonies of RCA Victor's radio show *Music America Loves Best,* a remarkably popular, high-budget program that continued for five years with me as MC. We engaged such diverse guests as Jascha Heifetz, Marian Anderson, Dennis Day, Licia Albanese, and Desi Arnaz. I was still cementing my two worlds, earning excellent money in one and prestige and deep inner satisfaction in the other.

A successful debut at the opera is good copy, and I received a great deal of publicity. By the time two weeks had passed—and I had sung my first Ashton with Patrice Munsel as Lucia—my radio reputation plus my fine Met send-off by the critics really put me into orbit. There was immense audience interest.

This *Lucia di Lammermoor* was another first for me, my initial appearance with that artist and dear friend whom I love to rib but really adore, that tenor (yet!) of some renown, Jan Peerce. His Edgar that night, like so many other of his roles, was sung beautifully. Patrice Munsel was a lovely Lucia, cooperative and outgoing. I was in the very best company, but from the outset, I loathed the role of Ashton. It is insipid and unsatisfying in every way. The only excuse for the opera is as a showcase for a diva and for its excellent last-act tenor arias; the baritone is a real stepchild. It went well enough that first night, but it was and will always be a bore to me.

One week later, I was lucky enough to sing my first Metropolitan Escamillo—faultlessly costumed this time—opposite Risë Stevens, an exciting Carmen. Like Licia Albanese, she helped her colleagues onstage, was part of the whole fabric, integrated into the entire performance, not removed from it. With Risë's help, I got another set of fine reviews. The critics were excessive in their praise, particularly pleased to hear "such a youthfully voiced Toreador." Well! Why not? I was a *kid*—and I had the world by the tail.

What a gratifying role that is, Escamillo! Small, it is true, but spectacular. More difficult than it seems, the "Toreador Song" drops into a very low register but remains lyric. It is impossible to bark the aria, even though it is bravura; if you push the low notes to enlarge the sound, then the high register will suffer.

In the first aria, the bullfighter faces his friends and *aficionados,* not the audience. I can't say I wasn't nervous, but I looked at the chorus cock-eyed and whispered, "Me? Fight a bull? I'd drop dead." The whole mob lit up, their loud cheers now supported by real mirth and excitement, all of them on my side—and I relaxed and let go. Everything fell into place. We repeated *Carmen* later in the week at a matinee that brought out the bobby-soxers and firmly established me as a drawing card.

At this performance, when I kissed Risë, there was a thunderous roar of approval from the balconies that was—in its lack of dignity but wealth of enthusiasm—a reminder of the effect a skinny young balladeer was having on the teenage audiences at the Paramount Theatre up the road a piece. Risë and I were both stunned by the commotion. This matinee was being covered by a *Daily News* reporter who was doing an article on children at the opera. He was as startled as we that they weren't so different from their swing-loving friends who congregated at the Paramount. The reporter's story created such a splash that Frank Sinatra, on his broadcast that week, wanted to know, "What's with these longhairs muscling in on my territory?" I became the Met's new Escamillo, doing the role seven times that first season.

I couldn't have been more pleased with the way things were going. My stars were obviously in good aspect. All was well at the opera, on the air, and in the concert world; I was now juggling three careers with one hand behind my back. These were the golden days, and I could do no wrong—or so I thought.

My latest bit of luck, I was informed, was that Jan Peerce and I were replacing James Melton and Francesco Valentino in a *Lucia* starring Lily Pons. I had never met Miss Pons, and soon discovered that I wasn't going to. She rarely came to rehearsals, and in this case she didn't at all. January 10, the day of the opera, arrived; I still had not seen the diva. The curtain rose, and after singing in the first scene, in which she does not appear, I was rushed to the lady's dressing room to be introduced.

When I entered her dressing room, there was no doubt I was in the presence of a star truly the toast of the opera. The tiny singer sat at her dressing table—glistening like a jewel. She was all sparkle and twitter.

My God, she is a star! She's actually twinkling!

She now extended her hand as if she were handing a coin to a beggar. "Eet eez a great plazure to meet you, Meester Merreel."

As if on cue, four Persian cats leaped at me from various directions. I was covered with cats pulling at my beard and wig, clawing at my costume and rubbing aggressively against my leg.

The lady ignored the assault completely; Mademoiselle had something else on her mind. "Just remembair, Meester Merreel, *nevair* move toward *me* on ze stage. *I* weel move toward *you*. You understand? Zat eez right. Now, somezing else. When I swoon, just make sure zat zere is a chair for me to faint. No? Zat eez right. *Merci!* Eet was lovely to meet you. *Enchantée.* I weel see you on ze stage. *A bientôt.*"

Who knew what *that* meant then? But I *did* know the sound of dismissal. She further helped with the French lesson by turning back to her toilette while one of her cats wet my shoe—for luck, no doubt. It was one of the unbelievable moments of my life.

That is all that transpired between us until we met onstage and sang a duet that went so well that you'd have sworn we'd rehearsed a month. With her voice and her flair, she was one of the few divas who could get away with it. But she was alone onstage—absolutely; a star, to be sure, but a lone one. There are many great singers who learn only their arias and manage to get through the remainder of their roles. I was to meet many and learn much; but I wasn't to come across many like Pons. She wasn't just a star. She was a whole darned constellation!

Not a day passed when I didn't learn something new at the Met. Papa Senz, the cherubic, jolly little makeup man, had worked with Caruso and Chaliapin. When I discovered he really had made up the divine Caruso, I almost collapsed.

"What do you eat, Mr. Merrill? Caruso used to have dee chicken-in-dee-pot—sent in from Del Pezzo—a couple of hours before he sang and den dee broth troughout dee opera. I can see him now, sipping dee golden likvood dat soothed dee golden troat."

The next time I sang, of course, I sent out for chicken-in-the-pot. The great tenor was known to have loved good food and appreciated the best. What was good enough for Caruso would certainly be good enough for me. It was delicious. Then, while Papa Senz made me up for Escamillo, I sipped "dee golden likvood."

I can still see those golden globules of fat floating on top of the broth.

"Drink!" commanded Papa Senz.

The broth almost killed my performance that night. There was so much fat in the soup that I got a frog in my throat and practically croaked the "Toreador Song." From the grave, these tenors can spot a baritone.

Caruso once, in *La Gioconda*, just before beginning his "Cielo e mar," discovered that he had a frog—no doubt from the same broth. He had to make a decision quickly, and walking upstage, he cleared his throat and spit upon the ship, returning downstage to sing gloriously. Such was the mystique of this man, so great his legend, that for years after his death, tenors, just before starting the aria, walked to the back of the stage and spat upon the scenery, as if the action had some profound motivation. Caruso had done it! Even so, I stopped "sipping dee golden likvood" after one try.

Papa Senz told me how Chaliapin would often arrive in his dressing room filled to brimming with vodka. He would sit before his glass in his undershirt and allow Papa to play Rembrandt upon his face. Suddenly he would bolt upright and stare at Papa with his falcon's eyes. "Vot are you making me up for, Papa Senz?"

"For *Boris*, Mr. Chaliapin."

"*Boris!*" he would bellow. "My God! Vere is dee score. Qvik! Give me dee score!"

But there was never need to worry. Chaliapin was a giant, magnificent on and off the stage. Not only was his voice like the winter's wind howling through the Kremlin, but evidently his stature was so heroic and his sense of tragedy so profound that he still stands irreplaceable. It's not often that I wish my life away, but if I were older I could have heard both Chaliapin and Caruso. Certainly, it is not just nostalgia in their still-living admirers; their recordings, though imperfect and scratched, secure their legend.

Again it struck me that I was *really* singing at the Metropolitan Opera, where they had reigned, that I was being made up by the same man who had transformed Chaliapin into Méphistophélès and Don Quixote, and Caruso into Eleazar and the Duke of Mantua. Overnight, I'd climbed from the Catskills to Mount Olympus.

With the ascent thus negotiated, I was now introduced to the most dangerous adventure of them all—the Metropolitan tour. Our 1945–1946 season—my first and the company's sixty-first—had been immensely successful, putting the Met in the black for a change. The greatest draw that season was the great *basso buffo* Salvatore Baccaloni, one of the sweetest men who ever lived. His popularity with the public was tremendous. His Don Pasquale, Dr. Bartolo in *The Barber*, Leporello in *Don Giovanni*, and Sacristan in *Tosca* were just a few of the brilliant portraits that made him so loved. Ezio Pinza's appearances hardly discouraged the customers either. His Méphistophélès in *Faust*, Don Basilio in *The Barber*, Figaro in Mozart's *Le Nozze*, and his perfect Don Giovanni had long since made this extraordinary artist a matinee idol. Jussi Bjoerling's glorious Rudolfo, Cavaradossi, and Manrico were just a few of the roles that made opera buffs out of anyone with ears. And the management's attempt to glamorize the opera by the addition of such slim, attractive young artists as Mimi Benzell, Bidú Sayão, Patrice Munsel, Risë Stevens, and Gladys Swarthout was paying off.

It was a happy and successful company that went out on tour that season. The very nature of such an excursion, with its forced intimacies, gave me my first realistic picture of my colleagues. These gods and goddesses were harried human beings, pushed and shoved, pushing and shoving, herded like cattle on the trek westward. The towns changed names—Boston, Cleveland, Minneapolis, St. Louis, Dallas—but once the pattern was established, nothing was really different for the six weeks we were out.

The Metropolitan traveled like a circus with high notes. One string of railroad cars housed the orchestra, ballet, scenery, and stagehands; another, the soloists, chorus, conductors, and management. As some of the most famous names in opera boarded the train, you could actually see the Pullman porters and waiters and conductors brace themselves for the onslaught. Already experienced, their memories of the last tour still raw, all their requests for transfer refused, these dedicated workers—the railroad's human sacrifice to the great god Dollar—now *earned* their salaries. They knew how overworked and undertipped they would be. Their very lives would be at stake in the hysteria that would now become their daily fare. From dawn to dawn there would be no peace. Everything was a crisis, and the simplest request—for a bit of paprika or an extra towel—was vocalized like a drowning man's cry for help.

The service was never quick enough or leisurely enough. The food never had enough pepper or always had too much pepper. Shades always had to be drawn or raised, chops rarer or better done—with the only alternatives suicide or murder. Since opera singers are the hungriest people in the whole world, the mad dashes to the dining car for the first sitting could be likened only to the panic that follows the cry of "Fire!" True, the second sitting often saw mezzos and tenors left unfed or, at least, not fed properly; but I was seldom one of the slowpokes.

"What's on the menu?"

"How can we keep up our strength with these small portions?"

"Hamburger again!"

"The hell with the waistline! They have Lady Baltimore cake."

"I'll have the liver, but instead of the grilled tomato . . . What the hell do you mean I can't make a change? I *detest* grilled tomato, and no one is going to force me to eat it!"

"Lima beans will be all right. What do you mean I can't?"

"Waiter, I asked for some more butter fifty miles back—and if I don't get it, Mr. Johnson is going to hear about it."

Then we were in the lobby of the hotel in each town, waiting for our rooms. The lines, the queuing up like schoolchildren waiting for a vaccination. Your hotel depended on your name and income. In any case, at the Y or the Palmer House, there was always the sextet from *Lucia*.

"But I made my reservation last month."

"Last month? *I* made mine last *year*. You promised me the same room."

"You don't understand, my good man. I never sleep in less than two rooms."

"No window? I'm a singer, not a coal miner. No, this time I'm through. Really through. If Gatti-Casazza were still . . ."

"What do you mean, no cooking in the room? I cooked there last year and fed half your damned staff."

"Well, if I can't sleep anywhere, I don't know how they expect me to sing. I just don't care anymore. I just don't care. I've had it."

It was—and it is—bedlam. Mr. Johnson, who traveled in a drawing room with a staff and a traveling office, had a fantastic organizational job, which Mr. Bing and Frank Paola, the tour director, have inherited and do so thanklessly.

Opera singers on the road should be tagged and labeled like children off to summer camp. There's always someone lost at the movies or in a department store. One miserly conductor used to stay at third-class hotels and would have to find his way to the rehearsal hall from one-arm joints on the other side of town. Others—some of the ladies—stayed at the very choicest hotels, in suites paid for by admirers who traveled with the company or discreetly alongside it. Sprawled over a city though the mob would be, everyone would gather at the converted ballroom or auditorium, where we would rehearse, put on our performances, and then disperse again. After three to five days, we would move on—all five hundred of us—and it would start all over again.

Two trains arriving in a station; bassos, sopranos, baritones carrying bags, posing for photographers, priming themselves for new battles at new hotels; everyone exhausted, but always the few who have rested and groomed themselves for the press. Never enough redcaps. Italian conductors screaming for their bags in Milanese or Neapolitan patois. Everybody fighting for cabs, and some splitting them to save money. Everybody yelling and screaming—except those who are singing that night and are therefore terribly refined and aloof. But the wives or husbands or lovers who were traveling with them would do the screaming for them and then be shoved into cabs to ensure the hotel reservations or register first at the best hotel. Chaos. It was absolute chaos. And I loved every moment of it.

The caste system is extant in the opera. And just as the choice of hotels and restaurants in the towns divided the stars from the chorus, so did the accommodations on the train. Then, within these groups, cliques would form. There was the oregano clique —the amateur chefs from Italy who traded recipes and made their own food over burners. Then the gossip clique—those who would first invent and then pass on the latest dirt about one another. There were the game players, who whiled away the time with Twenty Questions, Ghost, or a great quiz that went something like, "Who hit a flat C in *Butterfly* back in 'twenty-three?" Then there was the storytelling clique, which had much in common with the gossip clique, and screams of dirty laughter would rise from each group every few minutes.

I was not above joining one of these groups—the poker players. Pinza, Baccaloni, Ferruccio Tagliavini, and I were quite a quartet, though, I fear, not always in close harmony. Baccaloni was, of course, adorable, and Tagliavini vocalized by singing the words *Pepsi-Cola,* whose fascinating syllables he had learned in Italy from our GI's. His English was pretty good, but Baccaloni's was impossible. I rarely understood what he was saying. Since he was famous as a clown and I wanted him to like me, I laughed a great deal at his stories, and we got on famously. On one occasion, though, he went on and on, in his usual unintelligible way, and I kept nodding my head as his lovely eyes popped with excitement and his five chins shook. When he was through, I leaned back and roared with delight.

"*Ma!* Roberto," he stopped me in shock, "but he is *morto—* dead!"

Ah, Baccaloni! His poker was about as good as his English, but it was always fun being with him. As for Signor Pinza, he took the game seriously. He was frugal, Ezio, and carried a small purse that rather enhanced his sixteenth-century personality. He was a real don, and you expected him to throw the purse to the porter in reward for some small service. It never happened. The strings were drawn tightly, and the purse sat with his rising stack of chips on the table.

I was never lucky at poker, but the games were extremely pleasant. Both Pinza and Tagliavini were warm and more than friendly. I could say and do no wrong—until one night when I developed a winning streak. It can happen. I began filling inside straights and drawing third deuces. My luck changed completely, and so did the two signori, only Baccaloni remaining jolly—if unintelligible. Pinza and Tagliavini became so ill-tempered and rude that I half believed that in a former day—a bit further west —they might have run me off the train or engaged me in gunplay.

I was a novice with the opera and was scheduled to sing with these great stars, so I reversed my winning streak until I was even and then left the game. I never played with them again, even though once more I had become their favorite young baritone.

Once settled in a city, it wasn't all work. The company was entertained like royalty. Opera lovers across the country presented us with a string of breakfasts, lunches, midnight suppers, and buffets that were more lavish than I could have ever imagined. These marvelous people spoiled us rotten. One evening, uncharacteristically arriving late at one of these fetes, I approached a musician who, in New York, usually, after a performance, had a jelly donut and coffee at a cafeteria.

"I got stuck back at the hotel. How was it?" I asked.

The violinist shrugged his shoulders. "How was it? Caviar, lobster, terrapin, champagne—the same old crap."

In Atlanta, opera lovers gave galas that were incredible in their opulence. Without exaggeration, the countless molds of pâté and whole roast pigs and cold viands and salads would have fed a great army. Nevertheless, I took a risk if I stopped to shower and change: by the time I arrived at some of these bacchanals, the plague of locusts called the Metropolitan Opera Company would have stripped the once-groaning tables of all but the wilting ferns. I had joined the right company and met my equals.

One of our conductors looked like a whale in his tails, and

these parties helped keep him in shape. As for the singers, costumes got tighter and tighter as the season went on. One of our
tenors had a heart attack after one such supper.

If the gang was not wolfing food, it was preparing it. Once, in
Cleveland, Papa Senz, a great chef, was making a fantastic
spaghetti sauce in the wig and makeup room. The meat sauce
had been simmering on a Bunsen burner for hours, and the re-
sults smelled spectacular.

Since I wasn't singing that evening until nine-forty, I had a
light snack; and finding the food irresistible, I promised to be
back for more after the performance. But something struck me
on stage that night—and it was my Aïda, Zinka Milanov. Utterly
repulsed by my aromatic Amonasro, her nose wrinkling in horror,
Aïda, for the first time in the history of the opera, recoiled from
her father. When she slapped my face, she added, "And don't
you ever do that to me again!"

Between Caruso's broth and his own garlic sauce, Papa Senz
seemed committed to my destruction. Zinka was no weakling.
She packed a mean wallop.

In time, I came to expect such behavior and simply turned
my other cheek. Everybody was temperamental, and everybody
was eventually on the receiving end. The story went that Zinka,
at one time quite heavy, so irritated Toscanini that he pointed to
his head and shouted, "If you had here, Madame, what you have
here"—pointing elsewhere—"you would be an *artiste extraordinaire!*"

I survived her fury that first season, and through Papa Senz,
Zinka and I kissed and made up. There is always compensation,
however, and I was paid in kind for my lack of consideration. In
Houston, Texas, as I sang Amonasro in one-hundred-degree heat,
under lights that made the town's heat wave feel like a pleasant
zephyr—with audience and orchestra in shirt sleeves—I made my
entrance and within three minutes lost every bit of makeup; it
ran off me, leaving the whitest Ethiopian ever seen on or off
the stage.

By the time my second season was about to open, in October,
the road experience had made me part of the family and had
given me even greater confidence. I was ready for new roles and

straining at the leash in an effort to get Mr. Johnson and St. Ledger to let me do Valentin in *Faust*. Having shied away from minor parts from the outset, I had managed to secure myself three major roles that first season, two of which—in *Carmen* and *Traviata*—were building my reputation.

Forever being told that Valentin was coming up, I bided my time. Amonasro was my newest role, and I was scheduled to sing it with Ella Flesch. Other than that, I was told to be patient. It was difficult.

CHAPTER TWELVE

MY OTHER CAREER was doing so well that I was able to buy a house on Long Island and moved my parents and myself in after we burned all our old Brooklyn furniture. I was itching to spend money, and I took my mother to Sloane's on Fifth Avenue, where we started from scratch. We were now settled not too far from Gil, who had a small house and was now looking around to improve *his* lot. Gil had left the Brooklyn Navy Yard, and my old, dear friend Sidney Baron had recently been discharged from the navy. Sid and I had been friends since he had lived with the Margolises while studying conducting. He also played piano, after a fashion, and he used to accompany me on occasional club dates. He had played for me at Gil and Julia's wedding at the Château d'Or on King's Highway. Gil and Sid met again now and became friends.

Sid's brother was in steel, in Toledo, and Gil went out there to learn the business. The plan was that he then would return to the East and become Baron's New York representative.

Gil learned fast and became so fascinated with the field that he decided to become a steel broker. A broker needs an office, so Gil installed some phones in the basement of my house, invested twelve hundred dollars, and acquired a partner, a friend's father-in-law, who had capital. And so the Meldon Steel Company was born.

I introduced them to my local bank; and with that initial loan, they made their first purchase of steel, sold it at a profit, and they were launched. With Gil on his way, both Miller boys were now doing all right.

Although I was planting my roots in the opera, it was clear that I was reaching far afield for further nourishment. It may seem more understandable when it is considered that I was at that point making one hundred and twenty-five dollars a week at the Met and two thousand a week on radio.

It wasn't the need to support my family; that, I could easily have done on my Metropolitan salary and concert engagements. This was something else. I wanted all the good things for myself, and I loved the kind of mass adulation I could get in the popular field. I still loved "Show Biz."

It took a half hour to record "The Whiffenpoof Song" at RCA, after I sang it successfully on my program, and the first six months' royalty check was FORTY-FIVE THOUSAND DOLLARS—all in capitals. The record became number one on the *Hit Parade* and was played on jukeboxes throughout the country, pushing crooners, swing bands, and all sorts of entertainers that I had envied to second place.

Now that I had such celebrity in the popular field, the field that all the guys back in Brooklyn would really find worth conquering, my irritations grew greater back at the opera. Valentin in *Faust* was given to Martial Singher, an excellent baritone, who had preceded me into the company by three years. He had seniority, but my impatience knew no reason.

From the outset, I had shied away from any minor role, and now, through the salesmanship of Emil Cooper, one of our conductors, I allowed myself to be conned into taking one. Cooper was a Russian—dynamic and fast-talking—who had been at Salzburg for twenty years.

He came to me while he was casting *Boris Godounov*. "Merrill! You have got to do *Boris!*"

"Boris? You must be mad. I'm not a basso."

"Not Boris!"

"I could have sworn you meant *Boris Godounov*."

"I did, Merrill. But the part I want you for, it is not Boris. It is *more* important."

"Maestro! Please don't tell me that Moussorgsky named the opera after a minor character."

The conductor shook his head with a smile. "You are a funny fellow—everybody says. But you are also—even more important —a lovely baritone. I want that you sing the Tchelkalov."

"Tchelkalov? Who's Tchelkalov?"

"He asks me who is Tchelkalov."

"That's right, who is Tchelkalov?"

Cooper raised his arms as if he were conducting a symphony of agony. "Only the man who *makes* the whole opera."

"Please, Maestro, I must get to NBC."

"You do not know *Boris Godounov*, do you, Mr. Merrill?"

"Not to speak to," I answered.

"Ha, ha!" he laughed mirthlessly. "A very funny fellow. So let me teach you, young man. The baritone *introduces* Boris. The baritone *opens* the opera. The baritone is secretariat of the Duma."

I had never heard the whole opera; I had listened only to the Chaliapin solos. I knew that Pinza was singing Boris, and scuttlebutt had it that Cooper was assembling a fine cast. The way he was talking, and with Valentin out the window, it might be a good idea at that.

"He is?" I asked, not knowing what a Duma was.

"The audience will fall on the *floor*, Merrill! I am telling you. What a *gorgeous* music you will sing!"

The music *was* gorgeous—all sixteen bars of it. That was my whole part in *Boris Godounov*. I had been completely taken in by Emil Cooper, who could sell anything.

But it turned out well enough: the role seemed tailored to my needs. I wore a robe over my street clothes and an easily attached beard, and it turned out just fine. I was really lazy. After all, having the number-one hit record in the country kept me busy hopping to Lindy's and Colby's and the bank.

Then came the topper, the cherry on top of the sundae, perhaps the greatest moment in my life. In the midst of all this razzmatazz, Sam Chotzinoff called me. *The* Maestro, Toscanini, wanted to see me. An avid radio fan, he had heard me sing the "Di provenza." The Maestro and his NBC orchestra were going to broadcast *La Traviata,* and he wanted me for Germont. He had never seen me at the opera; he just wanted the voice after hearing it. This, it turned out, was typical of the old man.

When Chotzinoff first relayed Toscanini's request to see me, I almost fainted. I might have been feeling like a big shot around town and backstage, but this was the towering musical genius of my time. It was like being beckoned by God. *Toscanini!* He *had known* Verdi. When Chotzie passed me the word, we were at the radio station, in the studio, and I couldn't believe it.

H. Leopold Spitalny did not share my shock. He believed it. His comment brought me back to reality. "Chotzie! Ve must see dot he doesn't ruin dee boy's tempi!"

My *bar mitzvah* years before had been just an audition. My debut at the opera had been a dress rehearsal. *This* was the moment. Knowing the great man's reputation, I was aware that he could destroy the speck of ego I now possessed.

I'll die if he doesn't like me. If he doesn't accept me, I'll kill myself!

My call for the first *Traviata* rehearsal at NBC was in Toscanini's own studio on the eighth floor. Needless to say, I didn't sleep the night before. My anticipation of the worst kept me busy pacing. My parents heard me. Momma made tea and got some *hamentoshen* out of the cake tin, and Poppa joined us in the kitchen wearing the old Indian robe he wouldn't throw away. A whole house, and the three of us were still huddled in the kitchen.

Poppa tried to relieve my mind. "If he asked for you, Moishe, he knows what he wants. So what are you worried?"

"I know, Poppa."

"So, at your Opera House, famous they may be, but to me, one tenor in particular, I shouldn't mention a name, he sounds like he's *pishing* on a tin roof and they yell 'Bravo!' Another singer, I don't understand how a man can go a whole night without blowing the nose. So why are *you* worried?"

"Listen to the critic!" Momma interrupted impatiently. "Fought me every inch of the way to keep his son from being a singer. And now he's Olin Downes and Virgil Thomson together."

Poppa ignored her. "At the Metropolitan, all the time you sing

the part he wants, and the newspapers, God bless them, tell
the truth for a change and rave. So what are you worried? Here,
have a *bissel* tea and then sleep, mine boy. This walking like a
wild animal behind the bars in the zoo, up and down, is no good.
Listen to your Poppa."

My mother looked at my father in irritation and then jerked
her head toward him. "Does anyone except an artist know,
singer mine?"

Now, Poppa was a stranger.

"Toscanini asked for you after he heard your record, so he
likes you, already, and knows what he wants," she said.

"But, Momma, imagine. This is Toscanini!"

"He's a man like everybody else, Moishe."

"No, Momma, not like everybody else."

"He's a great man, Moishe, but he gets hungry like everybody,
and he's got ears and loves to make beautiful music and wants
you to sing for him. You'll help him, and that's why he wants
you. Here, take a fresh lemon—that's dry."

She now turned back to my father. "Abel *Hamentoshen* is not
a medicine—it's poison. Don't complain to me when you get
sick later."

"If it's poison, it shouldn't be in the house. If it's poison, what
is it doing here? A man can't take a *tiny* piece of *hamentoshen*
in his own kitchen?"

The next morning, I boarded the subway into Manhattan and
sat singing every note of the part quietly to myself. My heart
was thumping at the thought of meeting so exalted a musician. I
finished the "Di provenza" pianissimo and was shocked to hear,
"*Bravo, giovanezzo, bravo, bravissimo!*" I looked into a broken
overcoat button and then up into an old Italian man's face. He
was hanging by a strap and smiling. *Maybe it's an omen,* I
thought. I was always seeing omens.

On the eighth floor at NBC, a receptionist informed me that
the Maestro was expecting me. Expecting to find the entire cast,
I was stunned to see Toscanini sitting alone at the piano. He
looked up as the woman announced me, and I stopped halfway
toward him. He was wearing a linen Italian prisoner's jacket,
buttoned all the way down the front. Our eyes met. Never before

or since have I seen such eyes. They were like hot nails burning right through me. We stared at each other for an eternity. Then he twisted his mustachio and beckoned me with his second finger. Gingerly I moved toward him, sensing his disapproval. *Is it the way I'm dressed or my youth or my face? In everything there is chemistry, and if chemistry doesn't work between people, you can forget the rest.*

The longer I stood there, the more hopeless it seemed. He seemed to be sniffing me, the way an animal does. I felt myself diminishing under his scrutiny. I can never forget the man's presence; his beauty was astonishing, and energy radiated from him like a halo. He was luminous and almighty, and evidently this was Judgment Day—and I was being stopped at the gate.

His voice is going to be thunder and lightning! All Radio City will tremble with the fury of his pronunciamentos!

But his voice was pianissimo, almost gentle, actually plaintive. *"Ma!"* he began. "You are the Germont from radio, the man Chotzie speak of?"

"Yes, M-M-M-Maestro," I stuttered, for the first time in ages.

His head shook almost imperceptibly. "You make the 'Di provenza' for Red Seal?"

"Yes, M-M-M-Maestro."

A great sigh escaped him, followed by another silence. I half expected tears to fall from those eyes, they now looked so sad. *"Ma,* you are ten years old, Mayrrill."

"No, Maestro, I am twenty-eight, going on twenty-nine."

"Ma, he is a child," he complained to some Roman god who had failed him once again. *"A bambino!* He knows no suffering. He has not lived yet. Ah! He is just beginning." He addressed me again. *"Allora!* Do you *have* a son?"

"No, Maestro, I'm not even married."

The Maestro seemed to weary of me and turned back to the piano. It would have been his way of dispensing with me. I wasn't sure what to do. Then he began to play, and I recognized Germont's first entrance music. Toscanini proceeded to play the entire role. It was obvious that I was supposed to sing, and I did, trying desperately to keep up with him. Practically blind at that point in his life, the Maestro, though a genius, was not a pianist. Neither disability stopped him from forging ahead and, indeed, changing tempi, as Spitalny had suggested he would do. He never stopped once until I had sung every note of the role, and then this mad and maddening audition was over.

Toscanini closed the piano score with great ceremony and once more turned his penetrating gaze on me. I felt I had just run an Olympic race against Mercury.

The Maestro's eyes became alive with mischief. *"Ma!* Mayrrill, *you* and me together—I am going to make you a father!"

As long as I live, I will never forget the smile that followed.

The next morning, Chotzie called to say that the Maestro found me inexperienced, and terribly young, but capable of growth. He liked me.

For the next ten days, we rehearsed alone every morning before the orchestra and the other singers. Licia Albanese was again the Violetta, and Jan Peerce, a great favorite of Toscanini's, was the Alfredo.

During those rehearsals I saw the legend of Toscanini as a reality. Almost everything I had heard about him was true: he was the sun and he was a hurricane; he was kind, he was sarcastic; he was considerate, he was sadistic. There was only one cliché that I found without any basis in fact. The story was that he would explode in fury because of some disapproved mechanical subtlety in the singing or playing. This was absolutely untrue, although he did demand technical perfection. It was the emotional demands he made on his men and soloists that were inhuman.

His own vitality and passion were such that shallowness of expression, lack of vigor, poverty of soul drove him to near madness. He looked and listened always for the inner life. If this was not present, he was capable of the most satanic cruelty. If he was guilty of any mistake, it was that he expected of others the same divine urge and boundless energy that he was blessed with. With all his impatience and lethal wit, he was always saved from a rage by honest emotion, by heart. *This* lack made him lose compassion, thus lack of heart in a musician made him heartless. It was ironic.

During piano rehearsals, our Gastone in *Traviata* was not

getting the quality the Maestro wanted, and he was trying desperately.

"Gastone, I want you to laugh the notes, not sing them. *Laugh!*"

The tenor, through sheer terror, became more mirthless on each successive attempt. His voice was excellent, but he could not—through either fear or lack of humor—produce the light-hearted song the Maestro wanted for Verdi's music.

"Are you deaf?" he screamed. "Ha, ha—hahahaha-ha-ha!"

Poor Gastone, ready for suicide, was hardly in the mood to laugh. It got worse and worse, the laugh grislier and grislier until, in one last horrible salvo, Toscanini fired the poor guy.

If this happens to me, if he yells at me that way in front of everybody, I'll never sing again—anywhere.

I actually prayed—as the Maestro, with exactly the right air, laughed the notes and replaced the Gastone—that I would survive the purge and be the permanent Germont. Everyone was cringing in terror. He could do that to you then, when he was still a youngster—in his middle seventies.

One of his cellists, a poor schnook, was emaciated and seedy looking. To my ear he played just as well as the other cellists, but Toscanini would rage, "Live! Live! Don't just play the notes!" The man would play the passage again while the cast and the rest of the orchestra would wait in embarrassed silence. The guy would give it everything he had, and the Maestro would storm, "No! No! Have you no heart?"

Finally, the man took to keeping a bottle under his chair and peppermints in his pocket. It is true that a healthy man cannot be forced into self-destruction, but this particular musician was so hounded, so lacerated every day, that he eventually drank himself to death.

Toscanini, that beautiful Renaissance man, would jump up and down like a monkey, screaming and cursing, when the orchestra would not do as he wished, did not give reality to the music he heard inside his head. His men detested and adored him—even that cellist, whose escape into whiskey was literally a damnation, a self-inflicted punishment for not living up to the standards of his master.

What a temper that glorious man had! His head would rear

and his finger would point at the offender like a sorcerer's. The eyes would glow with hatred, the words were poison. He was delivering another curse! He had hundreds, each one more colorful than the last.

This to the strings: "Because you are all idiots and I can find no man anywhere who can play the violin, I am going to change professions. I am going to open a *whore*house, and when I do and I have the most *beautiful* women in the whole world offering their glorious bodies, not *one* of *you* will be allowed through the door!"

Concentrating his vitriol, he once collared a French-horn player who had fallen short of perfection. "Your mother, *imbecille*, should never have let you come out."

One morning, someone said that at the Metropolitan Opera House, the music was played a certain way. The mere mention of my opera company would literally drive him into a frenzy, and he would scream his favorite curse against the institution he left forever in 1915. "You talk of that place which I pray every night of my life that God will burn down," he began, taking a deep breath. "Starting on the roof, where the music is made filthy by their touch, then to the top floor, where the *artists* rehearse, and on down to where the conductors mislead their singers. And when all the floors are smoking and charred and in flames, it should burn to the ground floor, where the orchestra bastardizes the music from the roof and management sits making the place the *grave*, the *tomb*, of all beauty and honesty and heart. And when there is nothing left of this terrible place but ashes and bits of embers on Thirty-ninth Street, I would stamp those out with my *own two feet*."

He would then, in a purple rage, stamp his feet like Rumpelstiltskin. No one in his right mind would ever mention the Metropolitan Opera House a second time in his presence.

Whatever had been his battle with Gatti-Casazza years before, the Maestro had given up opera for symphony and had only recently, because of Chotzinoff, agreed to bring opera to radio. It had been an irreplaceable loss to the Metropolitan that this genius had exiled himself. The world should be forever grateful that Samuel Chotzinoff convinced the Maestro to interpret and record so many operas, especially those of his beloved Verdi.

Our *Traviata* was proceeding but with certain problems. The duet between Licia and myself had, all in all, gone well at rehearsal, and now I had my solo aria. There was a bass and cello introduction to the "Di provenza." The Maestro had talked at length with me of Germont's feelings concerning his son's future. He coached me tirelessly, wanting, demanding, more maturity than that of the Germont for which I had received such praise at "that place." I understood the men's adoration of him. When, at last, you got what he wanted, you realized a potential in yourself you had never even suspected existed. The Maestro made you better than even *you* thought you were. He made you float. He made the impossible come true.

I was ready for my solo, but we couldn't get past the strings. "*Basta!* I want more accent, *bassi!* Accent! Again."

The cellos and basses would play and my mouth would open to form the first note.

"*Imbecilli!* You don't know what *accent* means? *Feeling!* Again! You are amateurs, plumbers!"

Time after time, he stopped them just as I was about to sing. In this mood, he would cut me to ribbons. But on the umpteenth time, I began to sing.

"No, no, Mayrrill! *I* will sing until these butchers get it right."

Despite his failing eyesight, Toscanini saw everything, from every angle, from all sides. He knew when the trumpets, seventy-five feet away, weren't paying attention. His antennae picked up the slightest defection. The Maestro missed nothing.

Once, at a piano rehearsal—out of his eyeshot—with my hand under a table, I tapped out the rhythm on my knee. I was conducting for myself in four, or four beats to the measure.

When the rehearsal was over, the Maestro passed me and patted me gently. "Mayrrill! That part I always conduct in *two*, not four."

I would have died for him. He was a god. Now he was demanding celestial music from his ever-so-mortal musicians, and I waited, pulsating with the rest of the company. At last he was satisfied and pointed at me to begin singing. Completely unnerved I was palsied with fright, Still, it was impossible to forget what he had taught me, impossible to contain what he had demanded should flow. I felt my voice escape me and float free.

When the aria was finished, there was a terrible calm, and then the Maestro sprung from his podium and threw his arms around me. I was so grateful that my first rehearsal was over, so relieved that it had gone well, that I clung to him. Wrapped in each other's arms, we were for all the world a father and son reunited after a lifetime. In a way, we were.

"I make you a father, *caro*," was all he had to say.

It was a great moment. Maestro Toscanini had touched me with his magic, and I would never again be free of his presence.

In the great duet that Licia and I sang in the second act, there was one syncopated passage that gave me trouble: the bar starts with an eighth rest before the baritone voice comes in. Afraid of missing that moment, I kept anticipating it. This man of biblical rages would gently beat the time on my head with his baton to give me the proper beat. To this day, whenever I sing Germont, I feel the Maestro's magic wand upon me.

In two weeks, we broadcast the *Traviata,* and it was a smash success if not a perfect performance. There were minor mistakes, and though it had been taped at the studio, the Maestro would not allow it to be issued as an album, refusing to perpetuate the few tiny flaws. We were all greatly disappointed until—one night at Constance Hope's, where Toscanini, in the gayest of moods, was enjoying the champagne and soup he adored—an RCA executive told a group of us that the tape had been pirated and that copies were being sold in Europe at fifty dollars each.

The Maestro was furious. As hard as he could be, there was none more softhearted. "You mean that to hear Toscanini they pay fifty dollars?"

"Yes, Maestro."

"And without the fifty dollars, people cannot hear?"

"That's right, Maestro."

He shook his head. "*Ma!* The rich do not have better ears. Let everybody hear. Those racketeers cannot keep Verdi and these voices from the people."

And so it was released here. His son Walter, with whom he lived, had the original tape in the cellar of their house and now played it to see whether the errors could be erased and those portions redone. It was possible, but it was August and my hay fever was back. The Maestro, who suffered from ragweed also, was sympathetic. Therefore, the album was released as it was, even with the charming addition of his own voice singing along *sotto voce*.

This was my first operatic album and certainly my most memorable. It marked an association that added a few cubits to my stature as a singer. It added nothing, however, to my gray matter and erased any humility I might have had. Now a favorite of Toscanini, I might just as well have been knighted. My feet never touched ground, and Sir Moishe began flying in and out of the Metropolitan, barely bothering to rehearse properly.

From the peak of the Toscanini broadcast, I now entered the valley of my career. Moe Gale was tasteful enough to keep me from accepting engagements that were undignified, and certainly my club-date days were over. For better or for worse, I was a Metropolitan Opera star, and there were jobs—no matter how well paid—that were now beneath me. But there was one particular job that was obviously above me: the one I was too stupid to respect and work at. But no one could tell me anything.

I was drunk on my life, and this was my champagne period. Every night was New Year's Eve. Remembering it now, it is a senseless montage of snatches and pieces of what I thought was glamour: clubs and flashy girls and fan mail and bravos from my claque. It was my champagne period, all right—all bubbles and the worst of hangovers.

There wasn't much time for study, and I would wait until the very last moment before I began to prepare a role. Relegating my Metropolitan career to second place, of course, I never hesitated to use the prestige that accompanied it!

ROBERT MERRILL, YOUNG STAR OF THE METROPOLITAN OPERA HOUSE, WILL PRESENT A PROGRAM OF HIS SONGS

ROBERT MERRILL, METROPOLITAN STAR, GETS HIS HAIR CUT AT THE TERMINAL BARBERSHOP

BOB MERRILL OF THE MET AND DANNY KAYE OF HOLLYWOOD SURPRISE THE AUDIENCE AT THE PALACE

One evening, just before I was introduced at a *Night of Stars* benefit, I bumped into Danny Kaye backstage. He screamed in shock, "You! It's *you*, somebody Miller from Tamiment!"

"You! You were that skinny guy with the wife who played piano and wrote that funny stuff!"

"'Figaro!' I should have known. I was in my car one day and had the radio on, the top down—you know—my hair flying in the wind, when suddenly that voice came over the air. Robert Merrill! For Christ's sake. That's *you!*"

After the reunion, we became close friends. That season Danny, a brilliant comedian, was playing his first great engagement at the Palace, and we were together constantly. One day, I was watching from the wings, when he dragged me onstage. Typically Danny, he had been knocking himself out for the audience and wanted to change his shirt. He simply introduced me to the audience and left me onstage with his accompanist, Sammy Praeger, who was an old friend.

My shy days were over. "Sammy—do you know 'Deena'?" I asked.

I then went into an impromptu imitation of Danny, which worked so well that it brought the madman back onstage, fresh, dry, and at my throat. Choking me, he yelled that he would keep out of the Met if I would quit comedy. We did a duet, then ended a seven-minute spontaneous act with "The Whiffenpoof Song." I carried the melody while Danny, suddenly a small boy, bowed and closed his knees as if in a mortified attempt to hide the fact that he had seen his duty and obviously done it. The audience adored it, and Robert Merrill, Metropolitan star, was getting laughs as an entertainer and adoring it even more.

When I played the Roxy some time later—a return engagement, this time as the star of the show at seventy-five hundred a week —Danny, just arrived in town, checked his bags and came directly to the theater. When I saw him making faces in the wings, I pulled him out. The management couldn't have been more pleased when he ran into the audience, jumped over people's heads, and generally went berserk. Again we ended with the "Whiffenpoof" duet. There were those who said we had quite an act, and no one will ever know the satisfaction I got out of clowning around onstage.

Mr. Johnson did not think I was funny. I was depending more and more on prompters instead of knowing my parts thoroughly; and though I never neglected my voice or completely stopped studying—that was like brushing my teeth every day—I was really goofing off. I was being spoiled by my radio programs, where there was little discipline necessary. I was falling back on my natural singing ability, taking the easy way. It was possible over the air. It was not possible at the opera.

We were on tour, and I was sitting in the club car of the train with Mr. Johnson. His coolness to me had reached such glacial proportions that I asked him why. He was such a gentleman, Edward Johnson.

"Why do you imagine there is anything, Merrill? Are you guilty about something?"

"Please be frank, Mr. Johnson. It's important to me," I insisted.

It certainly was important that this man, who had always been so kind to me, also approve of me. He had never called me "Merrill" before, and it was awful.

"I know there's something, Mr. Johnson, and I'd love to clear the air. You know how important my work with the opera is."

That did it.

"If you wish me to be candid, that is exactly what I do *not* know."

"Mr. Johnson!"

"All right, young man. You've asked me to clear the air, and I will. I have lost all respect for you."

This I had not expected to hear.

"The Metropolitan is very important to all of us," he continued, "and I do not like your exploitation of our company for your own commercial purposes. It is not dignified."

"But I was on radio before I joined you, Mr. Johnson," I justified. "And I sing the finest music."

"Sometimes!" he interjected.

"But wouldn't you say that I was making a lot of new friends for the Met, Mr. Johnson? No, really! Millions of friends who hear an aria and maybe like it and then come to see opera for the first time."

"I never said that you were not nor could not be an asset."

"I would never do *anything* that would in any way hurt my career with the company. It's my life. You must know that. It isn't as if I were on *Lum 'n' Abner*."

"'*En l'homme honorable' quoi?*" my cultivated boss asked.

"Nothing will ever come before the Met," I said, trying to convince us both. "Please don't feel that way about me, Mr. Johnson, please."

"If all that you say is true, why are you so ill-prepared? There is never any complaint about your voice, but your attitude is something else again. You arrive late; you are flippant with the conductor and, at times, insensitive to the needs of other members of the cast. Just because it comes easily for you, you must understand that rehearsal and *serious* rehearsal is necessary for other members of the cast."

I was really getting it, and everything he was saying was well deserved. "I am genuinely sorry, Mr. Johnson."

"It is delightful that you have such high spirits, Robert," he softened. "But putting on opera is a serious business. I ask only that my company be disciplined and conscientious. You have a great career ahead of you if you don't let it slip through your fingers. This advice is for your own good."

"I won't fail you, Mr. Johnson. I promise you."

Our talk cleared the air, and it did pacify him. It also curbed my kidding around—for a while. Everything I had said to Mr. Johnson was sincere, but I really didn't understand the complaints. I *was* making friends for the opera through my radio programs; and as for my lack of preparation, it might conceivably have been hurting me but certainly not the opera. The audiences were great with me, and I was getting more than my share of the bravos. I was now singing Amonasro, Valentin, and the inevitable Figaro in *Barber*. Yes, I was getting more than my share of the bravos and saw no reason to worry.

It was difficult for me to be sedate, but I tried for a while. Almost symbolically, Danny Kaye visited me at the Met and went insane again. I introduced him to our conductor, Fritz Reiner, who was a tense, dedicated, no-nonsense character. Hungarian and explosive, Fritz could easily blow up, and Danny, to whom nothing was sacred, did everything possible to detonate the bomb.

Not since the Marx Brothers in *A Night at the Opera* was such mayhem and sacrilege committed at the Metropolitan. Danny was thoroughly outrageous as he joined Reiner up on the roof, singing everybody's part at the *Falstaff* rehearsal, throwing the music in the air, turning the whole session into a shambles, and forcing poor Fritz into good-natured surrender. Like everybody else, Reiner was wholly disarmed. Danny always got away with this disgraceful behavior by being the most charming man alive. His victims always wound up in the palm of his hand.

Much later, when I introduced him to Mr. Bing, Danny immediately called him Rudy. Rudy! I almost died. I would have been kicked right in the head, but Danny got away with it. Unbelievable!

It has always been difficult for me to understand people like Danny. With his assurance and self-confidence, Danny seemed never to be in doubt about anything; he could walk into any situation and command it. It was the quality I had heard in Titta Ruffo's Figaro, in everything he sang. Men like these never seemed to suffer from fear, from feelings of inferiority.

I was on my way up at the Metropolitan and had already arrived as a radio star when I sang at a benefit one night. Lawrence Tibbett and John Charles Thomas were standing in the wings, and you would have thought me an amateur or a child if you had seen my embarrassment. What was I doing, daring to sing in front of them? No critic, no conductor, no Mr. Johnson could convince me that I was good enough to take their place.

I certainly wasn't lacking in vanity; but at the beginning of my third season, in 1949, when Mr. St. Ledger called me to his office, he frightened me more than Mr. Johnson had on the train.

"Bob," he began with a great big smile, "we have a surprise for you. We want you to do *Rigoletto* this coming season. We think you're ready now."

Rigoletto! The greatest baritone role in opera! To be told you are going to do Rigoletto is like an actor being told he can do Hamlet. This Hugo-Piave-Verdi hunchback is *the* role, and its rewards are as great as its demands. My heart sank with the realization of my inadequacies. The requirements for this work are immense. I could kid the others, but I knew what my limitations were. Didn't they know I was just a guy who had struck it lucky? I couldn't take on such a big job.

"Gee, I'll have to think it over, Mr. St. Ledger."

"Think it *over?* I don't think you heard me, Bob. I said *Rigoletto.*"

"I know. I heard you."

"You've heard of the work, of course. It's only the best baritone role in opera." He thought he was selling me the idea.

All my childhood fear returned. *I can't ask them to turn all the lights out onstage! I can't ask them to let me sing it from the dressing-room john!*

"I know," I answered Mr. St. Ledger. "B-b-b-but I'll have t-t-t-to think it over."

The gentleman couldn't believe his ears. "Aren't you the same Mr. Merrill who refused to learn any part but a lead in his first season? Well, this is the *biggest!*"

"I know, Mr. St. Ledger, and I'll think very seriously about it."

"This is nonsense, Bob. You're going to do it, not think about it. I don't know what's on your mind, but we need you and you're ready and that is that, young man."

That night Moe Gale and I spent hours mulling over the possibility of my tackling the part. He too was convinced that I was ready, but I would accept no argument. At last he suggested that I take my problem straight to Edward Johnson, which I did.

"But I imagined you would be thrilled, Robert," Mr. Johnson said. "You're the heir apparent. Mr. Warren is doing concerts, and Mr. Tibbett . . . well, he has been with us for over twenty-five years."

"But I'm not ready, Mr. Johnson."

"I wouldn't allow you to sing such a major role as Rigoletto if I didn't think you were ready."

Major role! Rigoletto made Germont and Escamillo and Amonasro look like bit parts. The whole weight of the opera rested firmly on his hunched back. *They must be out of their minds. I'm a kid. I know I have a voice, but I'm a kid. How could they think I could follow Tibbett's performance?*

"I'm sorry, Mr. Johnson."

"Think of your career, Robert."

"That's just what I'm doing, sir. It may be a disaster. I'm just not ready."

Mr. Johnson looked at me hard. There was a flicker of recognition in his eyes, and at that moment, I believe he understood me: both the boy who was blowing his own horn loud and big and the young man who was terrified of real responsibility. "I suppose you're not, Robert. When you are, we'll *both* know."

It was simply a question of maturity—or lack of it. My God, I was still living at home with my parents like a child. Something had to be done about that! First things first.

CHAPTER THIRTEEN

ONE DAY, I was in the Met's rehearsal office and overheard someone at the telephone ask, "Is Tibbett there?"
There was a silence, and then this fellow said, "Well get that
bum over here and pronto!"

He was talking about the great Lawrence Tibbett, who was
at the sunset of his career. He was no longer *Mr.* Tibbett, he was
"that bum." Of course, it was nonsense; Tibbett would be celebrated as long as there was opera, and this little man's name
would be, and actually already has been, forgotten. But I got
scared. Just beginning my career, I thought of Mr. Johnson's opening-night bromide, and it was true. We were all part of the flow.
I would eventually inherit Mr. Tibbett's roles as he had De Luca's
and as De Luca had Scotti's. It was like the *begat's* in the bible—
only, in reverse.

*Someday somebody's going to say, "Get that bum," and when
he does, I want to be able to hold my own and ask nothing of
anybody.*

I was scared and began to buy government bonds; and then,
through some singer-turned-insurance-man, I began to take out
annuities.

I was buying bonds, but I was also taking stock. According to
all my buddies, it was time this bachelor had a bachelor apartment. Even Moe Gale said that it would be far more convenient
if I lived in town, and there was no earthly reason why I couldn't

keep up two residences—one for my parents and one for myself. That is, no financial reason. Even my father suggested that I take my own place when he saw what the tensions at home were doing to me.

Poppa's health was becoming progressively worse, and everything was going wrong with him. His diabetes and stomach ailments were real enough, but when I took him to the doctor, the diagnosis was not a physical one.

"Your father has to get away from home for a while."

"Okay, Doc. I'll send them off to Florida—or on a cruise in the sun."

"No, Bob, that isn't what I mean. *He's* got to get away—alone. Maybe to his brother Max, up in Utica. Doesn't he run a shoe outlet store now?"

"That's right."

"He's an easygoing fellow, as I remember."

"A very sweet guy."

"Well, there's your answer. You must get him away from your mother."

But Mom wouldn't allow it. "Get out!" she'd scream. "Let me alone! Let me have some peace." But she clung to her charge, imprisoning them both. Now I, for one, *had* to get out.

When one of the directors at RCA got himself married and gave up his apartment on Sixty-seventh Street, off Central Park West, I grabbed it. I grabbed it, all right, but it took me three months to screw up enough courage to break the news to my mother that I was really leaving. Now things got worse.

Pretending that the apartment was coming through in a week or so, I tried to convince her that it was not the end of the world. "Gil didn't disappear, did he?"

"Your brother's a married man," she answered, forgetting how she hadn't wanted that, either. "When a man gets married is time to leave his home."

"The boy has a right," Poppa said. "He pays the bills. He's the boss."

"So help me God, Abe, if you open the mouth on this subject! The boy is just talking. He's too smart to leave his home, this beautiful house. Is he crazy—with everything beautiful, and still new, and his mother to cook for him and make a home?"

"I'm not just talking, Mom. It's time I had my own place. *Everybody* says . . ."

"Everybody! Who? Bums and *bumikehs,* hall-room boys and *bumikehs!*" She now dropped all pretense. "Fun I can't keep you from having, but the safety of the home and the parents is something else after all the laughing. *Your own place?* What's in a New York City apartment that you don't have here?" She put her hand to her mouth. "Sh! The answer must be something you can't tell a mother."

"What are you talking about, Mom? I'm a man now—an opera singer, a star on the radio."

"And too important for your mother?"

"Lotza, the boy didn't . . ."

"It used to be your friends would come here and I'd feed them. How they loved it. And we'd sing all of us and have fun. What went wrong?"

"Nothing, Mom. I . . ."

"Do I annoy you, Moishe? Do I once ask for tickets to the opera? Always I wait until I'm asked. Am I like some mothers, wanting the child not to have a life? You don't enjoy yourself with the girls and your friends—God only knows where—till all hours so I don't sleep a wink?"

"You *sleep!*" Poppa interrupted.

"You *put* me to sleep," Momma lashed back. "So shut up!"

"Leave the boy alone, Lotza. *Oi!* Such a mouth. Moishe, listen to your Poppa. Go. Fly. Get out. She can drive a man crazy."

"Me drive . . ." My mother started to sputter with rage. "You'll drive me to the gas pipe. Don't you dare talk of driving. I became a nurse. *Not* Lotza, *Lillian Balaban, singer,* with her own program on the air! Who knows what could have happened? I became a nurse for an old baby who doesn't grow, still a greenhorn, who sneaks out of the house to *nosh* English muffins with orange marmalade, yet. *Poison!* Now he poisons the boy's mind. Moishe, Robert, singer mine, Moishela, why? With no reason to leave a beautiful home? Why can't you be satisfied where we're all happy?"

"Momma, this is pointless. It's not the end of the world if I move into town."

"It's not?" my mother asked.

"No, it's not. I'm not going to Mongolia. I'm going to Manhattan."

"It might as well be Africa."

"You'll change your mind, Momma."

"Never!"

"Go, mine son," Poppa cried. "Get out."

My mother now turned on my father. "You should be *cursed* for sending your own flesh and blood from the house *he* paid for. When were *you* ever . . ."

If I had waited another week, I would have gone out of my head.

After my Sunday broadcast, my mother called me at NBC.

"Hello, Momma. Everything all right? How's Poppa?"

"Hello," my mother greeted me calmly. "I thought I should tell you that I'm going to commit suicide. I'm taking the gas pipe tonight. If you don't want it on your conscience for the rest of your life, you'll come home right away."

She hung up immediately, knowing that no line could possibly have topped that little speech. That night I drove home and packed the little I'd left there. Poppa hadn't been feeling well and was asleep.

My mother sat, a portrait of tragedy. "You're leaving? You've made up the mind?"

"Yes, Momma. I'll be here Friday for supper."

"Friday I won't be here. Friday I'll be dead."

"Stop talking like that, Mom. It's not funny."

"Funny! You've always laughed at everything, you and your brother. My whole life, everything, the sacrifices, the work, the dreams. It was all a joke. Lotza Balaban, the comedian. Laugh everybody! And my funeral! That will be what you call the 'big finish' in your show business. We'll see how you laugh."

I had heard so many funny stories about the mother who won't let her sons go. My God, they're not funny, those stories. They're grisly. In some curious way, Momma's scene was making me

strong. I had always been indecisive, but she was now making
it impossible to retreat. "You're aggravating yourself for no reason, Mom. Now I'm leaving. I have to drive back now. There's
an early rehearsal call in the morning. Take it easy, Momma. The
whole business is ridiculous."

"I know your mother is ridiculous now that you're a big
macher, the famous Robert Merrill. If you walk out now, I have
nothing to live for. Who? What? Your father who steals candy?
A *goniff* who stole my life? If you leave, as God is my judge, I'll
kill myself. The gas pipe is the only answer."

I suppose that did it. "All right, Mother, you're right. But just
remember one thing. If you commit suicide, *I* will cry and Poppa
and Gil will cry and maybe a few other relatives—*and then life
will go on*. We'll bury you and I'll say Kaddish and we'll light
a candle on the anniversary. Is that what you want? A *yohrzeit*
candle once a year? Good-bye, Momma."

She refused to make my parting official by even answering
me. Recoiling at my attempted embrace, she sat stiffly at the
window and refused to look at me as I left the house.

I called Gil, whose home was in New Hyde Park, not far away.
He and Julia wished me luck and then went over to Momma's
"for a cup of tea" while I drove to Manhattan and my first apartment. This is the way I was forced to leave home.

In a sense, my mother was not just being dramatic; her threat
was not an empty one, for from that moment on, she tore her
health down and made both herself and my father wretched. A
fury raged inside her. Of course, by outer appearances, things
were normal. I went for dinner, she and Poppa came to the
opera, I spent time with them and shared as much of my career
as possible. At these times, my mother would almost recover
her old spirit.

At the Chambord or Le Pavillon or some such fashionable
restaurant, my chameleon-like mother, in all the finery she was
so proud of, would sit like a queen. The menu could be the
size of a billboard and all in French, but she'd point to the right
dish instinctively or outbluff the headwaiter. Nothing threw
Lillian Miller.

Poppa was a different story. Not able to eat certain foods anyway, he'd sit, my little father, dwarfed by the outsized menus and napkins, looking helplessly at the bill of fare. But he didn't have one grain of pretension.

"Moishe?"

"Yes, Poppa!"

"If I could read the French language, which I can't, I still couldn't read it in this darkness. No light. It's supposed to be romantic, maybe?"

"It's atmosphere, Abe," my mother explained with contempt.

"Atmosphere! Who can tell what you're eating if you can't even order? So I can't see!"

"Let me suggest something," I would say.

But he would have already collared the waiter, whose snobbery was destroyed immediately. Looking directly into his eyes would be this delightful man with raised eyebrows and a sense of conspiracy.

"Sir!" he would address the waiter. "Do you have, maybe, in this gorgeous, fancy place, maybe a little chopped liver? And maybe then some chicken? A half broiler would be lovely. Plain, no sauce. I'm not a well man, you know, but I can always eat a little something if it's cooked good. Mine son here, he says the food here is A-number-one."

He always got the best service: waiters can spot a phony a mile off, and they, like everybody else, immediately sensed Poppa's genuineness. He was authentic, my father. He was called the mayor of 169th Street in Kew Gardens. And Mom was jealous. She never understood why it was always Abe who was adored. He was so human, my father. He missed his boys when they moved away from home, but he accepted the inevitable, he never resisted what he knew was the natural thing. Boys crawled and then walked and then ran away from home.

Well, I had left home. The world was a big place, and now I wanted to broaden my horizons even further.

Licia Albanese and her husband, Joseph Gimma, a stockbroker, were off to Italy on a vacation and asked whether I would join them. The idea of a change of scene, now that the first act of my life was over, appealed to me. Now that I had left home, why not see the world? The idea of seeing Europe was exciting to begin with, but to see it in such congenial company made it impossible to refuse. Licia and Joe were marvelous. Joe had his car shipped over to Naples, where we picked it up. I couldn't believe I was on the Bay of Naples. Sorrento, Amalfi, Pompeii, Vesuvius, the San Carlo Opera! The home Caruso built for himself when he made it big! The sky was so blue, the buildings so pink! It was a Fitzpatrick Travelogue. It was marvelous. "See Naples and die." But it wasn't the tourists who were dying but the Neapolitans. Postwar Naples was in terrible shape. The natives were everywhere hawking, begging, some of the more desperate borrowing babies to soften the hearts of the "rich" foreigners. Children wandered barefoot, dressed in rags, but laughingly accepting gifts and hugs. Their poverty was no joke, but life is an *opera buffa* to most Neapolitans. War and peace, feast and famine are part of the same libretto. Naples has always been poor, but it is beautiful. Like grass that pushes its way up through concrete, the Neapolitans laughed and enjoyed—even then, in 1949—and their city, for all its war-torn areas, was anything but depressing.

Traveling with Italians was, of course, a help, and the Gimmas gave me Italy on a big silver platter. Joe had family in Bari on the Adriatic, and we made that our first stop. Then we crisscrossed the country on our way north, seeing places I had thought existed only in dreams. Rome, with its ancient and modern ruins, its great physical beauty and vitality, brought back memories of Ramon Navarro in *Ben Hur*.

Those cities! Verona, Assisi, Siena, Pisa, Perugia! I even saw Rimini, where Francesca came fom.

Verdi's home in Parma was a special pilgrimage. I had to see where such a man had lived and worked. Giuseppi Verdi had always been a favorite of mine, but Maestro Toscanini's adoration of the composer had increased my interest in him. The Maestro had also lived in Parma, studying at the Pagal Conservatory. Reading about the great Verdi and his sensual love of life and, in a sense, his slow maturity as an artist brought me even closer to him. He too preferred the contemplation of nature to the labors of his craft. I have always hated studying, whether it was at New Utrecht High School or the Metropolitan Opera House.

Deadlines! *Ugh!* I have always detested work. When you are young, you can often avoid doing the things you hate. But as you grow older, it becomes increasingly difficult to live on plain charm. As the years go by, you buckle down and you write *Otello* instead of *I Masnadieri.*

At this point in my life I was having fun again. Again? When had I ever stopped? Licia and Joe took me everywhere, from the baths at Salsa Maggiore, where we left smelling of acacia leaves, to La Scala. Unfortunately, the opera house was closed, but we spent hours in the museum. We were given a special tour of the opera house—stage, pit, and all—and I was enraptured. *This is where Toscanini conducted Verdi! It's been here since 1778!*

This trip to Europe was important in my life. For the first time, I became sensitive to the durability of art. In Florence, for instance, simple identification with the great beauty that surrounds them all day long has had a refining effect on the Florentines. "Breeding" suddenly became clear to me. When generations of a family or a community are exposed to grace and splendor, then it is reasonable that the offspring are thoroughbreds. Exposed long enough, for instance, to the symmetry and aesthetics of Florence, you've got to have some of your rough edges smoothed and beveled. *Culture* suddenly wasn't a stuffy, empty word but an atmosphere in which good and fine things could flourish. I thought of the cabbage-smelling halls of my childhood, the ugliness of Williamsburg. Florence was probably the furthest thing from Williamsburg there was.

We heard an opera there, in the exquisite little Pergola Opera House, an obscure Rossini work, heavy and rarely played; but the three of us were entranced by the young soprano. Her sonorous voice, her charm and beautiful presence made us search the program for her name. What a lovely discovery she was. We were so thrilled with her performance that we went back to congratulate the girl—whose name was Renata Tebaldi.

When we got to Venice, that most improbable of cities, I was greatly affected by the architecture. Venice is itself a work of such art that living in it must be like spending your life onstage in a sensational opera where everybody is a star.

We really lived it up, staying at the Royal Danielli Hotel, where my room hung over the Grand Canal. I thought it very romantic—until I closed my tired tourist's eyes, only to hear the cackling of angry voices. It was an argument interspersed with laughter, and when I looked out of the window, directly beneath me was a group of gondoliers dividing their take.

"Please be quiet!" I shouted, to no avail. "Shut up!" I then screamed. Knowing only the Italian from my operas, I attracted their attention with a double-fingered whistle and then yelled Tonio's "Si puo?" from *Pagliacci*.

It worked, and they stopped babbling and yelled back, "*Si?*"

I was then helpless. I could only continue, "*Signori, signori,* pardon me if I am alone. I am the prologue."

This insane introduction didn't impress them. Obviously thinking me *umbriago* and not responsible, they continued their chattering.

Then, in a brilliant flash, I shouted, " 'Tacea la notte placida'!" This is one of the soprano's arias in *Trovatore*, and it means "Peaceful was the night." I thought it an excellent choice, but they still didn't get the point. There was now only one language left. Taking my water carafe, I emptied it over the group and went to sleep.

The next day, bright and early, we went walking over and through the maze of streets and canals and took the inevitable gondola ride. Having negotiated a price—I wondered whether our gondolier was one of the noisy parties from the night before —Joe, Licia, and I got in, made ourselves comfortable, and tried to pick out the various *palazzi*. The trip was delightful, and our straw-hatted oarsman began to sing, for the tourists, a medley of P.S. 19 songs like "Santa Lucia" and "Funiculi-funicula." He was simply terrible, and as we were smiling our approval, I thought of the night before and winked at Licia.

"What about a little *Traviata*, honey? He'll fall in the water!"

Joe beamed expectantly, and Licia cocked her head mischievously. "All right, Bob."

Licia Albanese burst into most beautiful song, and then I joined her. Our unexpected duet rocked the boat. Our gondolier dropped his oar, almost losing it altogether, and was rendered silent—probably for the rest of the season. Other gondolas began to follow and glide abreast of us, and Licia and I just kept singing while people waved and swayed—like an old Grace Moore–Nino Martini movie. We'd never had such fun.

We met an American woman in the Piazza San Marco who told us that her daughter, Dolores Wilsoni, was making her debut at the opera as Gilda in *Rigoletto* that very night and would we please come? It sounded like a great idea. We got all decked out —Joe and I in black tie, Licia beautiful, terribly dressy, and elegant. We arrived at the little Teatro Malibran to find everyone dressed informally, the men in shirt sleeves like at a ball game. The asbestos curtain had advertisements for restaurants and barbers and markets and drugstores. It was a Venetian version of a second-rate vaudeville house, and *we* were dressed to kill. We were so ridiculous that we were part of the show—the curtain raiser. And then the tenor came out, and—*questa o quella*—I had never heard such an ovation anywhere. You would have thought Caruso had been resurrected for the evening.

"Who is that?" I asked.

"I don't know," Licia answered, looking through her program. "I think it was Pasquale something."

"He must be fabulous," I said. "Listen to them—here in Italy, where they really know opera."

"He looks very young," Joe ventured.

The boy began to sing, and the poor kid was—*questa o quella* —from fish. Nevertheless, when he was finished, the audience went mad. We could only assume that they were all deaf, until we discovered that he was a local boy from right across the canal.

Our young Wilsoni girl turned out to be a lovely Gilda with a beautiful voice and, especially for a debut, great poise. At the end of her duet with Rigoletto at the end of the third act, which went very well, the demonstration for the two singers was immense. Cries of *"Bis! Encore! Bis!"* forced the curtain up again to find only the young soprano onstage. The audience kept screaming as the curtain descended again. It rose once more, and now only the baritone was there and ready to repeat the aria. It was a comedy of errors. Lubitsch or Mack Sennett couldn't have directed it better. When both, at last, emerged together and

extended their arms to the maestro, *he* had disappeared. It ended
with the Rigoletto, all alone onstage, singing the duet by himself
—no mean feat, believe me.

But I envied this baritone because he was out there doing the
role that I didn't dare to try. A cloud suddenly hung over me as I
remembered Mr. Johnson's understanding of my fears. In an
effort to shake the depression, I thought, *No, when it's right for
me, I'll do it, not before. Courage and ignorance are two different
things.*

We took the successful young Gilda out for supper and wished
her well. All three of us felt that the girl had a career ahead of
her. "Work hard," I heard myself say. Then I suggested that we
go across the lagoon to the Lido. I was in the mood for some
roulette. I had dreams of going to the casino and breaking the
bank like Ronald Colman in the movies.

The casino had just opened, and sitting there at the gaming
tables with a glass of champagne in my hand, I fancied myself
an impoverished Russian prince who would save his whole
dynasty and the girl he loved through a streak of unimaginable
good luck.

Rouge ou noir! My fantasies were getting me nowhere, but Joe
couldn't make a mistake; it was incredible. From a very modest
start, Joe was now commanding all attention. Whether on even,
odd, red, black, or a number, his chips kept multiplying. Not
being greedy, he was willing not to press his luck and leave with
a sizable profit; but I needed some more drama.

"I'll take one third of your bets, Joe. Keep it up."

"All right," Joe announced. "Leave it all on red."

My heart almost stopped. We had a few thousand riding on
the red, and I watched the tiny ball spin around with a new sense
of urgency. This was really thrilling! Of course, Joe won again,
and with all my knowledge of roulette—acquired at Loew's Pitkin
and the Republic in Williamsburg, it is true, but from great
teachers like Mr. Colman and Cary Grant—I was now the junior
partner in a brilliant international speculation.

Joe and I kept winning, until our spiraling profits brought a
haggard and harried manager over. The poor guy was white.

He leaned over Joe's shoulder and begged us to stop. "I just opened, and you're breaking me. If this goes on, I'll have to close down tonight. Please, *per favore*, I beg of you—stop, enjoy your winnings, and let us buy you some more champagne!"

What a gay and happy night that was for all of us, including the manager now that we complied with his wishes. The evening was perfect. Crossing the lagoon, returning to the Royal Danielli, we made plans to go to Murano in the morning, since I wanted to send some glassware home to my parents. We left an early call, and I went to my adjoining room and got into a hot tub.

Lying there in that beautiful marble bathroom in Venice, I was blissfully happy.

Joe knocked on the bathroom door. "You in the tub, Bob?"

"Yes, Joe."

"Can I come in? It's important."

"Of course," I answered. "Join me. I'll get a sailboat from room service and we'll play together."

When Joe walked in, he didn't look as if he wanted to play. His eyes were filled with tears.

"What's the matter, Joe? Is Licia all right?"

"Licia is fine, Bob! A cable came. . . . They gave it to me and . . ."

"What is it, Joe?" I asked quietly, almost knowing. "You can level with me."

"It's . . . it's your father."

"Poppa!" I yelled. "What happened?"

"Here, Bob." Joe was holding out a towel.

But I didn't want to move. It was warm and safe in the bath. I was a kid again without any worries about parents dying. I knew. You always know. You just don't want to believe it.

"Tell me, t-t-t-t-tell me!"

"Your father . . . he passed away."

Joe broke down, and then I did. I let out a wail, and that's all I recall. I don't remember getting out of the tub, but I was wrapped in a terry-cloth robe and sobbing in my room as I tried to get the airport outside Venice on the phone. Licia, in her night-robe, was crying also. The three of us were impossible. I had to get home immediately, and it wasn't that easy, since it was necessary to get a reservation to the States from Rome; you couldn't get home from Venice.

What am I doing here in Italy? Why did I ever leave America? Why did I ever leave home?

I had to take a boat and a train and a plane and a cab. I would have run all the way home to Kew Gardens. Poppa! Oh, my God. That tiny little man who worked so hard and loved me so much that he begged me to leave home. I cried my eyes out while Licia and Joe managed to get me passage from Venice to Rome at 7 A.M., though from there on, everything was still doubtful.

The plane was a vibrating toy; how it got to Rome is a mystery. Haunting the TWA office all day, I would sob again as I recalled my father bent over his work at the sweatshop.

But why? Why now, when he can enjoy, relax, never have to work again? Why now?

There was one English-speaking Roman at the airline office, and he asked me what was wrong. When he heard my story, his eyes moistened. Those Italians! To them, every lost child, every sick Momma or dead Poppa is theirs. What heart they have! Through this fellow, I was squeezed onto an already full plane that night. In a way, my rush made no sense. Poppa was already dead, and there was nothing I could do for him. But I had to say good-bye.

The Pultisker Progressive Society, of course, conducted the funeral, and they had waited for me. "Where's Moishe?" they'd said. Moishe had been having fun again, but Poppa understood. He had loved it that I was going to Europe. "In my time, the thing was to come to America. Now everything is *moishe kapoy*. You make money, and instead of the mountains, you go back to the old country."

Poppa! He'd never asked anybody for anything in his life, and his children's success gave him nothing but pleasure. That overworked little body had been filled with pain for years; now it was free of misery. He was at peace, Poppa—as my mother never would be.

Both relieved of her charge and robbed of her mate, Momma was more guilty and bitter than ever. What had the world ever given her? Not much, I suppose, so I tried to make up for everything. She certainly was not neglected by her sons or her daughter-in-law Julia; but she preferred to suffer, my mother.

Once, at a *Night of Stars* benefit at Madison Square Garden, after my appearance, I called my mother up to the stage to sing with me. Looking radiant and running right up to the stage without coaxing, she joined me in a chorus of "Sweethearts." And she was great. She had come alive again, and it showed in her voice. I'm sure that the audience was surprised, simply expecting to hear Robert Merrill's mother carry a tune, but she was magnificent. Her large, dramatic soprano was as vibrant as ever. She had flair and a sense of drama, but this too helped to destroy her.

She was such a hit and seemed so happy that, in an attempt to engage her energy in something constructive, to fill her time, I introduced her to Mrs. Gustave Hartmann, the chairwoman of the benefit. Her husband, Judge Hartmann, was the cofounder of the Old People's Home. My mother could have done so much good there, occupying herself on the entertainment committee—something; but no, she went right back to her favorite pastime: eating herself up alive. She had her one night of stars and could again make me guilty for leading a life independent of her.

Gil and Julia now had two children. They were a family of their own and so had an excuse for not being at her beck and call. But I was the gay bachelor. My mother didn't know that I was lonely as hell, that to be alone was death to me, that I had to have people around me all the time, that I couldn't make a telephone call without having a pal join me in the booth. Now I understood why my parents had stayed together all those years. They had each other, my parents, to share their tortures, to feed and raise their family.

My apartment was filled with people and laughter all the time now. My mother would have considered it a halfway house or Grand Central Station—anything but a home. She was terribly suspicious of bachelor apartments, and rightly so. I'm afraid I wasn't studying too hard, either. I had a new role and kept putting off my preparation for it.

The Count di Luna in *Il Trovatore* is one of the most difficult

parts in opera. Bernard Shaw, when he was a music critic, said
that any baritone who attempted to sing it was insane. The role
is both dramatic and lyric, and the aria "Il balen del suo sorriso"
the most trying I have ever sung. And, again, you are on your
own. I kept putting off studying it, really learning the role; and
all of a sudden, there it was in the *Times*. In two weeks I was
making my first appearance as the Count di Luna.

I hate cramming, but cramming is what I had to do. I was
guilty of all the things that Mr. Johnson had accused me of. How
he tolerated it, I'll never know. Kidding around was one thing,
but giving the audience less than it deserves is another.

My first Count di Luna was disappointing. I got by through
sheer gall and the prompter's help. I relied completely on my
natural abilities and added nothing. And my acting! *Mama mia!*
Fortunately for me, Zinka Milanov and Kurt Baum were so
wooden that my own oaken performance wasn't singled out for
scorn. The three of us could have been the stars of a puppet show.
And to make it worse, it was a benefit for Hadassah!

The next season, I started off with my first High Priest in
Samson et Delila. This is another role I have never relished,
although I had an experience while singing it that I wouldn't
have missed for the world.

Kurt Baum, a giant of a man, was the perfect Samson, and
Risë Stevens the Delila. It must be said that Kurt, who had a
glorious dramatic tenor, was, like so many of his pitch, high-C-
crazy. He even had circulars printed: "Kurt Baum, the High-C
Tenor." Unbelievable! To begin with, poor Kurt was accident-
prone. Something always happened to him onstage; and in this
particular performance, it was while he stood as Samson between
the great pillars, blinded, shorn of his locks, his prayers about to
be answered. Singing away as he leaned against the columns
ready to destroy the temple and all his enemies, Kurt was
stunned when overzealous stagehands anticipated their cue and
brought the edifice down on the whole cast, Samson included.
The massive structure crashed before our hero was finished with
his aria. Kurt's reaction was singular. With the whole gang lying
dead onstage, Kurt, rising out of the rubble more like Lazarus
than Samson, girded himself and hit his high C as the curtain

fell. Risë and I were convulsed with laughter and could barely take our curtain calls. Nothing was going to rob Kurt of his favorite note, and nothing ever did.

When he wasn't making his own boo-boos, he was attracting them. As Don José, he bent over Carmen's dead body one night and his heavy hairpiece fell off—right on her face. Kurt was marvelous and had a magnificent voice, if little or no stage perception.

Kurt and Zinka Milanov were not overly fond of each other, yet they were fated to appear together constantly. Zinka would close her eyes in torture, as if to proclaim, "Everyone else gets a handsome tenor. *I* get Baum." Kurt would hear that they were cast together once again, and you could read his mind: "She is out to destroy me, that woman! I am never good with her!" The management, ignoring the feud, always had them sing together.

At one performance of *Trovatore*, Kurt, who prided himself on the fact that he could hold a high C longer than any other tenor, was singing his "Di quella pira" at the end of the third act. Kurt held the world's record of twelve seconds; and on this occasion, sword in hand, he hit a real beauty. With his luck, the curtain closed during the note; but Kurt simply walked through it with his sword and held the note until he was damned well through. His claque went berserk.

Kurt Baum was the tenor to end them all. When he first visited me, he walked into my still-to-be-decorated living room, which was curtainless and rugless but did have a piano. He went straight to it, struck his favorite ivory, and sang out his favorite note, holding it to my great pleasure. He commented on nothing in or around the house. Architecture, landscaping were lost on him. "Roberrrt! Ach! What a room for high C's."

That's all he ever thought of—that and his feud with Zinka. Since Milanov and he felt as they did, so, of course, did their claques. These gangs of professional adorers would shout each other down and often engage in all kinds of vendettas. Like everyone else, I had a claque for some time, until my disgust made me drop it.

In Italy, years ago, in order to educate audiences to a new opera, people were hired to cue the gallery and stalls to the end of the unfamiliar arias. This practice blossomed into the biggest racket in the music world. Realizing that power over audience reaction was possible, each singer began to hire his own band of devotees, who, for a price, directed the rest of the audience to adore him by creating a synthetic ovation.

The claque leader always gets free tickets and so much money a head. There are orchestra specialists, balcony noises, and standing-room bravos. I know one fellow who had cards printed announcing his trade: "Audience Enthusiasm." In Italy you can even hire booers to torture your archenemy. It is a most serious business there, and if a singer refuses to cooperate by paying a claque, he'll likely be beaten up after the performance, in much the same manner that Chicago hoodlums once employed to make vaudevillians and nightclub performers pay "protection."

Mussolini outlawed the claque, but it reemerged stronger than ever after the war. There are Italian claques, Bulgarian claques, German claques. I loathe them all.

Mr. Bing has tried to discourage their use here, especially when, just recently, Leonie Rysanek's life was threatened over the telephone a few minutes before the performance. These maniacs will obviously stop at nothing short of sopranocide. I got rid of mine years ago, after one of my lieutenants came backstage in Cleveland and threatened reprisals and repercussions if his ridiculous demands for a minimum amount of worshipers and a maximum amount of money were not met. It came to me that hearing bravos when I knew I had sung badly was pretty ridiculous, and this, together with the excesses of the ultimatum, made the whole business insupportable.

The Met knew that clients were solicited backstage, and individual claquers are now paid by check in order to keep it legitimate. Frankly, there are nights when my colleagues' demonstrations drown out my applause, and it *is* irritating; but I, at least, know that mine is from genuine admirers and not paid stooges. The claques don't like me, and I don't like them, so we're even.

One great tenor's claque always went into a frenzy the moment he walked out on the stage or tripped or blinked his eyes or just opened his mouth to take a breath. This army was well trained, and orders usually came from the general—the tenor's wife. One night, I overheard them as I was dressing. Frau Tenor was giving directions to a spy.

"When he comes out in the first act, everything you got! Understand? Then with the first aria, not *too* much but nice; and the second act, the little aria, a *little* more. In the *third* act, after the *big* duet, there I want a very nice hand."

"No!" I heard the tenor shout. "There and *everywhere* I want *alles bumbus*. *Everything* you got for the first, second, and everything!" Then he hit a high C just to keep in practice.

He wanted *alles bumbus* from the very beginning, and that's what he got from this balcony specialist, who now ran out into the field to deliver the latest orders. In the meantime, the tenor —and I saw this because I now went into his room—was on his hands and knees, undressed, as his faithful wife gave him a shot of B-12, which he was convinced was good for his voice. I always wondered why he didn't take vitamin C!

Whenever I think of manufactured "audience enthusiasm," I remember one particular *Bohème*. It is one of the great memories of my life. Jussi Bjoerling, Cesare Siepi, Licia, and myself all sang as we never had before. Jussi had had some bronchial congestion earlier in the week, but his Rudolfo that evening was fantastic. It was a date I will never forget: the first night of February in 1954, and all the stars were really in harmony. Siepi was divine, Licia maybe even better, Jussi absolutely miraculous, and I—if I may say so—didn't need any claque to tear down the house, which is the whole point of the story. The audience that glorious night applauded until midnight, *and it was real*. No one wanted to leave the theater. It wasn't a question of piercing screams of ecstasy emerging from isolated spots in the house. *No one* in the whole place moved from his seat. It is not often that an artist feels that he has worked at the top of his talent with others who have done the same. In that *Bohème* all New York was our claque!

When Jussi hit a high C, the audience, needing no artificial stimulation, was moved to demonstration. Jussi could do this with a B or an A—with any note. He was not high-C-crazy. He was an artist.

I know of one tenor whose maestro informed him that he was

conducting the "Di quella pira" from *Trovatore* in B flat. The tenor was unimpressed. "Maestro, you play in any key you want. *I* singa in high C." Tenors are dedicated men; on occasion, they meet audiences equally dedicated. In Parma, a tenor was so detested by the public that he was forced to leave town in the dead of night through his hotel window. In Parma, they take their opera seriously. When the poor guy, fearing for his life, got to the railroad station, the porter recognized him and hissed, "Carry your own bag, you butcher!"

But in Parma and elsewhere, I must admit, it is not only the tenor who gets it. Legend has it that a baritone in *Pagliacci* was so bad in the "Prologue" that the house rang with the boos. One Parmigiano began to yell, "*Bis! Bis!* Sing it again!" The baritone did an encore, and it was worse, if possible. Again cries of, "*Bis! Bis!* Once more," came through the hisses. A third time the terrible Tonio sang the "Prologue," and a third time came the requests for an encore.

The exhausted baritone poked his head through the curtain with his eyeballs popping. "I cannot sing it again," he gasped. "*Per favore,* I cannot."

"You will!" screamed the audience. "You'll sing it until you get it *right!*"

In Parma, they don't kid around. The opera is a serious business.

Something was to happen that seemed designed to teach me just how serious opera was in New York City as well. Edward Johnson's fatherly and permissive role in my life was being recast by the Fates and the retiring gentleman himself. As singer and then manager, Mr. Johnson had been with the Metropolitan Opera House since 1922; he was now looking for a successor. He found, in Rudolf Bing, who was visiting New York with England's Glyndebourne Opera Company, a perfect candidate. Through the board of directors, he approached Mr. Bing, whose eventual acceptance of the exalted post was to change my life dramatically. With Mr. Johnson's retirement in 1950, another chapter of my life was definitely ended.

CHAPTER FOURTEEN

I WAS USED to Mr. Johnson; indeed, we were *all* used to Mr. Johnson. His departure was something of a shock to the whole company. Our boss had been a singer and understood a singer's needs. He was an American and had done everything he could to help American artists and bring them into the company. We were all sorry to see him go. Rudolf Bing was an *X*, a great big *X*; and I was not alone in being apprehensive.

Slim and elegant, sharp-eyed and sharp-featured, polite and rather aloof, Mr. Bing cut through the red tape—and all sorts of rituals—like a brand-new pair of scissors. In a medium where great names abounded, our new general manager decided to play down the star system. The opera was the thing! Tonight—*Traviata!* It didn't work, but he tried.

With a great surge of energy and daring, Mr. Bing immediately engaged the legitimate theater's Margaret Webster to direct a brand-new production of Verdi's *Don Carlos*, with sets by Rolf Gérard—introducing Cesare Siepi as Philip II, Fedora Barbieri as Princess Eboli, Jussi Bjoerling as Don Carlos, Delia Rigal as Elizabeth, and me as Rodrigo.

Rodrigo is an excellent and noble part, with some of the opera's most lyric passages. Two of the baritone's arias, not well known, are exquisite and far more beautiful than the more popular "Di provenza" from *Traviata*.

I was flattered that Mr. Bing thought enough of my work to make me part of his first opera at the Met, his first opening, the very first innovation of his regime. It was clear that he liked me, and I was grateful that my luck was holding out. This young man was vibrant and courageous, and he had all sorts of marvelous plans for the company and me. From this particular production, it was clear that Mr. Bing intended to dispel much of the recent criticism concerning the visual tackiness of the Met productions. Later in the season, he was also presenting a new production of *Die Fledermaus,* for which he engaged the brilliant Broadway director Garson Kanin, who had both written and staged the classic *Born Yesterday.*

Much as we missed Mr. Johnson, it was difficult to grieve when there was so much activity and such hope for the future. Here, obviously, was a man who was going to get things done, and he began, most pleasantly, by raising salaries. When he arrived on the scene, I was making four hundred dollars a week. Now, beginning with five hundred per *performance,* my salary began a steady rise.

The job of running the Metropolitan Opera House is one of the toughest in the world. It is almost impossible to handle all the temperament, which does not begin and end with the singers. The conductors are the biggest prima donnas of them all. It is almost impossible to keep the peace and not to lose the excitement, to make the thunder without the rain, to balance the productions without damaging the Dresden egos of the artists. He has to make enemies, this man. It is important only that he not make the wrong ones permanently. Very few have the gift.

The weight of the opera world is on his shoulders, and the overhead is always greater than the take. There are one hundred and twenty musicians contracted for the season, ninety chorus people, twenty to thirty highly paid stars, six or seven conductors, and as many international directors; there are seventy-five stagehands, whose salaries average two hundred a head per week. Add to all this the makeup men, the assistant conductors, the ballet corps, the wardrobe mistresses and electricians, the painters and ushers, the office and box-office staffs and you may get an inkling of the budget and size of the Graustarkian kingdom that Mr. Bing has to govern.

No country on the eve of war ever had need of greater diplomacy and tact than this gentleman, who must cast a couple of dozen operas and try always to blend a beautiful voice with a beautiful figure and four to six principals who are congenial. Zinka and Kurt were the loving Lunts compared with some of the natural enemies who clasp each other's waists just a bit too tightly and still thrill the balcony with their duets. After all, there are just so many first-rate sopranos and tenors and baritones and bassos and contraltos. If Mr. Bing had to cast only with singers who adored one another, it would be the end of opera. He has a tough job, and he walked into it with eyes open and shirt sleeves—only figuratively—rolled up. He is quite a stylish gentleman. I must say I liked Mr. Bing immediately, but I was not yet as much at home with him as with Mr. Johnson.

When Danny Kaye came into town again, it occurred to me that he would make a magnificent Frosch in the brand-new *Fledermaus*. Mr. Bing was looking for a nonoperatic comedian for the part, and I thought it could be a tour de force for Danny and a great draw for the Met. I arranged a meeting at the St. Moritz, where we had cocktails. It was here that the irrepressible Danny called Mr. Bing Rudy and got away with it.

Nothing ever came of the Frosch idea, although both men seemed tickled by it. Jack Guilford eventually played it very effectively in a production that was a great success. Both Patrice Munsel as Adele, the maid, and Risë as Prince Orlofsky were delightful; and Ljuba Welitsch, whose debut the year before as Salome was nothing short of sensational and who as Aïda, later that season, was so dynamic that she practically knocked me off my feet on my entrance, was equally abandoned as Rosalind.

Things were really jumping at the Met that first season of Mr. Bing's reign. Two other singers made their successful debuts that year—Victoria de los Angeles, as Marguérite in *Faust,* and Roberta Peters, whose last-minute replacement of the indisposed Nadine Connor as Zerlina in *Don Giovanni* proved the making of her. She was quite the talk of the opera and, with excellent reviews tucked underneath her arm, was cast as Rosina in

Barber that February. Mr. Bing wanted me as Figaro, so I met the pretty young lady.

As young and as innocent as could be, wide-eyed Roberta was dedicated to her career, a very serious singer. I was pleasantly surprised to discover that her real name was Peterman, and having more in common than I had thought, we started seeing each other.

Things were happening for me at that juncture. On my return from Europe, I'd done a concert at the Hollywood Bowl and had received a phone call the next morning that I didn't take too seriously. Mark Newman, composer Alfred Newman's brother, was on the wire asking whether I'd be interested in a screen test. A year or so before, while having dinner at Danny and Sylvia Kaye's with Louis B. Mayer, I had sung for the great producer, and Danny had tried to talk the head of Metro into giving me a contract. Mayer was not unimpressed, but he had just signed Mario Lanza and didn't know how *he* was going to work out: opera on the screen had departed with Pons, Moore, and his own studio's MacDonald.

It was amusing in a way. I knew Lanza; we had met on Fifty-seventh Street in New York when he was still a serviceman. He wanted to be an opera singer, and after hearing him sing, I took him to Mr. Margolis. He did an aria from *Turandot,* and we were both impressed. Mario had a wonderful natural voice and not the slightest inclination to polish it. He asked for advice— "Should I learn sight reading? Should I get a coach? Should I study with this Margolis character?"—but he never took anyone's counsel.

A sweet guy and a real peasant, he had a terror of singing in front of a large audience. He played at studying for a short while and then quit; he had even less sense of responsibility than I. Compared with Mario, I was a conscientious student. From the beginning, with all my nonsense, my voice was always the most important thing in my life.

Mario, who wanted the Met so badly that he'd say, "That dump! I wouldn't be seen dead there!" was destined to become, before his early death, a movie star of the first rank. Yet he would have given up everything else to sing on Thirty-ninth Street.

"The Maestro, Toscanini, wanted to see me." Here at his home in Riverdale, New York, with (left to right) Norman Scott, Nicola Moscona, George Cehanovsky, myself, Jan Peerce, Lawrence Davidson. Seated with the Maestro: Virginia Haskins and Herva Nelli.

With Jussi Bjoerling (far right) and Nicola Rossi-Lemini backstage after our opening in *Faust*, 1953.

"What a pity Momma couldn't have heard Sutherland. How she would have *kvelled* from that voice and my singing with her."

Wagner International Photos

Leontyne Price, "the greatest Aïda I ever worked with!"

Wagner International Photos

"I bumped into Danny Kaye.... He screamed in shock, 'You! It's you, somebody Miller from Tamiment.'"

Wagner International Photos

Louis Armstrong. "We had a ball, Louis and I. He's a great artist and never says an unkind word about anybody. He's a beautiful human being."

CBS-TV photo

Years after I ate his prop donut, Red Skelton invited me to appear as a guest on his television show.

CBS-TV photo

Tonio in *Pagliacci*

J. Abresch

Gérard in *Andrea Chénier*

Louis Mélancon

Escamillo in *Carmen*

Bruno of Hollywood

Don Carlo in *La Forza del Destino*

Louis Mélancon

The Barber in *The Barber of Seville*

Sedge LeBlang

Renato in *Un Ballo in Maschera*

Sedge LeBlang

Amonasro in *Aïda*

Germont in *La Traviata*

Rigoletto in *Rigoletto*

Lord Ashton in *Lucia di Lammermoor*

Rodrigo in *Don Carlo*

Iago in *Otello*

"I had proposed. Marion had accepted."

Lizanne, Marion, "Singer Mine," David.

Wagner International Photos

At home with the Merrills.   *Wagner International Photos*

At the Voisin, celebrating opening night, 1964. Johnny Carson and his lovely wife, Joanne; Vice President Humphrey (then in the middle of his campaign) and his lovely wife, Muriel. Standing next to me is Leonard Goldenson, president of the American Broadcasting Company.   *Wagner International Photos*

Opening night is always exciting at the Met, even when I am just a guest and not singing.

Wagner International Photos

"I will be a good boy, Mr. Bing."

Wagner International Photos

Actually, he had all the basic ingredients for a great operatic career—except self-discipline. He also had glamour, with or without that hundred pounds he'd shed and regain every six months or so. He was a wild one, Lanza, but he was now the possessor of the one thing I had dreamed all my life of having: a Hollywood contract.

When Mark Newman called me at the Beverly Hills Hotel and asked whether I was interested in a screen test, I let out a whoop.

The next morning, I met with Bill Micheljohn at Paramount Pictures, and he took me into makeup. Before I knew what was happening, I was on a set—a living room. There I was introduced to an assistant director, who placed me on a couch next to a phony fireplace and then had lights and camera arranged around me. An off-camera voice asked me questions about my opera career, the Brooklyn Dodgers, and my impressions of Hollywood; then an accompanist sat down at a piano, and I sang "Figaro." It all seemed too easy and not very promising, too good to be true. Shades of my old dream of being another Bing Crosby. It was even the crooner's home studio. Everyone thanked everyone, and after the usual, "We'll call you if anything happens," I returned to New York to rehearse for my first season under the new regime.

But miracle of miracles, Moe Gale informed me that the test had been a success and that director George Seaton wanted to see me in New York at the Paramount Building on Forty-third Street. Paramount had a film for me—a wonderful script called *Anything Can Happen*. If another test in New York was successful, they would sign me to a contract. Moe and I were both thrilled, and we agreed with alacrity when we were told the picture would be shot in the summer.

The new test was also successful, and I signed a contract with Paramount that was beyond my wildest dreams: sixty-five thousand dollars for ten weeks' work! In my hysteria, I imagined that the ten weeks would neatly follow my Met tour, which always started in April. But things now took a strange turn.

I wasn't used to the ways of Hollywood. José Ferrer, an Oscar nominee, whose *Cyrano de Bergerac* was playing all over the country that year, was what they called a "hot property," and my script went to him.

That was where things stood while I was dating Roberta. Everything was up in the air, and we were both light-headed with our good fortune and our new romance.

With the exception of Zerlina in *Don Giovanni*, which she repeated, Roberta was doing only the Queen of the Night in *Magic Flute* and spelling Lily Pons as Rosina in *Barber*. My schedule had become fairly routine now—the Count di Luna, Germont, Escamillo, Tonio in *Pagliacci*, and, of course, Figaro. The season was going well for us both, and we were having fun, especially with that pink, hazy Hollywood future of mine looming on the horizon. Then the dawn came up like thunder.

One morning as I read the *Times*, a little item hit me in the eye: "Robert Merrill, young star of the Metropolitan Opera, will make his motion picture debut in *Aaron Slick from Punkin Crik*, to start shooting in April."

April! That was impossible—the Met tour began in April. A quick phone call confirmed the news. Moe Gale and I had a little conference. My contract with Paramount was ironclad. Certainly, Mr. Bing would understand my dilemma and release me from the tour, thereby ensuring himself a famous movie star as a drawing card the following season. Obviously, Mr. Bing would see the advantages for all concerned.

All this was obvious to everyone except one person—Rudolf Bing. The tour was set, and he found it impossible to release me from my obligations. I, in turn, now saw my one chance for Hollywood fame and fortune slipping through my fingers. It wasn't only the sixty-five thousand dollars; that was chicken feed compared with what I would make once I was a great movie star. And there was no fame like Hollywood's. Tibbett, Pons, and Moore had become household words through motion pictures. Their brilliant Met careers rested on the strong foundation of international acclaim gained by their screen appearances. This would be impossible for me to give up. This was and always had been my first dream. After all, Crosby had preceded Bonelli.

Mr. Bing was evidently bluffing, and Moe and I decided to

play his game. "He'll come around, Moe." Famous last words!
Mr. Bing was adamant. I was scheduled to appear in eight performances on the tour, beginning with *Don Carlos,* for which
I was already advertised. Moe and I tried everything. I still have
the letter Mr. Bing sent me. It reads:

Dear Mr. Merrill:
. . . Please let us not waste any more time, either in this
letter or in further conversation, and accept the fact that with
the greatest regret it is absolutely and completely impossible
for us to meet with your request for release from the tour.
. . . Frankly, as I said to Mr. Gale, I don't think it entirely
reasonable to make such a request about eight weeks prior to
the commencement of the tour. As you know, this is the first
tour under a new management, and changing of casts for tour
cities as against New York performances is one of the most
important features that can establish or spoil the relationship
between management and the committees of the various tour
cities. We really have no adequate replacement for you, and
even if we had such a replacement we would be failing in our
duty if we considered it. We have no justification for offering
any of our tour cities such a change at this late date when
your name has been announced and printed in the various
touring publicity and prospectuses. So, in short, let us forget
about it. I fully understand the disappointment it may be to
you and I regret it, but we all occasionally have to face up to
the fact that we cannot have everything we want. We must,
on the other hand, discuss at an early date your appearances
at the Metropolitan for next season. We have big plans for
you and I hope your next season will be as successful and
interesting as this one was. Kind regards.
Yours sincerely,
Rudolf Bing

<u>Put that in your pipe and smoke it.</u> The letter was softened
only by that bit about the next season. I was bound, but I refused
to be gagged. Nobody was going to stop me from singing my
way into all the theaters of the world. Only motion pictures

really circled the globe. Mr. Bing would have to understand and forgive.

"It's the gold ring," Moe said to me, "but there's always the chance Bing will get difficult."

"If I miss this chance, Moe, I'll never get over it."

"I know, Bob, but . . ."

"There are no *but*'s, Moe. This is what I've been dreaming about all my life."

"I thought you were always dreaming of the Met?"

"I did, but it came true. Can't a guy have more than one dream? You know how I've always wanted pictures. Now that I'm with the Met, if I make my name on the Coast, that's it. It's the gravy train, everything! Bing'll be the first one who'll be grateful, because it'll bring them in at the box office. When did a movie name ever keep anyone away? On Broadway or at the Met? Since Danny became a movie star, he can name his price in New York and London!"

"Bob," Moe implored, "don't think I'm not eager to have you make it big out there. . . ."

"Well, then?"

"You've trusted me up to now, and things have gone well—"

"So well," I interrupted, "that we've reached this fork in the road. What can Bing do? Give me a demerit? He says himself that he can't replace me. The tour will be water under the bridge. The picture will be over, and everything will work out. I've got to go, Moe. There's just no stopping me."

"Well . . . I think we can manage it."

"We've got to. This is the jackpot!"

I volunteered to pay for any replacement, even offering to import an Italian baritone, but Mr. Bing was not interested.

"He's got to release me, Moe!"

But Mr. Bing was not so inclined. Convinced that I could outbluff him—that he was trying to hang on to his cast but really understood—I not only ran out on the tour but, in my desperate rush, also skipped my last Figaro.

Hollywood had beckoned, and I dropped everything. No sacrifice was too great for me to make on my way to the top. Paramount! The very word means "above all others in rank, supreme."

Paramount. That snowy mountain peak surrounded by stars was a symbol of everything I wanted. It was my original dream. Damn it! Nothing was going to make me miss the bus.

My first stop was the Château Marmont and a four-hundred-and-fifty-dollar-a-month apartment that was a movie set itself. It was the foyer of my new life, the entrance hall to Wonderland. I was so impressed with the apartment and with myself that I almost lost consciousness. My first caller was Western Union. It was not a singing telegram.

Robert Merrill   Robert Merrill
Château Marmont   Paramount Studios
Hollywood, California   Hollywood, California

I have made many efforts to reach you by phone both yesterday and this morning which you have evidently avoided. Must therefore repeat statement made to your representative last night that unless you fulfill your obligations to perform on tour beginning Monday consider contract breached and all possibility future association Metropolitan Opera ended. Must ask for telegraphic notice of your intentions by six P.M. New York time. Greatly regret that you have forced me to such extreme measures but serious situation leaves me no alternative. Rudolf Bing—Metropolitan Opera

It was not only prudent but extremely astute of him to have sent his wire to both addresses. I was obviously not only in two places at once, with two dreams; I was actually two different people, and I always had been. And one of them was now wretched. Mr. Bing had up and fired me—a possibility that had never even occurred to me! This was a price I wasn't at all prepared to pay, even for Hollywood.

Didn't anybody understand? I wanted both worlds—not in collision but neatly orbiting around each other. The heavens were so designed that everything managed to avoid hitting everything else; why couldn't my universe be arranged as efficiently? There was nothing I wouldn't have thought up to rationalize my behavior.

Moe Gale was more practical. He wrote Mr. Bing immediately:

Mr. Rudolf Bing
Ritz Carleton Hotel
Boston, Mass.

Dear Mr. Bing:

I was, as you can imagine, terribly sorry to see your announcement in Saturday's paper regarding Bob Merrill.

Since then, I have been bombarded by the press for a statement. As I would prefer not to have this dispute bandied about in the press, I would appreciate it if you could arrange to see me in Boston on Wednesday to discuss the matter.

I believe that a meeting at this time would be to our mutual advantage since there are several vital facts which I feel you should know and which have direct bearing on the situation.

> Sincerely,
> Moe Gale

Mr. Bing's answer came by return mail.

Dear Mr. Gale:

If there are any "vital factors" of which I am unaware, you should have given them to me before. Now the damage is done and I cannot see any useful purpose to our meeting.

I cannot take seriously all this business about "misunderstandings." The whole matter is as clear as daylight. The Metropolitan Opera Management has been misled all along and Mr. Merrill has in cold blood broken his contract with us and is continuing to do so. The matter is closed as far as I am concerned.

> Yours sincerely,
> Rudolf Bing

I tried to justify my actions by claiming that the Met had failed to pick up my option for the road tour. I insisted that while I might be *morally* guilty, there was no *legal* contractual bond. I didn't have a leg to stand on. Even if I was in the wrong only morally, how much wronger can anybody be? But I was compelled to pursue my course, and there was no stopping me. Paramount would sue me if I breached that contract, and I might have chanced that; but I preferred to continue my quarrel with the Met, feeling that it would all somehow come out well in the end.

Lying around that absurd six-room apartment, I proved conclusively—if anyone ever doubted it—that I had left New York for a fool's paradise. *Don Carlos* opened in Cleveland with Frank Valentino taking my place as Rodrigo, and the papers were filled with the news of Mr. Bing's fury: "A singer's relations with us cannot be a one-way street. If we honor our obligations, they must do the same."

"Bing Fires Merrill" were three little words that flashed around the country and were understood by everyone except me. Well! I would show them all. I was hardly condemned to oblivion by the Metropolitan's rejection. My star, far from having fallen, was truly in the ascent.

The next day, I went to the studio and met with the other members of the cast: Alan Young, a nice lad whose recent appearance in Shaw's *Androcles and the Lion* showed real promise; Dinah Shore, a lovely girl whose great popularity on radio was obviously just a prologue to a great film career; and Adele Jergens, my love interest in the picture and evidently a new name in the making. Claude Binyon, our writer, greeted us by saying, "This is a great cast, and it's going to be a great picture." Produced and directed by the very successful Perlberg and Seaton, with a score by Livingston and Evans, whose "Mona Lisa" was up for an Academy Award, there was no doubt that it was going to be a sensation. This was the only thing that kept me from complete depression. The film had the sweet smell of success.

Paramount used my split with the Metropolitan for publicity and photographed me with Crosby, whom I never expected I would meet *this* way. The caption of the publicity shot was something like, "Paramount's Bing likes him even if the Met's doesn't." The whole episode was a nightmare.

I was now thrown into an exhausting routine of color tests, costume fittings, and rehearsals, which happily filled the day from seven in the morning until ten-thirty or so at night. In a state of fatigue, it was difficult to dwell on my own little dream.

Then I discovered that Dinah Shore had twelve songs, while

I had a chorus and a half. It was senseless. Perlberg gave me my first lesson in Southern Californian logic when I approached him.

"Bill, I'm an opera singer. That's what I do, or did. Why don't you give me some songs to sing? Or let me do 'Figaro' in that sequence when . . ."

"But, Bob," Perlberg explained, "the public knows you're a singer. That's the whole psychology!"

Nothing else was making sense, either. Claude was constantly telling me that I was projecting too much on camera. This was a new medium to me. In opera, the gesture is large and aimed at the topmost gallery; like the makeup, it is devised to project for a city block. The camera evidently picked up your innermost thoughts; and at this point, that was something for me to worry about.

I was now transformed into a glamour boy. Via Paramount and its publicity department—with a lot of help from the newspapers—I became Hollywood's official escort. Invited everywhere, my dates were a movieland who's who. I danced with that gorgeous, sweet Lana Turner, dined with the ravishing and *gemütlich* Marlene Dietrich, partied with Yvonne De Carlo and Sheilah Graham. The opera singer, the Metropolitan name, was always respected; there was always awe for opera singing. One night in a furry, blurry drive back from a party singing "Sweet Adeline" with Judy Garland and another couple, I remembered in misery that I was through, finished, washed up at the Met. The lure of Hollywood had done what my mother, poverty, and wild horses couldn't do: it had stopped me from singing. When Mr. Bing mentioned my name—in fact, when anyone did—in the press, it was (at Mr. Bing's request) as "Robert Merrill, *formerly* of the Metropolitan."

I pushed these thoughts out of my mind while I continued my whirl. Danny and Sylvia Kaye gave a party for the visiting Oliviers, and it was the gala to end them all. I sang "Figaro," Jascha Heifetz played the "Hora Staccato," and forty fiddlers floated throughout the house playing all night.

Vivien Leigh was bewitching. As for Sir Laurence, he unwittingly opened up all my wounds by pumping me about the opera. He was a frustrated singer. "How I envy you, Bob!" he said.

Envy me? He's the most famous actor in the world!

Olivier loves music, especially Handel, some of whose arias he sang for me that evening.

"I'd sell my soul, Bob, to sing like you."

But you don't become Faust that easily, and we both knew it. Still, I was flattered.

Olivier, Danny, and I joined forces and sang opera all evening —to our own delight, at any rate. Danny had a great voice and, had he studied, might easily have had a career in serious music. But, then, he also could have become a chef, preferably a Chinese chef. He is the most wonderful Oriental cook; I can still see through his transparent noodles.

All Hollywood set a feast before me, but I was starving to death. What the devil was I doing out there, so far from home, in that strange, unreal place? One morning—really, at dawn— when I arrived at Paramount to be made up, I sat in one of several chairs before a long mirror. A very pleasant character actress walked in and sat in the next seat, a towel around her head, ready for the makeup man. She nodded very warmly when she saw me, and I smiled vaguely, too tired to talk and not re- membering where I had ever seen her.

She probably just recognizes me from the newspapers, or maybe she has a bit in my picture, I decided.

Dozing with fatigue while the men worked on us, I would occasionally open my eyes and look at the bit actress in the glass. She seemed more and more familiar to me, but I couldn't place her. *Where in the devil have I seen this woman?*

Later she rose, now fully made up, an absolutely ravishing young beauty. And why not? It was my dinner companion of barely a week before, Marlene Dietrich, who must have thought me the rudest man in Hollywood.

I was certainly the most wretched. When I took Hedda Hopper to the Shrine to hear Lily Pons do *Traviata,* the music, the Germont, the whole evening brought home to me exactly what I had done to my life. If I'd been a drinker, I would have gotten plastered. As it was, when I got back to my apartment at the

Château Marmont that night, being an eater, I groped my way
to the icebox but found nothing. My whole life was as empty
and cold as that refrigerator. I was alone—with no opera, no
wife, no food, and no one to take care of me. In every way, my
life was one big bust. When I turned on the radio, there was a
benefit opera performance from the East. The whole world was
conspiring to help me drown in self-pity.

During the last two weeks, I had earned thirteen thousand
dollars extra for overtime and worked for four hours being
chased by a bull. Now I began to dub the sound—"looping," as
they call it—synchronizing the words with the action. It was all
very technical and very boring, science and not art, talking and
not singing. There was not one solitary second of self-satisfaction
in any of it. The last fillip was my appearance at the Motion
Picture Academy Award Presentations singing Livingston and
Evans' award-winning "Mona Lisa." As I sang the song, my mind
wandered to another stage, with a gold curtain and a giant pit
in which the orchestra was playing Verdi.

I'm out of my head. What in God's name am I doing here?
If I don't become a great movie star, then I've just flung myself
into space and I'm lost forever.

When I left Hollywood to do a series of broadcasts with the
San Francisco Symphony Orchestra, Paramount gave me a lovely
birthday cake but neglected to pick up my option.

Five years after the war was over, Hollywood created, in
Aaron Slick from Punkin Crik, the biggest bomb ever to hit the
movie theaters of the world. And Robert Merrill, "formerly of
the Metropolitan Opera," became part of the history-making
event. Alan, Dinah, and I had joined hands to make a completely
forgettable movie.

So the comet returned to the East with its tail between its legs.
Putting all pride aside, I now used every method of communica-
tion to reach my old boss—to no avail. He would have none of
me. I begged, I pleaded, but nothing would alter his decision.
And so—a tendency to excess being one of my many flaws—my
world was ended with both a whimper and a Bing.

CHAPTER FIFTEEN

WITH MY FUTURE still up in the air, I flew to Frankfort for the USO and toured all the army camps in Austria and Germany. Picking up a Dutch band and a private car, I traveled the length of the Rhine Valley, entertaining at everything from an opera house that seated eleven hundred to an improvised clubhouse, for audiences composed wholly of GI's. There were few streets in war-ravaged Munich, but a new opera house was already under construction. It was shocking to see nothing but rubble and dried wreaths over improvised graves. My first reaction was exultation—my enemy was dead. Then the piano player in the Munich pit, a squat, bull-necked little German, told me his story. He had gone out to lunch while five thousand Allied planes bombed Munich. When the raid was over, Fritz ran breathless through an obstacle course of smoking, gaping holes in a mad race to reach his family. He ran in circles for hours. Not only was his home and his family wiped off the face of the earth, but he couldn't even find his neighborhood— it no longer existed. His whole world had disappeared in a few minutes.

As he told me the story and recalled his own bewilderment, I no longer exulted. If I didn't believe he could feel what I felt, then there was no point to anything, and we might all just as well vanish in a mushroom cloud. What a horrible story it was. Yet six million Jews had been erased like chalked figures on a blackboard. I would never be able to solve the riddle: how can you hate a people and love humanity at the same time?

But the same afternoon that he related his saga, I visited Dachau. It was a kind of compulsion that I see all the horror. Memories of Passover at Uncle Looey's came back to me in a rush. Forty or fifty of us would sit in that tiny apartment, all of us waiting impatiently for the prayers and songs to be over so that we could enjoy the feast of the year. The rituals were a bore to us kids—only the food was remarkable.

Religion meant so little to me, and in my childhood any brush with it had been unpleasant. Now, in Germany, bits and pieces of the Seder, the Passover service, fell into place. The whole ceremony, a commemoration of Moses' leading the Jews out of Pharaoh's Egypt and into freedom, was so apt. Was any Pharaoh ever as terrible as Hitler? These Jews of Germany and Poland and all of Europe weren't led to safety by anybody. This consciousness at the scene of the crime made me really aware for the first time. Tradition and ritual were not always empty, barbaric, and outdated. It was important to remember these things, but there was a way of remembering without forgetting the rest of the world.

My children not only have the beautiful and happy Christmas tree and gifts I missed, but they also enjoy something else I never enjoyed. Being Jewish to them is not what it was to me— something separate from the *rest* of the community—but part of the whole.

My life had changed so much since Williamsburg. I had moved far from that ghetto. The little boy who could only see a ball game in a counterfeit Boy Scout uniform had sung for the President of the United States.

President Truman used to fly me to Washington in his private plane so that I could sing at his parties. He had first heard me when I sang the Lord's Prayer and "Eternal Father, Strong to Save" in the Senate on the first anniversary of President Roosevelt's death.

When FDR was alive, I had flown up to the White House to sing "Home on the Range," reputedly his favorite song. I was informed that he detested the piece, and I quickly changed my program, earning with my "Figaro" a loud, delighted Presidential bravo. I sang for Roosevelt only once, but I was a frequent visitor at Blair House, where his successor lived.

The President's daughter Margaret and I sang countless duets, with Mr. Truman accompanying us or simply turning the pages if José Iturbi was at the piano. Vice-President Barkley was another frustrated baritone, and we used to sing together, the President, the "Veep," and I, making me feel like one of the musical Cabinet. We would really raise the roof with "Wagon Wheels."

"Thank you for being so sweet to my baby," the President would say after I would sing with the delightful Margaret. That warm and lovely man!

Harry Truman was the man who dropped the bomb on Hiroshima, who finished the war against these Nazis. Could my parents, my grandparents ever have dreamed that such a thing was possible—that Moishe would dine and make music with the President of the United States?

I then thought of General Eisenhower, whose army had swept across Germany, who was then the Supreme Commander of Western Europe. I had first met him when I was singing with the Denver Symphony Orchestra, in that amazing amphitheater carved out of Red Rocks Mountain. When the summer skies opened suddenly, prompting the audience to rise for cover and refunds, I had led an impromptu community sing that kept them at their seats. The whole Eisenhower family not only joined in a chorus of "Down by the Old Mill Stream" but—after the storm passed—congratulated me on my "typically American initiative." *Eisenhower! He made it possible for me—little Moishe Miller—to be driven up the Rhine in style—by an ex-Nazi.* Life was really astonishing.

The Twelfth Army might have won the war, but Operation Snafu was still the order of the day, and USO Headquarters at Nuremberg seemed to do nothing but goof. Things were so badly organized that on more than one occasion I traveled high into the Alps to a remote installation that not only didn't have any facilities but, more to the point, not one single soldier. We actually traveled five to six hours to arrive nowhere or at a camp just vacated, ashes in the ashtrays, wilting food in the iceboxes. It was enraging. We eventually crossed the Alps into Austria and landed in Salzburg, where we played our last camp.

Salzburg—a fairy-tale village. It is truly an ancient city, and I took in the surrounding wonders, including restaurants high in the mountains, accessible only by cable car. But the most interesting sight of all was Mozart's home. It was pure *Zauber*— absolute magic. *What ever else he did,* I speculated on my way back to the Goldener Hirsch Hotel, *he always worked at the very top of his talent, Mozart. He never threw it away. He never left the opera for Hollywood.*

Terribly depressed on arrival, I showered, dressed, and went down to the lobby. And there was Herbert Graf, one of my directors from the Met. My heart swelled at the sight of someone from home.

"Dr. Graf, what in God's name are you doing here?"

"Bob! *I'm* working in the Festival. But you? What are you doing here? The devil with that! What happened between you and Bing? You know he's here, don't you?"

My heart began pounding hard. "Here! *Here?* You mean he's here in Salzburg?"

"Right here in the hotel. It's not so strange, you know. He's scouting some singers. Would you like the number of his suite? Or should I give him yours?"

"You're a nice guy, Herbert, but I'm afraid that Mr. Bing already has my number! I'll call *him.* Thank God I bumped into you."

Nervously I went to the desk and asked for Mr. Bing's suite. My hands were ice cold. I half wished he wouldn't answer.

"Hello! Hello!" Mr. Bing repeated impatiently. "Is anyone there?"

"Yes, Mr. Bing. This is B-B-Bob Merrill."

There was silence. For a moment I thought that he had hung up, but the wire, cold as it was, was still open.

"Please, Mr. Bing, may I speak with you?"

"What are you doing in Salzburg?" he asked idly.

"I'm here with the United States Army," I answered.

"Ah, so," he said disinterestedly.

"May I speak with you, Mr. Bing? If I could see you—"

The tone was glacial. "There is nothing to speak about, Mr. Merrill."

"Not even for five minutes, Mr. Bing?"

"I do not see any purpose in any discussion. I hope you enjoy your stay in Salzburg with the army," he added with distressing politeness.

He could have been on the planet Mars. "I didn't join up, Mr. Bing," I volunteered. "I'm singing with the USO."

The sigh was audible. He was bored. "That's nice, Mr. Merrill. Now, if you don't mind, I'm dressing for dinner."

"Please, Mr. Bing? After all, for old times' sake?"

"Old times' sake? That is a most peculiar thing for you to rely on, Mr. Merrill."

The gentleman had every reason to treat me this way. Why shouldn't he be aloof, remote, disinterested, bitter, bored—in truth, fed up?

But I was willing to beg. "I beg of you, Mr. Bing. Just five minutes of your precious time. That's all I'll take, and I won't bother you again. We both happen to be far from home in a strange place—"

"I am Austrian, Mr. Merrill," he interrupted with impatience and some condescension. "I do not consider this a strange place."

"You know what I mean, Mr. Bing. It's too much of a coincidence that we're both here."

"I fail to see any irony or design in the accident of our mutual presence here at the Goldener Hirsch. Each of us has made his choice in life, Mr. Merrill. It is as simple as that."

Again, there was a dead silence.

"I'm alone in Salzburg, and just to speak with you for a few minutes, I'd be so grateful," I said.

The silence somehow seemed less empty.

"Well, perhaps some coffee at six-thirty, and then I must rush."

"That's wonderful, Mr. Bing. Thank you."

"In the dining room at six-thirty, then."

I walked around the streets in a sweat. At six-twenty, I was in the dining room staring at my wristwatch.

Will he really come, or was he just trying to get off the hook?

But Mr. Bing was more dependable than I. He arrived at the stroke. The two hands of the watch met; like me, they were praying.

Tall and straight, looking slim and fit, his face was as stern and as clean-cut as his sentences. He bowed slightly and sat down, drawing the chair beneath him all in one gesture. Like his name, Mr. Bing was all economy.

"Now, then," he opened the conversation in a frightening staccato. His voice softened noticeably as he ordered coffee.

"I'll have a cup of tea, please," I said to the waiter.

"Well, what is it, Merrill?"

"I'll be very frank, sir."

"Well, I should think so. I certainly haven't time for games."

"I want desperately to sing again."

"Have you stopped?"

"I mean at the Metropolitan, sir."

"Never, Merrill. Never, as long as I am general manager."

"But . . ."

"*Never*, Merrill!" And he smiled faintly for the first time. "Do you find the coffee not to your taste in Salzburg?"

There was something wonderful about his unyielding judgment, something almost biblical about the finality of his decision. His edict was carved in stone like a commandment: *Thou shalt not work at the Met again!*

That evening at the opera, we sat three seats from each other, at Mozart's *Idomeneo*. No one could tell me the Fates weren't throwing us together! Hilde Gueden, the soprano, was splendid. Her voice was velvet and effortless. She was the one that Mr. Bing was scouting.

He bowed a greeting. "How do you like Miss Gueden, Merrill?"

"A very beautiful woman with a very beautiful voice. She should make quite a Sophie!"

"Yes," he nodded pleasantly. "A lovely artist. She should make a wonderful addition to the Metropolitan—a lovely artist and a *serious* one."

"I sure would love to work with her back on Thirty-ninth Street."

Mr. Bing's smile couldn't have been more gracious. "Never, Merrill, never!"

And that was that.

On my return to New York, the press bombarded me with questions. "Are you going back to the Met?" was answered by a plaintive, "I certainly hope to," which was followed by the returning Mr. Bing's broken record, "Never while I am manager."

In September, I recorded *Carmen* for Victor with Risë Stevens and Jan Peerce, under Fritz Reiner's direction. Keeping my split personality intact, I also appeared with Milton Berle, then undisputedly Mr. Television, although even I objected to making my entrance with a golf ball in my mouth while Uncle Milty waited on the tee in plus fours. Legend had it that they used to determine Berle's rating by simply counting antennas. Milton used to rehearse with a whistle around his neck, and he'd run around blowing it at everybody. He rehearsed the orchestra, the actors, the lighting men, everybody. He was top banana, and he blew his whistle at the world. Berle hated fresh air—in fact, any kind of ventilation. I almost choked whenever I worked in his studio or sat in his office. But he was considerate to me, and I was able to convince him that the presentation of an opera star—whether "formerly at the Met" or not—with so little dignity could backfire and make him look bad, so he rewrote my entrance.

When his budget could afford it, I also worked for the perennial Ed Sullivan. Despite my doldrums, I was keeping active enough. But my mother wanted to know what was happening on Thirty-ninth Street. She wasn't impressed with anything else. One night when I was at Momma's for supper, Tante Lesser was there too. Now very old, she had seen me on television that week.

"So! I saw you on Ed Solomon's show on Sunday."

"Better he should be opening next week at the Metropolitan," my mother said.

"How did you like me, Tante Lesser?" I asked to divert my mother. Tante Lesser was a great critic.

"You looked beautiful, Moishe. It was a pleasure, so neat and clean and, *umberschrien*, healthy—even with the lines on my set. Also I saw you with 'Dahlink' Talullah. You looked marvelous. Mrs. Horowitz came over with some prunes, and I was so proud.

Nobody she likes, and she also thought you looked neat and clean."

She never mentioned my singing once as she continued. "Lotza, darling, it's wonderful to have such *naches* from the children. Look at him—a *mensch*, already, and a Hollywood actor. Tell me, Moishe, is it true Irene Dunne is a Jewish girl?"

"I never met her, Tante Lesser, but I don't believe so."

"Funny." Tante Lesser pulled the corners of her mouth down. "I heard from Mrs. Horowitz that she knows someone in Paterson, New Jersey—*epis*, a Dunne also, maybe *mishpucheh*. Well, who knows? James Cagney I heard, also. No? Ach, Lotza, what a country we live in." She looked around my mother's house. "It's hard to believe there was a day when you didn't know how you were going to feed them. And now look!"

Tante Lesser raised the palm of her hand and shook it at my mother in disgust at all the ugly memories. "Ach!" she grunted. "You've got good sons, Lotza. But why not?"

"I've got nobody," was my mother's answer. "What? He's here for supper tonight? I see Looey's Sidney more than I see my own." She raised *both* her palms to the Fates, washing her hands of the whole business of living. "Tante Lesser, you don't get what you deserve in this life, and there is no other one, so what's the *naches*, what's the pleasure?"

"Mom!" I objected.

"I tell you, Tante, I wish I could change places with Abe," she continued, warming to her favorite subject. "He's in his grave, and it should have been me. With Looey gone now, I have no immediate, you'll forgive me."

"Are you crazy, Lotza? It's a sin to talk so. Grandchildren from Gidalia, a fine boy and so successful; and Moishe a big star on TV and everything? A beautiful home, a woman who cleans and lives here when you want. Who ever imagined? And the Florida sun when you're cold—do you remember before you had steam? Lotza, I'm taking such an inventory I'm afraid to *beshrie* you." Tante Lesser spit in the air.

"Don't be afraid, Tante. I was cursed years ago. Money is nothing. Success does not mean happiness always. Success," she now announced, "can be failure."

"Mother," I said, "I didn't come all the way out here to listen to such nonsense."

"To Hollywood and Germany is nothing to mine world traveler, but to come and see his mother is a big *tsimmis* like the North Pole."

Whenever my mother chose to speak of me in the third person, she was really in a state.

"He used to bring his friends here—all the boys to *fress* and sing."

"Mom, I told you. We're all grown up. The fellows are married, working out of town, busy living."

Tante Lesser didn't seem as large and redoubtable any longer, partly through my growing up, partly through her growing older. She had changed, but she was as wonderful as ever. "Lotza," she now said, "your boy is a man—well known—a big man. He didn't have to be here tonight. Mrs. Horowitz's son is *nothing* in handbags—and she could die, he wouldn't know for months. Moishe is *here*. Him and Gidalia, they aren't ashamed like some with the fancy-schmancy. What are you going on, when you have such good sons? You should do some charity, maybe give more time to the Pultisker Society—and that gorgeous voice you got. . . ."

"I've begged Momma to do something. I've introduced her to Mrs. Hartmann in New York. She could help entertain the old people. . . ."

"The old people, the old people. Which is worse—to die young before the dreams come true or grow old when everything turns sour and nobody wants you and nobody cares?"

Tante Lesser shook her head. "Lotza, a woman who eats herself up is on a diet of bitter herbs. Count the blessings!"

"One, two!" my mother cried hysterically. "My grandchildren. Gidalia is married. A boy till he gets married should live at home. He doesn't run like a thief in the night."

"Ah!" Tante Lesser sighed knowingly.

I shrugged my shoulders and closed my eyes in distress.

"So when are you getting yourself a nice Jewish girl, Moishe?" Tante asked.

My mother's anger was now directed at both of us. "A wife?

What are you talking? He can't even keep a job, my comedian."

My mother's pain at my dismissal from the opera was second only to mine. Perhaps it was even greater; for her, no other success could ever compensate for that loss. My mother was certainly gratified by my radio and television appearances; and if the Hollywood venture had not been made at such a sacrifice, she would also have been thrilled at the money and the prestige. But unlike me, she found these nonoperatic pursuits nothing by themselves. To Lotza Balaban, even if I had become an international movie star, I would still have been a baritone out of work. Only now did I understand how permanently set my mother's sights were. Also, she had identified with me so completely that she felt she, Lillian Miller, was no longer with the Met. She was once again reduced to Lotza the housewife, with no family to take care of. We were both suffering at this point. As the days went on, it grew worse.

The opera was to open on November 13 with *Aïda;* the previous spring, Mr. Bing had told me he wanted me to appear as Amonasro. I had gone my merry way, and now I not only had cut myself out of the opening-night cast but had actually presented the Met with a brilliant substitute.

Some years back, Constance Hope of Red Seal Records had called to ask whether I would present a protégé of hers on my radio program, *Music America Loves Best,* in order to give the lad a send-off. Connie was a good friend, and I took him on her word. He wanted to sing "Ol' Man River."

"How well does he do it, Connie?"

"Very well!"

"Okay, he's in."

"Thanks, you're a darling."

"What's the guy's name?"

"George, Bob. George London."

When I saw the opening-night advertisement, I was chilled by the irony of the situation. I was supposed to have opened in the new *Aïda,* directed by Margaret Webster and decorated by Rolf Gérard. Looking to see whether Guerrera or Valentino was singing the role of Amonasro, I saw the name London. Mine was still Mud—and now on two coasts. Early and frighteningly accurate reports of *Aaron Slick* landed me right up the Crik. The movie was such a clinker that it prematurely aged Alan Young and sent Dinah Shore beating a retreat to other media, where she fortunately prevailed. As for me—I had been a human sacrifice to a false idol. I had sung my swan song at the Met, and I was rewarded with the biggest turkey in Hollywood history.

Now a great young baritone was making his debut in my place. I was beyond suffering. Since it was the end of everything, I decided to go in style. I got two good tickets to the opening and took Claudette Colbert, whom I had met through the Jack Bennys in Hollywood. Claudette was charming and chic and also warm and understanding. She knew what I was going through and helped keep my spirits up. I gave my best performance that night. We dined at Sherry's, holding court while autograph hounds, friends, colleagues, and first-nighters stared at Claudette in envy and me in pity. Mr. Bing sat elsewhere.

Memories crowded in on me as I looked around the room and thought of the welcome I had received here six years before, when I was first engaged by the Met, when everything I had dreamed of had come true. The champagne I'd drunk that first day was fresh and bubbly. This Piper Heidsieck was the best but tasted flat.

Claudette touched my hand gently, as if she had read my mind. "You'll be back here, Bob. You'll see."

Everyone said this—except the one person who could make it happen. My heart beat faster as we went to our seats and the lights dimmed. The Aïda was Zinka Milanov. At her best, Zinka was the most glorious dramatic soprano I ever sang with. I thought with nostalgia of the time she had clumped across the stage in her thick wedgies and stomped right on my foot, almost crushing it. Not only did I see stars from the agony, but she had broken the buckle on my sandal as well, so that when I moved, it flew right into the orchestra pit. Some eager beaver in the pit thought he would save the day by throwing the sandal back onstage! We would still be having a catch if I hadn't stopped. Dear Zinka! For all her vocal magnificence, she was not the most graceful woman onstage, nor had she ever really contacted me before in any role.

Will I ever sing Amonasro with this marvelous woman again?
Will I sing it with anyone again?

I thought of Ljuba Welitsch, who did nothing *but* contact me onstage. She used to go so wild that her Aïda was actually dangerous. She could knock you down when she came rushing toward you screaming, *"Padre!"* I used to plant my feet as firmly as possible, brace myself, and then pray I'd survive her attack. For some reason, Ljuba would grab hold of you for dear life. She was uninhibited as Aïda, but her Egyptian princess never topped her Musetta in *Bohème.* One night she jumped into Marcello's arms with such suggestive abandon that management was shocked and furious. She never did it again. Ever since her smash hit as Salome, the attractive redhead abandoned everything but the stage whenever she appeared. She was quite a woman and the opera's Gabor.

I also thought of Stella Roman, a beautiful soprano and an excellent Aïda. She was a fine artist, and I'd enjoyed singing with her; but to me, the most glorious Aïda of all time was Elisabeth Rethberg. What a divine artist she was! After hearing her sing with Gigli, her voice lingered with me for days. The woman could sing Wagner one night and Verdi the next. Fantastic! Robert Merrill couldn't sing *anything* anymore—on *this* stage anyway.

The lights lowered and Fausto Cleva, the maestro, walked through the pit and turned to acknowledge his applause. And then the opera began—without me.

My first surprise was the Rhadames. I had never heard Mario del Monaco before.

My God! Here's a thrilling tenor. I'd love to sing with him.

As for London, he was wonderful; it was altogether a splendid debut, my loss being his gain.

We toasted Mr. Bing in Sherry's between acts. He was really consolidating himself as the new general manager. This *Aïda* was just one of the four new productions Mr. Bing planned for the season. *Rigoletto*, designed by Eugene Berman and directed by Herb Graf, turned out to be another triumph for him. Our Salzburg discovery, Hilde Gueden, made her debut as this Gilda.

Then Alfred Lunt's brilliant direction of *Così Fan Tutte*—designed by Gérard with greater success than he'd had in *Aida*—proved to be a real feather in Mr. Bing's cap. It was a tremendous hit. Under the new boss, the Metropolitan seemed to be undergoing a complete rejuvenation. His employment of such offbeat, nonoperatic directorial talents as Webster and Lunt and now Tyrone Guthrie, who staged the new *Carmen,* promised to create a wider audience appeal.

The season had opened and now continued most auspiciously for everyone connected with the Opera House. I attended about three performances a week, always sitting at Sherry's between the acts, as near to Mr. Bing as I could manage. It was quite a romance. And I must confess, I was more desperate in this suit than in my growing courtship of Roberta Peters, whose lovely Gilda and Zerlina and whose Lauretta in *Gianni Schicchi* were helping to consolidate the position she had won with her dramatic last-minute replacement of a star a year before.

Whether I was with Roberta, with my mother, with Gil and Julia, no matter with whom I was sitting at Sherry's, I would flirt outrageously with Mr. Bing. No matter where he turned, I caught his eye. I was forever bowing and smiling and nodding and winking. I popped up everywhere—in the aisles and in the boxes, in the bar and in the john, and, of course, in the lobby. Robert Merrill, formerly of the Metropolitan Opera, had become the biggest lobbyist outside Washington, D.C.

Our relationship, Mr. Bing's and mine, became almost intimate in its polarity. Words were unnecessary. Our eyes would meet across a crowded room, and my pulse would quicken. My smile would plead for reconciliation, my eyebrows would raise in happy expectancy. I knew that he knew what the message was. It was now the gentleman's turn to smile; but it was a remote, tolerant, self-contained expression that—accompanied by an almost imperceptible shake of his head—meant eternal refusal. The quest and the rejection. It was our ritual, played out for all to see. My courtship was public, my ardor unashamed. He knew that I knew that he knew that I knew. But with all his aloofness, as time went on I detected less and less irritation with my suit. It occurred to me that if I were missing one night at Sherry's, the gentleman might crane his neck to find me. But I was usually there.

One night, his back turned to me, Mr. Bing must have felt my eyes burning holes in his neck. Deep in animated conversation with a stylish group of bigwigs, he became a trifle ill at ease. His straight back remained elegantly in position as only his head turned slowly to find the penetrating gaze. My very best choir-boy smile greeted him as he found the offending stare. He closed his eyes in ennui. The expression said, "I should have known. It's *him* again!"

My smile became brighter. "Good evening, Mr. Bing," I called out heartily.

"Good evening, Mr. Merrill," he answered politely.

"The new production is beautiful."

"Thank you, Mr. Merrill."

"Mr. Bing, please, let me talk to you. Please! I've got to come home!"

"Perhaps in my office, Mr. Merrill. Not here," he reprimanded. "Perhaps we can chat about it in my office—sometime."

I winced with happiness. The thaw had set in. There was a crack in the ice. Edelweiss had sprung up in a field of snow.

"When, Mr. Bing? May I see you tomorrow?"

"Yes. Perhaps. Perhaps tomorrow. Call me."

With my foot in the door, I now used every bit of salesmanship in me. The gentleman knew the product; he was just worried about delivery.

When I went to see him, all stops were out. I was never more sincere in my whole life. "Mr. Bing, you are right. I am wrong. What I did was unforgivable, and I won't even try to justify it. All I know is that, more than anything in the world, I want to come home to the Met. I couldn't be more sorry—and if you give me another chance, *you'll* never be sorry."

Mr. Bing listened patiently. "I think you mean what you say. If you write all of this to me in a letter, we will see."

I thanked him profusely and then ran up to Moe Gale's office, arriving breathless and hysterical. "Moe . . . I . . . think Bing'll take . . . I think . . ."

"Relax, Bob. Sit down."

Poor Moe had been terribly worried about the way things had gone. He was convinced that his permissiveness about my Hollywood adventure had killed my career. More than a manager, Moe was a friend. He now listened to the latest development.

"Bob, I want you to apologize publicly. That's obviously what Bing wants, and that's what he deserves."

"I'll do or say *anything*, Moe."

"Okay, kid. We'll work out a letter."

The New York Times and the *Herald Tribune* published my note:

Dear Mr. Bing:

Having had ample time to reflect upon the unfortunate incident last spring, I express to you now my deep regret for my action and the inconvenience it caused you and my colleagues.

I know what the Metropolitan has meant to me as well as to many others. I realize the complex nature and many problems of its operation. I realize that the success of the Metropolitan depends greatly on the sincere cooperation, loyalty and self-discipline of its artists. I also understand your action, in striking my name from the roster of the Metropolitan for not participating in the spring tour, and appreciate that you had no other alternative.

Singing at the Metropolitan has been my life. Should you be willing to consider my reinstatement, which I most sincerely desire, let me assure you that your trust in me will not be misplaced.

Please feel free to use this letter as you may think fit.

Sincerely yours,
Robert Merrill

Mr. Bing had demanded absolute surrender, and he got it. I had begun to know him. Unswerving in his loyalty, unyielding in his honesty, he expects the same of others.

He accepted my apology in a letter—again making front-page news. Our exchange was meant to be public, my repentance well publicized. My redemption was now equally advertised.

Dear Robert Merrill:

To admit one's mistakes the way you have done is a sign of moral courage and decency. I shall be willing to forget the past.

Rudolf Bing

Alone with Mr. Bing, he thawed further, although his index finger was like an icicle pointing at me. "You'll be a good boy now, Merrill?"

"I will be a good boy, Mr. Bing."

You would have sworn I was three years old; I certainly felt it. I wanted to jump with joy. A contract for the balance of the season and the spring tour was immediately drawn up.

"You will open in *Trovatore* on March eleventh," Mr. Bing announced curtly. He was once more himself.

"Yes, sir. Whatever you say."

He looked at me, not without warmth. Then he cleared his throat and busied himself sorting out some papers. "Welcome home," was all he said.

CHAPTER SIXTEEN

AND SO THE prodigal son returned. Nothing else much mattered to me; I was home, and there was no doubt from my first piano rehearsal with Fausto Cleva, our maestro. It was wonderful to be back in harness. Del Monaco was singing his first Manrico in *Il Trovatore*, so we rehearsed together; when he opened up in that room, he sounded like a trumpet. What a voice! I now had two reasons for being as good as possible.

My mother, who had been eating herself up alive in Miami instead of Kew Gardens, flew north for my return. This, she wouldn't miss. My reconciliation with the Met did please her greatly. Everyone whom I had burdened with my grief now shared my joy. Wires from all over the world made the evening gala, and I was more nervous than I had been at my debut. The house was jammed; backstage, all my friends in the cast and crew made me feel they were glad to have me back.

Mr. Bing must never be sorry he relented. I've got to be twice as good tonight.

The ovation that greeted my entrance almost threw me. It was a welcome home so touching, so heartening that I could do no wrong from there on. From my first note to last, the music floated. "Il balen del suo surriso" tore the house down. I had thrown myself into my work as never before; my performance that night was a love letter to the Met—management, audience, ushers, everyone. Its answer was a deafening acceptance of me.

Standing alone in front of that curtain, hearing my name shouted over and over again, I swore that never, under any circumstances, would I ever betray this trust. Nothing would ever come before my first love. I swore it. Nothing!

My career was back in order, and something in me cried out for stability in every department of my life. The role of the playboy had become a bore. Sick to death of running around, I narrowed the field more and more to Roberta, whom I now introduced to my mother at Toots Shor's.

I studied my mother studying Roberta. On the surface, the girl was everything that Lotza had wanted her to be. Roberta was young, gifted, and pretty. She was in the opera. She was Jewish. Maybe if I was married, my living away from home wouldn't seem such an insult to Momma. It would be what they called "natural." At the time, it was a great shock that my mother did not seem to object.

I was equally surprised by Roberta's mother. Mrs. Peterman did object—and strongly. Fancying myself as quite a catch, I couldn't understand it. Roberta was a kid and was duly impressed with my station. Her admiration, almost teenage adulation, was exactly what the doctor ordered as far as I was concerned. After all, I did have position—further elevated by my recent return to the Opera House. And aside from that, I was an extremely successful singer. I was what mothers called "a good provider." Roberta, on the other hand, though she had scored an immediate hit, still had to build a repertoire before she could be assured of a career. One dramatic substitution did not accomplish this. I really couldn't understand the Petermans' disapproval. It was shared, it seemed, by Sol Hurok. The impresario was Roberta's mentor, and he had high hopes for her future. Evidently he did not fancy me as part of it.

While he doodled his name incessantly on a piece of notepaper, Papa Hurok insisted that this marriage would nip Roberta's career in the bud. Every time he said this, Mrs. Peterman would get a *shreck*—like someone sticking a knife in her heart.

I didn't understand this point of view, since at no time did I expect Roberta to give up the opera. But Mrs. Peterman—like my own mother—had slaved to bring Roberta *this* far, and noth-

ing was going to halt her progress. She had sacrificed everything
—the smallest pleasure—to school her daughter for her career.
She had literally done without so that Roberta could become a
singer. Her husband, my future father-in-law, was a shoe salesman, and there was talk that I would set him up in business.
Both Roberta and I had known want; both our families had
sacrificed for us. Certainly, they deserved the best we could give
them.

Roberta was a sweet girl, and I was terribly infatuated with
her. Our need for each other was mutual; and by the time the
press got through with us, we were convinced we were in love.
Despite the Petermans and Papa Hurok, we refused to stop seeing each other; we became a romantic entity because of the
pressures that surrounded us. The newspapers found us great
copy and created a glamorous and storybook romance that we
couldn't recognize as synthetic, as fraudulent as a press agent's
dream. We were having fun—singing together, dancing and dining at the best places, brightened and blinded by all the flash-
bulbs. We couldn't go anywhere without landing in the papers,
and we loved it.

Roberta was a kid; that's her excuse. I was an idiot; that's mine.
The whole relationship was unreal from the beginning. Anyone
who voiced an objection only threw us closer together. It was
time, I decided, that the *baritone* got the girl. Roberta agreed.
With great haste—as if we had to meet some kind of deadline—
we announced our engagement and made plans to be married.

RCA Victor summoned us both to its studio to record a series
of love duets. It's lucky they recorded them immediately.

Roberta and I were married at the Park Avenue Synagogue
on Eighty-seventh Street, in one of the biggest productions on
record. Both our families, half the society and opera world, and
what seemed to be all of New York attended. Now that our marriage was to be an accomplished fact, Papa Hurok wanted to
handle the seating. The list of one thousand guests ran the gamut
from Mrs. August Belmont to the Brownsville Feldmans who had
had steam heat before my family did. Eleanore Ross was the maid
of honor, and Gil was my best man. Driving to the temple, Gil, my
pal Paul Richards, and I ran right into the Greek Independence

Day Parade on Fifth Avenue and were a half hour late for the ceremony. The place looked like the High Holidays. I never saw so many people. It was bedlam.

Not since George Gershwin's funeral service at Temple Emanu-El was a synagogue so jammed with gentiles and sightseers. *Yentas* came from the Bronx and Brooklyn with folding chairs and, just as at Elizabeth II's coronation, sat outside for a glimpse of the celebrities, finishing off their day with a soda at Schrafft's on Eighty-sixth Street.

The front pages were filled with us: "Baritone Robert Merrill and soprano Roberta Peters, the two young, rising stars of the Metropolitan Opera, give their storybook romance the perfect ending today. Always in close harmony, the handsome couple plan a permanent duet."

Romeo and Juliet were being wed under God, and our families sat on either side of the aisle glaring at each other like the Capulets and the Montagues. Roberta looked divine, and I was nervous as hell as I heard Rabbi David Putterman say, "The two of you have been blessed by God with an art inexplicable to man. In every ritual of Jewish life, there is song, and no faith can last that does not sing. . . ."

What a far cry this synagogue is from the shulles *of my childhood. What a lovely man the rabbi is, and how shiny and understandable everything is here.* It was Moe Gale's temple, and I had attended a *bar mitzvah* and some services there. My mind stopped wandering, and I glanced at Roberta standing next to me. She looked exquisite and poised, as if for a music cue. It suddenly came over me that at any moment she was going to join the rabbi in song, that he would cue us and we would separately go into our arias, ending appropriately in our "permanent duet."

I started to cast a production that could be called *Roberto and Roberta.* Jan Peerce could be the cantor, and Chaliapin the rabbi. Lotte Lehmann as my mother, Maria Jeritza as hers, De Luca as Hurok, and Schumann-Heink as Tante Lesser. We were obviously doing a scene from some opera.

The voice droned on, and then I heard Rabbi Putterman announce that he had performed many ceremonies and that this was a very special one that made him extremely happy. "I have a perfect record," he announced.

My mother should have pulled his earlobes and spit in a high wind.

The good rabbi had hitched the two songbirds, and, properly mated, they now kissed as Mendelssohn's joyous music broke the solemnity and the audience became unruly. Leaving the temple was almost an impossibility because of the congregational riot. We were obviously a hit.

"Look at them, Sadie. A prince and princess!"

"They'll sing all day long, God bless them."

"Do you notice, the mother don't look so happy?"

"Isn't that Richard Tucker there? Look. And Licia Albanese?"

We were happily racing down the aisle.

"Good luck, Bob."

"Do you remember me? I used to sit in back of you at New Utrecht."

"Your father, *olivah sholom,* should only have lived to see this day."

A cheer went up as we reached the street, and people waved handkerchiefs and pushed autograph books at us. The police were trying to hold them back; they seemed to want to tear us apart in their affection.

"They're the perfect couple. *Oi!*"

"She doesn't *look* Jewish!"

"How natural they are. Just like real people. They got everything, lucky stiffs!"

Some stocky woman pushed a policeman out of the way with remarkable strength as she screamed, "Cossack!"

She now aimed her camera at us as we struggled toward the waiting car. I can still see that sunburnt, leathery face, still hear that rasping voice. "The whole thing's a fairy tale! Abner, the whole thing's a *fairy* tale."

And that's exactly what it was, the whole thing—a fairy tale, an opera, a storybook romance, a production; and we got made-in-heaven reviews the next day. We went off to honeymoon at the Hampshire House beautifully costumed, lighted, directed, blessed, and under contract. We were scheduled to play our wedding night and then join the opera tour in Boston, which we did, like two good little children.

It began well enough, and we were both having fun in our new roles. But, actually, Roberta and I had only two things in common: we were both singers, and we were both Jewish. That seemed quite binding for a few minutes there, but then, all of a sudden, it was not enough. Still drugged with the fanfare, I was hardly unhappy but rather dazed that we were married. We both were. It was fun, but it was odd.

In Cleveland, away from home for the first time, alone with a stranger, Roberta seemed to spend all her time on the telephone talking to her mother; and whenever she hung up, she seemed somehow changed—a little self-conscious and remote. As for me, the minute the courtship and ceremony were over, the second we were offstage, I felt equally self-conscious with her. The press had fancied us as Romeo and Juliet. I'm afraid we were more like Hansel and Gretel.

Knowing how I felt, I can imagine the panic and the bewilderment of a kid like Roberta—sheltered, inexperienced, away from her family for the first time. Her conversations with her mother became more and more frequent and more and more secretive. And now the Fates intervened: she was contracted to go to Hollywood to appear in a movie about the life of Sol Hurok. It seemed only fair, the way he had appeared in ours.

The terror that Roberta might become a mother and be forced to retire from the opera made me the heavy in the piece, the archvillain, the latest baritone role in my repertoire. Fond of each other, Roberta and I were not allowed to try to settle our own problems. Decisions were made without us, and the fact that we *allowed* such nonsense speaks for itself. We never should have been married in the first place. I had swept her off her feet, but now we were both off-balance.

When Roberta and her mother left for Hollywood, I, of course, continued the tour. The separation proved a permanent one. It is perfectly true that I was hurt by the news that my wife was not returning; there had been no hint at all—strangers though we were—that everything would not continue and eventually relax. But now it was *kaput!* Roberta, safely with her family, was asking for a divorce. Before a day had passed, I realized that my pain was wounded vanity and that was all.

This "permanent duet" had made several professional commitments, which we now honored, appearing on Ed Sullivan's *Toast of the Town,* on *Music Under the Stars* for Israel, and at an Ebbets Field concert, where we sang "Sweethearts" and "Kiss Me Again" as if we meant it. No one knew at that point that we were finished, that our marriage had ended after ten weeks.

We sang on a temporary platform at Ebbets Field, just where second base was. It is was all so symbolic. And there we talked, the two of us, about our mistake and about our future—which could be extremely uncomfortable unless we were prepared to be sensible and friendly. We were not to continue as husband and wife, but by the nature of our ambition, we would always be members of the same family, and this we had to accept. Each of us had made the Metropolitan Opera his home, and we were fated for the rest of our lives to work together.

We looked at each other, Roberta and I, and we were strangers who wanted to be nice. And that was that. Arrangements were made to dissolve our heavenly match, and we both returned to earth.

I had never suspected how much I could suffer from plain, stupid gossip. The press simply had us "agreeing to disagree," "hitting a sour note," and "ending our love duet," but the velocity with which our marriage sped to its end pulled tongues and sent imaginations plumbing the lower depths. I was suddenly regarded with the most outrageous suspicions. The public doesn't like its romances shattered and looks for romantic reasons. It was all so clear—in a muddy sort of way. My young wife had fled from my side, making me some kind of monster. Heads moved closer together when I entered a restaurant.

"They were married five minutes, you know, and they say . . ."

It has always been a mystery who "they" are. Certainly "they" are usually less informed than the most remote fan to whom the gossip trickles down. And these experts, these *mayvins,* always have the ear of the willing listener. I was accused of everything unholy. "Poor Roberta" seemed, in this fiction, to have been somehow victimized. The whole affair was a kind of royal scandal, with me in the dual role—take your choice—of brute or innocent, either part subjecting me to ridicule. The truth was so simple, but people are not. For a while, I went through hell, my spirits sinking to complete despondency.

On my return to New York, my apartment was lonelier than ever, my life emptier than it had ever been. There was only one thing to do, and that was to throw myself into my work. This was the time to conquer a new role and a great one. Rigoletto! If I wasn't ready now, I never would be. What I had been through would help. Much had happened to me in the last couple of years that would allow me to approach the role with real understanding. Still a bit cautious, my intention was to try out the part in Cincinnati at the Zoo Opera. Once before, when I approached a big one, I had "opened out of town," as it were. I couldn't help but wish that this time I would also have such excellent preparation.

In my second season at the Met, *Barber* was a lot for me to chew. Despite my fame with the "Figaro" aria, doing the entire role was a different story. I had gone to Montreal and sung at the Malsum Stadium, after diligently studying the role with probably the greatest Barber of them all, Giuseppi de Luca.

De Luca had made several farewell appearances. One as Germont, in 1940, at the age of sixty-four, was a sensation: the quality of the legato, the nobility of concept, and the dignity of his presence were unforgettable. Now, over seventy, resting on his laurels and counting his lire, De Luca was an adorable man with sparkling eyes and a gay and open face. With his fringe of white hair around his shiny pate, he looked like a sweet and jolly Benedictine monk. He had had a poverty-stricken childhood. With that kind of past, you either throw money around like it's going out of style or you become like De Luca. He was absolutely obsessed by money.

I met him one afternoon on Sixth Avenue lugging two heavy suitcases filled with programs for his farewell concert at Town Hall. The man was over seventy and flushed with the strain, but he wouldn't spend the money to send them or have them delivered. Figuring that it was better to get him to the theater before he became an emergency case, I said that I was on my way downtown and asked whether I could drop him. He gratefully jumped into the cab, after I relieved him of that ton of programs. Incredible!

He charged me twenty-five dollars an hour, and I took sixteen wonderful lessons from the old man. He was worth every penny.

"Remember, Roberto! Inside the head, the Barber is always thinking, planning; his brain never stops. He misses nothing; the eyes catch everything and sends the message to the brain. His head is rubbing its hands together, always—*capisce?* It never sleeps, always works."

That first *Barber* was a nightmare. Ezio Pinza was the Basilio, Baccaloni the Dr. Bartolo, and Bruno Landi the Count. All three men had played the opera so many times for so many years that they knew it backwards—which is how they sometimes sang it, just for the hell of it. I, on the contrary, was so new at the role that everything had to be letter perfect, every cue crystal clear and in its proper place in order for me to survive the debut at all. If one person blew a line, I would be sunk. Wilfred Pelletier was the conductor. His assistant stood in the bushes in this outdoor production, ready to prompt me.

I was in my usual state of panic, but everything went well until Signori Pinza and Baccaloni began to kid around. This opera is filled with recitatives—bubbling, glib patters—which these gentlemen now ad-libbed in their native Italian, with a gleeful, conscious mischief meant to throw me off my course.

There wasn't one cue that sounded even vaguely familiar, and my nerves got the better of me. The little boy in the bushes was screaming my lines, and there I stood with egg Florentine all over my face. It was disastrous. Baccaloni, contrite as he could be, began to feed me my lines—and, in the process, forgot his own. This struck Pinza funny, and he threw both of us our lines, but the wrong way around, and then, in half-controlled hysterics, he had to fake his own. Somehow we pulled out of it.

The press, evidently and gratifyingly not understanding Italian, ignored the verbal spaghettini and recalled in my singing and acting—quite understandably—memories of the great De Luca. They should only have known what an ordeal it was.

My first Rigoletto at the Cincinnati Zoo Opera went quite

well, which is to say I got through the part without a hitch. Stevenello was our director, and the Gilda was a gorgeous Czech soprano named Eva Likova, who had a superb voice and landed in the City Center Opera.

Performing in a park near the menagerie, this company was called the Zoo Opera most appropriately. There were times when the animals unexpectedly joined the chorus.

"Ho-ho-ho!" sang Enzio Pinza one night as Méphistophélès in the "Song of the Golden Calf." "Quack, quack, quack!" answered the ducks to the delight of the audience. "Rrrrrrrraourrrrr," roared the lion to everyone's horror. Performances were always interesting in Cincinnati, and the trip diverted me from my recent unhappiness.

On my return to New York, I went out on the town as never before. This was my social period as well as my blue one; it was the blending time for everything, even notoriety and celebrity—and coming from the Zoo Opera, I was now lionized. Success is a great leveler. All barriers are broken down, and those who have arrived all toast one another at the top of the heap. It doesn't matter what road you have taken; all roads lead to the great plaza, the *étoile*, the great square. In a sense, this is the greatest democracy of all, and I'm the guy who can prove it.

Cardinal Spellman asked whether he could make me his own special spaghetti and meat sauce. Winston Churchill treated me to a great cigar, and the Duchess of Windsor scrambled eggs for me. "You're my favorite baritone," she said as we danced. "And you are my favorite duchess," I answered. The Duke was writing his memoirs; I was still living mine. The Huttons, the Donohues, Elsa Maxwell! After I became friends with Elsa—she played the "Di provenza" for me one night—she introduced me to everybody. One night at Jimmy Donohue's town house, there was a full orchestra on each floor. I was living it up, dressing to kill, running around like a chicken without a head—and getting lonelier every day. Only my work kept me sane.

While I was rehearsing for the new production of *Faust*, Pierre Monteux, our maestro, approached me at the end of a long day. He looked at me quizzically. "Tell me, Mr. Merrill, where do you come from?"

"Brooklyn," I answered.

"Ah!" Monsieur Monteux was no longer puzzled. "That is why your French sounds so funny."

So much for all my new social pretensions.

This promised to be a beautiful opening-night production, with the new Gérard sets and Nicola Rossi-Lemeni making his debut as Méphistophélès. Victoria de los Angeles was the Marguérite and Jussi Bjoerling the Faust. The fine soprano Thelma Votipka, one of the loveliest women at the Met and certainly the least expendable, was the Martha. Tippy always sings magnificently. Whatever the role, she's the best help another singer can ask for. She is the female counterpart of George Cehanovsky, who had been a leading Russian baritone years before and, aside from being Elisabeth Rethberg's husband, knew every single part of every single opera by heart. More than once in my early, lackadaisical years, he gave me my lines. Once, when he was Wagner and I Valentin in *Faust*, because I was too far away from the prompter, he turned his back to the audience and gave me *every* line. He could have done the same for Faust—or for Marguérite, for that matter. What a pro!

Some of these less-than-world-famous singers at the Met help keep it the great organization that is. Alessio de Paolis, to me, was always one of the great artists of the company and a great loss to us all since his death in 1964. Once a leading tenor at La Scala, De Paolis had been the romantic lead in *Falstaff* with Toscanini conducting. Unfortunately, he developed Parkinson's disease and gave up leading roles for secondary parts so that he would be less likely to jeopardize a production. And so this amazing man created sparkling gems of such parts as the Philistines' Messenger in *Samson*, Basilio in *Nozze*, the Messenger in *Trovatore*, Sergeant in *Barber*, Borsa in *Rigoletto*, and Gastone in *Traviata*. Everything he sang was perfection, and he could steal a scene from Raffles himself.

Some of these magnificent performers seem never to hit the heights and are never celebrated by the public, but without them there just wouldn't be an opera. Some of them seem to go on forever. They have long since outlasted Rossi-Lemeni, who debuted that night in 1953 with an exquisite voice, which did not hold up very long—no doubt because of improper technique.

I distinctly remember his beautiful voice—and his makeup, which made him look more like Uncle Sam than Méphistophélès. The whole setting of the opera had been moved up from the sixteenth to the nineteenth century—to no advantage whatsoever. Poor Rossi-Lemeni should never have made his debut in this role; he was not at home in it. His voice was gorgeous and unwieldy and evidently beset with problems that made his career so short. Unlike Chaliapin and Pinza, with whom I sang in *Faust,* he did not sing correctly. Durability is the acid test of your training. These men grew in stature through the years; they sang well—as well as brilliantly. And it all begins, like everything else, at the beginning. I am often asked how a young singer can make a career in opera, and I always begin by wishing the aspirant luck in his choice of a teacher.

There are very few good voice teachers, more's the pity. Most teachers are not even singers and therefore lack the understanding of the singer. Often they are accompanists, pianists who find it more lucrative to coach voice. If you are the kind of person who goes to a dentist for an appendectomy, don't screen your teacher. And if you do not know whether the teacher of your choice is right or wrong for you, don't waste your time planning a career. You know, that's all—the way I knew that the first coach my mother took me to was strangling me.

It's not easy to be sure all the time, but nothing in the arts is easy, and I wish the novices luck. There is an instinct that most artists have. Without it, there isn't much likelihood that anything very promising can develop.

On one of my concert tours, after speaking at a conservatory, I was asked many questions concerning technique.

"What do you think about when you prepare to project the high A flat in the 'Prologue' for *Pagliacci?*"

The question was a wild one and deserved a wild answer. "I cross my fingers and pray," I replied.

"Oh?" was the fascinated response. "Which fingers, Mr. Merrill?"

A few months later, in a periodical, I read a description of how Robert Merrill prepares for a high note: "The Metropolitan baritone presses the index finger against the third . . ." Could they have been serious? They were! As for the student who originally asked the question, could he ever have believed that you could create a vocal tone by pressing your fingers together? Yes, he could. It's easier than working for years; it's the promise of Instant Success! As to whether this student could ever become a singer—no, he could not!

It is true that emotional stress hits the voice first. If my wife or children are ill, I immediately feel a constriction in my throat. Going on because you're a trouper is often cheating your audience of a good performance. An emotionally upset dancer does not usually lose the ability to point his toe and move, but every human being who has suffered knows how choking a lump in the throat can be. Imagine having to sing, no less speak, under great emotional stress.

An acute case of nerves and strain can still any voice; but the better a singer's training, the less likely it is that there will be extended periods of poor voice production. Years can pass and the voice will perhaps darken with time and tragedy, but it need not lose any of its flexibility and power. After many years, Jan Peerce still sings the Duke of Mantua in *Rigoletto*, and his voice is as bright and sunny as a boy's. He knows how to sing and does not allow his problems to interfere with his voice—which is easier said than done. To me, Renata Tebaldi is the *grande dame* of the opera, an artist of remarkable vocal gifts, elegant taste, and incredible consideration. In a medium where—unless you have neglected to cue your fellow singers—they won't even notice whether you've fallen through a trapdoor, Renata Tebaldi stands alone.

Gracious and sensitive, she not only shares her floral tributes with me, she shares everything. She is always in contact with you, on and off the stage. It is perhaps this very depth of feeling and expansiveness of soul that recently and temporarily affected her voice. The loss of her mother and the spell of ill health that followed her loss really threw Renata for a while. When you feel as deeply as she does, it is difficult not to have it tear you apart. It is gratifying that she is singing divinely and is herself again. How well I remember a *Don Carlos* sometime back in which

I performed poorly. My brother Gil had been taken to the hospital, and I was terribly worried. Why is the performer the only person expected not to react like a human being? The President of the United States will cancel appointments if there is a family crisis or tragedy. But to the guy in the theater, the show must go on. Why?

When your heart is in your mouth, how can you sing? I can conquer a cold or a pain or an irritation but not a nagging fear for those I love. Gil was sick. My brother Gidalia, the harmonica player! Who the hell felt like singing? It turned out to have been a bad virus, but we didn't know it then. Still, only Marion, my wife, understood my ghastly performance that night before I ran to the hospital. Even Moe Gale always said "that awful *Don Carlos*." I was expected always to be good, always to be superhuman. I am not. What was there to sing about?

Often, when I have not felt well vocally—and there is such a thing as being in good voice or bad, depending on weather, mood, or pressure—I have tried to make up for it histrionically. But opera is, despite all the talk, primarily singing. The great performer who is not a fine singer can be successful in *buffo* roles but not in *bel canto*. On the other hand, the *bel canto* singer, whose purity of tone and easy flow are so delicious to the ear, can get away with less than superb acting.

Jussi Bjoerling in *Faust*, as in everything, was always in good voice. The exception to almost every rule, Jussi could not sing badly—it was impossible. But our dueling scene in the new production, as in the old, was something else again. A fencing teacher had been brought in to coach us, but Jussi couldn't move too much and sing also. His choice was the right one. He was an opera star, not a member of the Moscow Art Theatre. Jussi's singing always came first onstage, although, I must say, he was never as indifferent to his colleagues as Corelli.

Franco Corelli is the ideal romantic tenor. The voice is wondrous, the face and figure princely. Still, he is the typical tenor. Completely detached from the opera, thrown by the Fates into the midst of these strangers on the stage, Corelli stands alone and aloof as he builds his fortress of high notes around himself.

It is hard to find a tenor with a sense of humor, and that is why I treasure Jan Peerce as a friend. He is a serious artist, but he does not take himself seriously, which is quite a different matter. One night in *Traviata* while Violetta was dying and Alfredo, my good friend Jan, was weeping, he couldn't resist whispering with mock impatience, "When is this babe gonna drop dead?"

Jan wasn't sure how I would react, but I topped him. "She ain't, kiddo. The penicillin is on its way."

That was the first of many laughs we've had on and off the stage since. It's lucky for me that he's a tenor, so we've been able to work together a lot. If he had been a baritone, it would have been tough.

I still wasn't satisfied with my work as Rigoletto. De Luca always said that when a singer gets through with a performance, he should feel as if he has spent the interest on his money and not overdrawn the principal. Allowing for the financial flavor of his simile, it made sense. After my first Rigolettos, I felt depleted —broke. I still had to learn to conserve my energy. It was also true that the critics felt that my "matinee-idol personality" broke through: "His charm is not lost in the role, and always there is lurking the wink of an enormously talented boy." It was obvious that I had to reflect and grow.

This was impossible with the social life I was leading, so I called a temporary halt. My apartment on Sixty-seventh Street became not my castle but my monastery. I had recently done an ad for Campbell's Soup, and the company sent me cases of it. My kitchen was filled to bursting with Campbell's Soup. I literally had closets filled. No matter where you looked in my small apartment, there were the familiar red-and-white labels, offering everything from Scotch Broth to Pepper Pot, from Green Pea to Vegetarian Vegetable. After my childhood, you don't throw stale bread away without kissing it, and you certainly don't ignore one thousand cans of soup. I stacked them in designs and made a game of choosing a flavor each night.

On evenings when I wasn't singing, I would open one of these tins and then take a walk down Fifth Avenue or across Fifty-seventh Street to see a movie at the Little Carnegie or see what was up at the Russian Tea Room. I had a woman who came in to clean for me an hour a day, and she would often supplement my diet by fixing me a steak and some sliced tomatoes, which I really looked forward to. Gussie Rock, a terrific dynamo who had been recommended to me by Mary Margolis, now became obsessed with my bachelorhood.

"You was meant for marriage, Mr. Bob."

"*Oi!*" was my only response.

"Oh, I reads the papers. So you made a mistake, but you the marrying type, and Gussie knows it. You can't sit around drowning yourself in all them cans. You think you're in the soup, but I got somebody for you."

"Please, Gussie," I pleaded. "You're a lovely person, and you are all I need to make me happy."

"You should meet her. She's the one! I works for her, and she is the *prettiest* girl and plays the piano something beautiful. She lives just six blocks from here, so you wouldn't have to go gallivanting. She's just your type, Mr. Bob."

"You're my type, Gussie. And I love the bachelor's life."

"No, you don't. And you wouldn't catch so many colds! Her first name is Marion. Sweet? And if you got married, she could play the piano for you when you practice and all. Miss Marion is the kind of girl who becomes a missus."

"Well, you just killed that deal, Gussie. Forget it."

But this advance publicity went on for quite a while. One day, Gussie actually handed me the telephone as she finished talking into it. "Hello, Miss Marion. This is Mr. Bob. Mr. Merrill, this is Miss Machno. You both lovely people, so talk now!"

I know now that Miss Machno was just as ill at ease on her end of the line.

"We seem fated . . . that is, Gussie seems to think we should meet, Miss Machno. I hear you're at Juilliard."

"I was. I'm teaching now—piano, that is."

"Well, how nice. I'd love to have you come to the opera some night."

"That would be nice."

"What about Tuesday? I'm singing."

"Oh, dear! I'm so sorry. I have an audition at NBC practically at dawn, and I have to practice all evening."

There was a silence that promised to be permanent. It was obvious that Miss Machno wasn't that fascinated by the idea of meeting me. And I wasn't fascinated by the idea of being rejected. That was that.

Gussie tried harder than ever to play Cupid, but it wasn't working out. She relayed an invitation to a brunch the young lady was giving. Paul Margolis, my teacher's son, would be there, but I just happened to have a matinee of *Carmen*. The months went by, and I did nothing to pursue the matter further. Miss Machno struck me as being a rather cool and dedicated musician.

Gussie insisted that Miss Marion was really Miss Right. "She's the salt of the earth, Mr. Bob," she advertised.

I steered as clear of Miss Machno as I could and neglected to call again. My wounds were still open from my last encounter with Miss Right, and the one thing they didn't need was salt.

CHAPTER SEVENTEEN

F AR BETTER for my health and ailing ego was the news that, after all these years, Toscanini had once more asked for me, this time for his broadcast of *Un Ballo in Maschera*. I had waited for another opera with the Maestro impatiently, worrying about his seeming neglect. But the Maestro always knew what he was doing: he cast his operas by balancing voices and complementing timbres that only he could hear.

When Chotzie had, at one point, recommended me for the jailer, Rocco, in *Fidelio*, Toscanini shook his head. "No, no! Mayrrill's voice is too pretty. I want the voice of a dog!"

Toscanini could not always get equal quality or phrasing by this method, but he did try to shade the voices like instruments. Anyway, there was no arguing with God. The important fact was that he wanted me again, and, of course, I was available. "Yes!" I screamed to Chotzie when he asked whether I was interested. I didn't know the role of Renato and began studying the part even though the Met season was just getting under way.

One November morning, while I was working at home with Gussie buzzing around me with the vacuum cleaner, the phone rang.

"Hello, Mr. Merrill? This is Marion Machno."

"Oh! Hello there."

"Please forgive my disturbing you, but is Gussie there? I've been looking everywhere for her. It's quite important."

"Yes, she is. Just one moment."

Gussie got on the phone and began ohing and ahing. "You poor thing, you. Of course, I'll be over. Mrs. Margolis will understand, and so will Mr. Merrill. He's *very* understanding. Here he is now, Miss Marion. Mr. Merrill, Miss Marion hurt her back and needs me. Say hello, now, while I dress."

The young lady had evidently sprained her back and was lying there helpless.

"Please don't let Gussie leave until she's through at your place. I didn't mean to—please understand, Mr. Merrill. It's just that I can't move and wanted to make sure she'd come in today sometime."

I didn't understand why if Toscanini was impressed with me, Miss Machno was not. I decided to give her another chance. "Gussie seems to want us to meet. Could you dine with me one night?"

"Why, yes. That might be very pleasant. Let me see—I'm free Friday evening."

"Good. It's a date."

But perhaps, as Gussie had said, just because of my bachelorhood, I caught an awful cold. When I called to postpone our engagement, Robert Merrill sounded more like Louis Armstrong.

When she realized who was calling, she laughed. "I think the Arabs call it kismet, Mr. Merrill."

"The Jews call it *beshairt*, Miss Machno. But let's fight the Fates—whatever they're called. Why don't you come right over here and visit a sick man? He'd love it—and Gussie is here, so it's okay."

"Well—all right. I will."

And so Marion Machno walked into my life bearing a jar of chicken soup, and it seemed that she had been gone for only a moment. She already belonged. Gussie went completely crazy; she heated the broth and ran around the apartment clucking, "I got my children together." And what a match it was! Marion was wearing a gorgeous deep-purple coat, and she had eyes like olives warming in the sun—and warming an already merry face. But when she gave Gussie her things to hang up and emerged from all that purple, she was bent over from her pulled ligament—a hunchback. She looked like a female Rigoletto. For my part, I was feverish and hoarse. I had a cold sore blooming on my upper lip, and I smelled of Vick's Vaporub. We were right out of Charles Addams or *The Enchanted Cottage*.

"If you rub my back," Marion said with a twinkle and no self-consciousness at all, "you'll get your wish."

"And all you have to do," I croaked, "is study with Sam Margolis for years and you too can sound like this."

Our meeting could not have been less romantic and more marvelous. I fell in love with Marion Machno immediately, and we began gabbing as if we had left off our conversation someplace, sometime, somewhere before. We belonged together. Instead of treating me like a celebrity, Marion barely acknowledged my position in the world of music—a world that she loved as much as I. We talked of her studies and of opera and of the Margolises, whom she knew almost as well as I did. Time flew, and suddenly she had to leave.

"Please come back for dinner, Marion. There's so much I want to know about you. Please come back."

Gussie was all ready to call off her time at the Margolises, to shop and cook for us, but Marion had an appointment that evening. The doctor arrived to give me a shot—I was scheduled to sing *Trovatore* with Milanov and Baum the next night—and in the confusion of his coming and her going, we didn't make a date; we just agreed to speak on the phone and arrange something.

I was certain that this *gemütlich* and warm girl would call the next day to find out how I was. It came as a shock when I didn't hear a word.

I could have died in my sleep. It could have turned to pleurisy or pneumonia. I can still have a relapse! The more I thought about her indifference, the more upset I became. *Of course, it's always possible that she called the wrong number. Or maybe she called while I was in the shower.* But I doubted this.

I gave her a couple of days to check on my health, and then I called *her* to make sure *she* wasn't on *her* deathbed—which seemed the only logical reason for her silence. She was in excellent health and was busy practicing! The girl worked fourteen hours a day on her piano when she wasn't teaching, and she wouldn't break the routine for one Good Samaritan call to a sick man.

"I'd love to see you for dinner, Marion. . . . I must say I thought you'd call, just to see if I survived that shot the doctor gave me."

How reasonable she made it all sound. "But, Bob, I barely know you. I thought it would be a presumption to call you—you know, rather pushy; and besides," and her voice now became a little edgy, "I don't believe in calling men on the phone." It now softened again; she was such a mixture of shyness and pertness. "I certainly cared how you were. I thought you knew that."

We went to Vorst's Grill on Columbus Avenue and picked up where we had left off, babbling about everything under the sun and fighting for the last soda cracker in the bowl. Marion relished good food as much as I did, and we talked our way through a feast. I had never felt more comfortable with anyone in my life. It was unbelievable. Marion had a roommate, Maria Caruso, who was an opera student, aside from her own musical interest, she was wonderfully versed on my favorite subject. But, then, she was well versed on everything.

When I suggested that she come back to my apartment to hear the newest rage, Tebaldi, do *Butterfly* and *Bohème,* she was thrilled. She had heard a great deal about the new soprano and could hardly wait for her debut, especially after my recommendation.

This was our first official date. Dinner and recordings, food and music—two of our favorite things and the very best of both. I found myself discussing life as I never had before—life and my own fears and hopes. I dropped the mask, the act, the defenses and found myself confiding everything to this girl. It was marvelous, the whole evening—until the phone rang. It was Anna-Lisa, Mrs. Bjoerling.

Jussi was under the weather, and she was worried about him. Was he with me? And could I check on him, because it was essential that he be in good shape for *Bohème* the next night? Devoted and understanding, Anna-Lisa was a remarkable woman, a great wife to Jussi, whose genius was a burden he sometimes relieved with the grape. He was a wonderful father and husband, but occasionally he escaped the pressures of this world through a glass darkly. I knew he'd be all right, that Anna-Lisa was worrying unnecessarily; and when she was convinced, or pretended to be, I hung up.

When I went to turn the Tebaldi recordings over, I found Marion putting on her things.

"You haven't heard the whole opera."

She seemed oddly and suddenly embarrassed.

"I know. I have to be up very early, Bob."

"Did something happen? I don't understand."

Marion has never played games. "It's just occurred to me where I am. It's ridiculous. There are etchings and there are records. I hate to sound old-fashioned and all that, but I feel far too much at home here—that is, you make me feel too much at home. . . ."

"But, Marion, everything is so pleasant—and perfectly correct."

"Of course, Bob. And the recordings were divine. She's superb, Tebaldi. . . . I do hope we see each other again."

Suddenly she wanted out. Every parting from her was irritating to me. The next night I was singing at a benefit and then I was doing a matinee broadcast of *Faust*. I had to think fast.

Texaco, sponsor of the opera broadcast, was giving a cocktail party, and I asked Marion to join me for this, for dinner, and then for a telethon late that night. In fact, I even asked her to accompany me on the piano at the telethon.

"You know 'Ol' Man River,' don't you?"

"I certainly do. How marvelous! Oh—well, what time *is* the telethon, Bob, because I'm afraid I can't have dinner with you."

"Why not?" I asked furiously.

"Because I have a date, Bob. And that's nothing to get angry about. After all, I barely know you."

"I wish you'd stop saying that."

"Well, it's true."

"It is not! We're old friends now, and there's no fun in being at the opera, going off somewhere, and then meeting me late."

"I'm sorry, Bob, but I just don't break dates with people."

"Who's people?"

"He's someone I've been seeing for over a year and—"

"And you barely know me!"

"That's right. I'm sure he'll understand and drop me at the station for the telethon."

"That won't be necessary. If you can't make it for dinner," I heard myself say, "then forget about the telethon." If I had had a mustache, I would have been twirling it menacingly.

"If that's the way you want it, Bob," Marion said coolly. "But I don't just drop people or break dates when something better pops up—and, what's more, I hate people who do."

"I don't have your character, I'm afraid."

"Am I still invited to hear *Faust?* Or is that off too?" Her lips were pursed somewhat petulantly.

I was being a rat. "Of course not. I want you to hear it."

"Then I'll see you tomorrow. Good night, and thank you for everything."

In the morning, she called off the opera date too. Ossy Renardy, the violinist, the husband of her best friend, Suzy, had just been killed in a crash while on tour. The news had come over the radio, and Marion, typically, was rushing to her friend's side.

It was odd. Years ago, my first recital was sung with Ossy Renardy. Suzy knew that Marion was seeing me, and just a couple of nights before, when Suzy had heard me sing at the Weizmann dinner, she had decided that I would be a permanent part of her friend's life. Marion didn't tell me any of this until months later, but it was true. Suzy was known for her second sight. This particular vision, if I'd known about it, would have both pleased and petrified me.

Suzy was an intelligent girl with a delicious French accent. Completely desolate now and in a state of shock, she became part of our evenings. Marion didn't want her to be alone, so we included her in all our dinners. I felt affection and sympathy for Suzy, but I also wanted to share Marion's friends.

In 1953, the Metropolitan still used to move a whole production to Philadelphia and give five or six Tuesday performances at the Academy of Music, and I was scheduled to travel there for a *Faust*. Since Marion had missed the *Faust* matinee, I now invited her to come to Philadelphia. Her reaction was ridiculous. "What do you think I am, Bob Merrill? First etchings and now the state line?"

I thought I was going out of my mind. "Etchings?"

"So—Tebaldi records! A variation on a theme. It's all the same thing."

"What are you talking about, Marion? I'm not suggesting a night at a motel. The *whole company* is going. The *whole cast* is going to Philly on a special train. You'll be chaperoned by a cast of thousands—and Pierre Monteux," I added. "He certainly knows how to *conduct* himself, even if I don't!"

"What am I supposed to say now? 'Take me to your leader'?"

"What are we arguing about? This is ridiculous."

"Tsk!" Marion tsked. Her eyes were lowered in exaggerated disbelief, her mouth pulled to one side in caricatured skepticism. She was impossible.

"Do you realize, my dear girl, that you are not talking to Jack the Ripper or a ribbon salesman but to one of the stars of this *Faust*, to Marguérite's dear brother, the noble Valentin?"

"My funny Valentin!" said Marion. "Everything's-a-laugh-Merrill-including-maybe-relationships-with-people-but-not-me-Thank-you-very-kindly."

She was, of course, possessed, but I adored her. If my brush with Roberta, now my ex-wife via a Mexican divorce, was all lights and music and fantasy, my romance with Marion was utter reality. From that first crippled, germ-infested, Vick's-smelling meeting, there was a tension, a resistance and attraction, a pushing and pulling—a relationship. Most irritating of all was Marion's candor, especially in the negative.

Far from flattering me, she often heard me at the opera without commenting on my performance at all. I would wait for some mention of my high A or my curtain calls or my legato, and I would wait all night. Little Miss Honesty obviously didn't like me that particular evening.

What does she know about opera? Another expert in my life! She gets an expression like Momma's when she disapproves of something. Who does she think she is?

And yet she would say nothing! And I wouldn't ask because I was sure she'd tell me.

Not that she never complimented me. She did. But not often enough. Well, Valentin was a favorite role of mine, and I was sure she'd love me in it. If she liked me with a heavy chest cold, this death scene would certainly clinch things.

She interrupted my thoughts. "I don't want you to think I worry a lot about this sort of thing. I don't."

"I know, Marion."

"You make me sound like some kind of fanatic," she went on, "like I'm some sort of puritan or something. It's ridiculous."

"I know, Marion."

"But you've gotta get up pretty early in the morning to fool . . ."

I adored this girl. "Marion! I swear to you that the whole trip will be as pure as a Deanna Durbin picture."

"What's a Deanna Durbin picture?" the suspicious child asked.

"A movie with a hundred men and a girl and Leopold Stokowski."

"What's so pure about that?"

"It was a children's picture!" I screamed.

Marion was somewhat taken aback. "After all, Bob, you *have* been around and you *do* have a reputation, and even Mary Margolis told me you're a wolf."

"She's *English*," I explained. "Now, listen to me carefully." I was becoming angry. "We board a train with Mr. Bing himself, Pierre Monteux, Rossi-Lemeni, and a million others, and we ride a few hours to Philadelphia, where we go to the theater and put on a performance, which you will watch—and I hope enjoy—and then we get on the same train and come home."

"All right, already!" Marion said.

She came to Philadelphia—and with Gussie Rock's blessings. While she was discussing the trip with Gussie, she picked out a trim little suit to wear, but Gussie quickly exchanged it for a very dressy little white affair.

Gussie then cut through all the nonsense. "Miss Marion, put on your glad rags and you go!"

This command was almost countermanded by Mary Margolis when Marion, accompanied by Gussie, called for me at my lesson. While I was finishing my session with Mr. Margolis, Mary looked at the dressed-up Marion and listened to the latest proud bulletin from Gussie.

Mary Margolis was shocked that the young, well-brought-up Marion was boarding a train—no matter how crowded—with what she called "a very good old friend, but nonetheless a wolf."

Marion almost had a change of heart, but the lesson over, I rescued her from Mary's Victorianism.

The junket was, of course, wonderful, and Marion couldn't have been happier that she had come and worn her "glad rags." After dinner at Bookbinder's, Mr. Bing invited her to join his Main Line guests in his box.

It was, all in all, a most successful performance and adventure. On the way back to New York, all of us except Pierre Monteux had sandwiches and coffee. Although we were arriving home at two-thirty in the morning, Madame Monteux had a special supper waiting for her husband. Evidently, there were *some* marriages that were happy ones. The first time I had called for Marion and spent some time at her place, chatting with Maria and her, she had gone to the icebox and cut big chunks of Muenster cheese and rye bread to munch on. I had grown used to girls who diced everything, and I thought, *She's passed another test.* It was now clear to me that Marion was the type who would fix a late supper that would put the Chambord to shame.

She lived only six blocks away, and I was on the phone every five minutes. "You start walking downtown and I'll start walking uptown and we'll meet in the middle."

I didn't like her being with anyone else at all. The next time I asked her to break a date—while we were having drinks at the Russian Tea Room—and she refused, I insisted. This time she did what I asked. Progress was being made, but I wasn't certain how far I wanted to go.

Marion ordered a new car, and her father—a violin and piano teacher—and mother drove it in from Detroit for her, taking the opportunity to visit their only child. I was sold on them immediately. Mr. and Mrs. John Machno were a lovely couple. We had a pleasant visit, though I'm afraid I whisked Marion off to the opera with me rather than share her even with them for their short visit.

On New Year's Eve, I took Marion to El Morocco and realized that unless great care was taken, I would be hooked. She had become as much part of my life as lessons with Mr. Margolis and brushing my teeth. I needed Marion, and I was scared stiff. Old memories of my parents and the recent echo of Roberta made me shy away from the idea of marriage.

The Met gave me some time off, and I now kept an old appointment with Danny Kaye and my brother Gil, and we left for Boca Raton for ten days of golf and sun prior to the Toscanini broadcast. I really fled to Florida, not quite knowing what would happen if I stayed in town. I felt that I had to detach myself. I was getting awfully used to talking to this girl until three in the morning. Her intelligence, her sympathy, and her warmth and interest—ever her mute criticism—made me feel oddly safe, really unalone. Of course I fled.

But when I arrived back in New York to begin my piano rehearsals with Dick Marzzalo, Toscanini's coach for the singers, I ran right back to Marion to continue my crazy courtship. Her company was now so essential that I divided my time between *Ballo* and her, hounding the poor girl day and night, trying my best to interfere with her work and practice schedules. But Marion was fantastically disciplined. She would have none of me when she was working.

One rainy day, while visiting with Marion and horsing around at the piano with her and Maria Caruso, I was having so much fun that I didn't want to leave for a rehearsal. For a change, Marion happened to be free and all caught up on her work. I called Dick Marzzalo and said that I was ill, and suddenly I saw something go out of Marion's eyes. I didn't relate the two things until later: women and their moods were always a mystery to me, and *that* would never change.

Maestro Toscanini was eighty-seven years old, and although the sparkle was still in his eyes, he looked bent, bleached out. During the *Traviata,* we would rehearse for hours and all fall exhausted while he planned still another try. Now we would rest on the hour, and the Maestro would reminisce. He told me he hadn't conducted *Ballo* in forty-five years. In some ways, though, the old man hadn't changed.

"Ah, Mayrrill," he would sigh, "I will never forget the first time I see *Ballo*. I was little boy, and Verdi himself conduct. The Oscar—ah, *madonna!*—that soprano, she had such beautiful legs!"

This time we rehearsed at Carnegie Hall, and I brought Marion, who sat up in the balcony right near Dimitri Mitropoulos and Fausto Cleva, who were unabashedly studying the Maestro. There has never been another like him, though Leonard Bernstein has the Maestro's fantastic energy and authority.

The melody sings in Bernstein; he catches fire, and it spreads to the men and soloists. I eventually sang Ernest Bloch's awesome Sacred Service under Bernstein. It is a masterpiece of liturgical music and almost Verdi-like. Bernstein conducted the Community Church Choir, the Metropolitan Synagogue Chorus, the musicians, and me with such white heat that he welded us together and wrought an altogether remarkable performance.

Conducting for singers is entirely different from symphonic direction. The conductor must never accompany the soloist but be in complete command. Mitropoulos, for some time, was too kind and allowed the artists to take over, thereby letting their performances suffer. Eventually he grew to be a superb operatic maestro. Fritz Reiner was excellent also, but he seemed very often to lose interest during a performance, and his beat would become so small that you couldn't feel it. Then the mood, or whatever it was, would pass and the pulse would revive. It was a frightening experience.

But, to me, Arturo Toscanini will always stand alone. He was the perfect artist, always painting a masterpiece, balancing, blending all into one immense canvas. Though his powers were now failing, he was still greater than anyone else. His temper was still prodigious too. When a photographer sneaked into Carnegie Hall and took a flash picture, hurting the old man's eyes, Toscanini blew up in a rage worthy of a thirty-year-old. He ran after the fellow, chasing him from the theater. What a temper and what energy!

I once saw him jumping on and off the podium, rehearsing the exact degree of rage he wanted to convey. His son Walter confirmed that he rehearsed that tirelessly too. He was a perfectionist in everything.

Jussi was set to sing in this broadcast, but he had gone back to Sweden. The Maestro received reassuring cables, but Jussi was nowhere to be seen. Because of his absence, I was singing without the tenor; and because of my own failings, I was still using the score, which irritated the Maestro. Always temperamental, he was now touchier than ever.

Three days before the broadcast, there was still no Jussi, and it was clear that he would have to be replaced. The Maestro wanted a favorite of his, Jan Peerce; but Jan, slighted at being second choice, refused to substitute for Bjoerling. The Maestro now would have no one but Jan, and Jan was having no part of the whole business. I called my friend and pleaded with him to join us, to no avail. Jan's wife, Alice, wanted him to do the Riccardo, since it might well be Toscanini's last opera, and it was Alice's insistence—actually, her threat to walk out of the house if he refused—that made Jan relent. Herva Nelli, another favorite of the Maestro, was our soprano.

We now had three desperate days of rehearsal, in that spacious house overlooking the Hudson, with the Maestro bringing us trays of coffee and relaxing by talking of the past. He hated *Lucia di Lammermoor* almost as much as I do. He detested the music and had refused to conduct it, until one clever impresario begged him to make "that lousy opera" sound good for a change. "So I do it and make Donizetti's score sound like fine music."

His authority and gigantic ego were so enviable that I would sit in wonder before him. He never sounded vain or conceited; the facts were just as he related them. I remembered that with our *Traviata* years before, he had changed a few words.

"Verdi is greatest genius, but he was lazy and make the mistake here. Now they fit the music. I know he approve of change!"

I'm sure he did.

His memory seemed to go back to the beginning of time. His stories were endless, his point of view always original. He remembered Caruso as a young boy. "A very lovely, lyrical voice but bad musician. He work very hard and then sang beautiful. I didn't see for long time and then meet here in New York at *that place*. I conduct and don't believe my ears how Caruso became baritone, with the voice big and dark. He was difficult man."

Perhaps, but so was the Maestro, and their fights at the Met were, and still are, legend.

These days and their aftermath with Marion were marvelous. My young Juilliard graduate was in seventh heaven when some French-horn player smuggled her into another Toscanini rehearsal.

But then Chotzie called me. Suddenly, the Maestro was calling off the whole broadcast; he had dreamed that he forgot the opera. This fading giant, who conducted everything from memory, had awakened in a sweat from this worst of nightmares.

Underneath his screaming tyranny, the Maestro had the softest of hearts, and when Chotzie spoke of the great disappointment the artists and public would suffer, Toscanini braced himself and decided to continue.

Marion was there for the performance, given in two successive Sunday sessions. The Maestro, for the first time in his life, hesitated a few times, but he collected himself immediately. No one noticed, and the performance went brilliantly with everyone at his best. We had to be—or else!

Before we began, Toscanini had said, "Mayrrill, do not, please, sing too loud." After the opera was over, he proved that he still saw and heard things usually denied mortals. An E flat is a fine baritone sound, and though I wanted to sustain it, I didn't dare suggest such heresy to the Maestro; he would have drawn and quartered me.

"Mayrrill!" he now said, smiling impishly. "I see you take a long breath and I figure you want to hold the E flat, so I give you the chance. Beautiful sound. Beautiful!"

He missed nothing, the Maestro, especially pretty women. When I introduced Marion to him later, at a private reception at the Barberry Room, he said, "Mayrrill! You are verrry lucky man!" He then patted Marion's bottom, which she immediately interpreted as an accolade—the equivalent of knighthood or something. She called Detroit immediately.

"Mother, wait—you'll die. Toscanini just—that's right, *Toscanini*—just patted me on the fanny. I'm Dame Marion Machno now—you know, like Myra Hess! Mother it was *thrilling!*"

But Marion—delighted as she was by the glamour and excitement of the broadcast and party—had been, I believe, quite put out by the interruption of my courtship and by my stag trip to Boca Raton. Since I was about to go to Rome for my first Italian recording session—*Manon Lescaut* with Licia and Jussi—in June, I asked whether she and Suzy would like to come to Europe.

"Bob Merrill!" Marion exploded—and the use of both my names was a very bad sign. "When I want to go to Europe, I'll go. I don't need you to suggest it. As far as I'm concerned, you can drop dead."

This because I asked her to come to Italy!

"Who needs it?" she continued in the same unreasonable fury. "Big deal. I'm supposed to follow him around the world, yet, chaperone included!"

"Marion," I was very calm, "I didn't suggest Devil's Island. What's so terrible?"

"*You* wouldn't understand!" was her only reply. "You just wouldn't understand *at all!*"

Some vague fear was gnawing at me, and in a way, I was glad that I had to take flight again. I was due in Las Vegas, and I flew. It was the perfect place to divert myself. It was my first appearance at The Sands, and I followed Talullah Bankhead.

Moe and I had not been sure about club offers until now, but we figured it would be all right if Melchior, Traubel and Pinza, as well as Bankhead and Noel Coward, were succumbing to the money and glitter of this brand-new world. I had been offered a very flattering ten thousand a week and a five-year deal, which I signed. I could only hope—and press index finger against . . .

From one hundred and twenty musicians to seventeen is quite a change. I was back to clarinets and saxes after all those years, and when I asked for three strings, I was refused. When I offered to pay for them myself, The Sands imported three fiddles from California. My new orchestrations of "Figaro" and "Toreador Song" were excellent, and I had a large repertoire of show tunes.

It had been quite a while since my old Bing Crosby–show-business self had been allowed center stage, and I was in seventh heaven. Of course, I was a nervous wreck when I walked out on the floor and was greeted by an audience that included half the celebrities of Hollywood and New York. *Both* Bob Merrills were gratified that night, because my arias brought down the house and shouts of "Bravo!" filled a nightclub. The ovation was really something, and I loved conquering another medium. I wouldn't have missed this engagement and the ones that followed for anything.

My only mistake was going to the blackjack table immediately after my first performance. Flushed with success, I became a big-shot spender. Lou Costello sat next to me, and while I was playing for two dollars, Lou was gambling twelve hundred on a card. So I was embarrassed into raising my bet to fifty dollars, thereby losing eight hundred dollars by dawn.

When I got up to my room, the light was coming through my window and my makeup was clogging my pores. In a state of exhaustion, I stared at myself in the bathroom mirror. What a mess! "Idiot!" I yelled on reflection. "Are you out of your ever-lovin' mind? At one time you could have lived off that eight hundred dollars for a year. There are people who need money."

Many actors have left their salaries in Vegas. I vowed I never would, and that was my last slip. After that, I limited myself to twenty-five dollars a night and usually broke even. But there were other troubles in the cards for me.

Dolores Wilson, the soprano we had seen do Gilda in Venice —with an *i* at the end of her name—had just made her debut at the Met, and some press agent had joined our names, creating publicity for both of us. My phone rang; it was Marion. Innocent as I could be, I was thrilled that Miss Independence had called all the way from New York.

"Honey!" I screamed. "What are you doing?"

"I am reading the papers," was her cold answer.

"What does *that* mean?"

"It means that it says here in great big bold print that you and *lovely* Dolores Wilson have been billing and cooing."

"When?" I asked her. "I've been with you. And you believe such nonsense?"

" 'Such nonsense' has broken up many a friendship. I am furious, Bob. I've given you a lot of time."

I promised to be home in a couple of days, and again I asked her to come to Europe with me. Once more she refused. She was being ridiculous. I knew marriage wouldn't work. I was too bitter for that.

At the Russian Tea Room, over early supper one night, Marion gave me Norman Vincent Peale's *Power of Positive Thinking*, which had just come out, and then she dropped the bombshell. She and Maria Caruso were going to drive to Washington, D.C., with a couple of friends to see the cherry blossoms.

"You're what?"

"We thought it would be a lovely outing."

"What is this—out of left field? The cherry blossoms!"

"What's so strange?"

"May I remind little-Miss-Emily-Post-old-fashioned-girl-De-anna-Durbin-picture that Washington, D.C., is also over the state line?"

"But *you* taught me how ridiculous it is to worry about such things. Anyway, there's safety in numbers."

"Three is safety. Four is two couples out for no good."

"Well! Look who's become a mathematical wizard and a jumper to very nasty conclusions. How dare you? The *chutzpah!* With the life you've led!"

It was not a pleasant supper that evening, but before the coffee, we made up. I was doing my first new *Barber*—directed by Cyril Ritchard—that night; and afterward, I was taking Marion and also Margaret Truman to a party at Leonard Lyons' house. The whole evening was crucial, since Marion was meeting

my mother, Gil, and Julia for the first time. They were all
sharing a box for the performance.

The opera went off beautifully. Siepi was in great voice,
Roberta was an excellent Rosina, and Alberto Erede conducted
flawlessly. De Paolis as the Sergeant, Cehanovsky as Fiorello,
and our director, Mr. Ritchard, himself as Ambrogio, were all
marvelous. The new production was quite a success, and I
believed myself excellent that night. My reviews were certainly
raves.

But Marion waited until after my family left and then started
storming. "You were a disgrace, Bob Merrill. A disgrace! And
you break appointments for rehearsal."

"What?"

"That day at my house when you called Marzzola and
played sick. How could you? If I had a gift like yours, I'd
never stop working. I don't stop *now* except to see you, and
what's the point of *that?*"

"Marion, what happened?"

"What happened? You're lazy and you won't work and you
have no sense of responsibility and you didn't know one damned
word that anyone else was saying on that stage tonight. Oh,
sure, you knew what *you* were singing. But did you listen?
Do you ever listen to anyone else on the stage?" She was almost
in tears.

"Have you gone crazy? Did you hear the hand I got? And
the bravos?"

"Oh, Bob," she said, grabbing her forehead. "Your voice will
always get you bravos, but not from *me*. I *know* what you can
do. I want you to be an *artist*, not just a singer."

I wondered how long she'd been saving this up. She turned
to leave. "Go with your Margaret Truman and your fancy
friends," she said. "Don't ever improve yourself. Go on—have
fun and settle for just *all right* and a few bravos! But I can't
watch it."

"Marion! Don't go, please!"

She was shaking with emotion, and I was all confused. There
was a knock and the door opened; Margaret walked in, and it
was impossible to continue the scene. In order to save my face,

Marion came to the party that night. The next day, we tried to talk the situation out as we drove to visit my mother on Long Island. Momma was playing the dowager empress and patronizing Marion. She was very pleasant to her at the opera and again at the house, but I heard that she had asked a close friend, "What do you think of this Marion?" The simple question was sullied by a grimace of such distaste and disbelief that I had to burst out laughing on seeing an imitation of it. It was *so* my mother. There was a resistance to Marion that she never had to Roberta, and it didn't occur to me then exactly what it was. Lotza knew immediately what I was trying, with less and less success, to fight. Marion's outburst could have been duplicated by only one other person in the world—my mother. I felt the familiar tugging again.

Now that my mother had reacted in her polite and rigid way to Marion, I was shocked by *her* mother's reaction to our continuing friendship. The Met tour was starting, and I wanted to hang on to Marion a little while longer, so I asked her to be my accompanist at a concert date I was playing during my week in Cleveland. She would make some money and have a chance to visit with her parents. Marion accepted.

At dinner with the Machnos, who had come in from Detroit, Marion left the table, and her mother started a whole spiel that really threw me!

"She's much too young for marriage, Bob. And I want you to be honest. Would you want *your* daughter to marry a divorced man? Please don't rush into it!"

Rush into it? I was running from it. Who asked *her?* I was scared stiff. Mothers! Women! The idea was frightening me more and more.

A new recording of mine, "My Love Is Like a Red, Red Rose," had just come out, and Marion wanted to get in touch with some of the Detroit disc jockeys she knew so they would plug it.

"Whoa!" I yelled. "Wait a minute, Marion. RCA can handle that."

It was my mother all over again. *She's taking over, and she'll be even more efficient than my first manager! I've got to get away.*

The tugging got worse and, as always, the flight followed. Only this time, I wasn't alone. Marion came back to New York with me. I was to join the opera in Boston, but I stopped off at home first. I insisted that Marion come to Boston for the weekend; after all, when I left Boston, I would be all over the map from Toronto to Cuba, and I wouldn't be able to see her again before traveling to Rome. She agreed to come up with me, and I made all kinds of plans. After my matinee performance of the *Barber,* dinner, then *Pajama Game,* the musical that was shortly to open on Broadway. It was all going to be very light and very festive. But suddenly I turned very green and came down with an illness that defied all diagnosis. I became terribly sick, and nobody knew what was wrong with me except Marion, who kept her own counsel.

She got me back to New York, and I had to cancel a week of appearances in the Deep South while various doctors stood bewildered at my bedside. Now I drove Marion out of her mind from my sickbed. Studying her damned teaching schedule, I called her every five minutes. Her pupils and their parents thought me mad.

I was furious at her indifference. "How can you leave me like this? Are you heartless or something?"

"Bob, I work for a living. You have your career. I have mine."

"But I need you."

"Gussie is stopping in, and I left food—"

"When are you coming home, damn it."

"Home?"

"When will you be here?"

The days were going by, and I was due to rejoin the company in Dallas on Monday. I would fly there while Marion would be in Englewood, New Jersey, with some kid who probably dreaded the piano lesson to begin with. There we were at the wire. We wouldn't see each other again for four months or more.

My God! Anything can happen in that time, with cherry blossoms and French-horn players!

Marion had just reheated some broth for me that she had

made the day before. It was late Saturday night, and I heard my voice as if it were somebody else's. "I suppose we'll have to live here."

"I suppose so. It could be worse."

I had proposed. She had accepted. All the symptoms of my mysterious malady disappeared. I felt great. Great? Glorious! I had never felt healthier in my whole life.

The next day was Mother's Day, and we ruined two mothers' afternoons with the great and happy news.

CHAPTER EIGHTEEN

LILLIAN MILLER was never a stereotype. Just when you thought you could anticipate her reactions, she would fool you all over again. My mother was really something. I could write a book about her.

While I went off to complete the tour, she telephoned my fiancée and asked her to drop in. Marion had several pupils out on Long Island, so she was able to make a package deal one afternoon, and the two women went to a Chinese restaurant where, Momma insisted, the "kreplach" was excellent. Over a couple of bowls of won-ton soup, I was dished by my own flesh and blood.

"So, has he picked out the ring yet, Marion?"

"No, Mrs. Miller. As a matter of fact, everything happened so fast . . ."

"I know."

". . . that we haven't even thought."

"Well, think!" my mother now directed.

What psychiatrist or sage could figure her out?

"Pick out a big one, mine girl," she conspired. "Carats like from the grocery in a bunch. He's got plenty, my son, the singer—plenty," she said as she stroked the collar of her mink coat, still around her shoulders on that warm spring day.

Marion was stunned. Who knows what was on my mother's

busy mind? One cannot say certainly, but I had my suspicions.

Since Marion wanted a religious ceremony, it was necessary that aside from my "shocking" Mexican divorce, I also obtain a *get*—a special Jewish divorce that would sanction my remarriage in the eyes of God.

Marion's folks still had their reservations about the marriage, but they accepted the inevitable. My mother was numb.

It was just the immediate family who joined us in the rabbi's study on Eighty-sixth Street. Mr. and Mrs. Machno, Momma, Gil and Julia, and their son Sammy, my only nephew. His sister, three-year-old Abby, slept in the car outside, tended by Grandma Turetsky.

Our mothers held up the corners of the traditional canopy over our heads, and for *mahzel*, good luck, I crushed the traditional glass beneath my foot. Gussie Rock, our matchmaker, had, of course, been invited but had declined. She had had some wine with us the day before and cried with joy at the success of her plot. Her "children" were getting married. She was certainly happier about it than our parents.

After the simple ceremony, unattended by the press in general but covered by some reporter who had checked at the license bureau and now took a few pictures in the street outside the synagogue, we stood like fools. No great reception had been planned—in fact, nothing, because of last-minute date changing. Relatives had flown in from all directions. But you just didn't say "so long" to the family. You had to have some kind of celebration. There we stood—a little band of people on Eighty-sixth Street. Since Julia's mother was kosher and Marion's father was a vegetarian, our choice of restaurants was somewhat limited. We decided on Steinberg's, a dairy restaurant on Broadway in the eighties, and after a feast, Marion and I picked up our bags and left for a honeymoon in Miami. We then went on to Cuba, along with Richard and Sarah Tucker, for ten days. There I sang the *Barber*. My first wife, Roberta, was the Rosina.

Up to this time and ever since, Roberta has almost vied with me for who could be more civilized and professional about our broken marriage. Professional she was, but she never mentioned my remarriage at all then, which seemed to carry discretion to the extreme. The ladies never met in Cuba.

Then Marion went back to New York to close the apartment and prepare for our trip to Europe. RCA had found it could put out great albums far more economically in Rome, and this was my first recording session there. A most pleasant part of my life, every year these Roman sessions last about ten days. RCA has a modern, air-conditioned studio now, but Angel and London Records hires the whole opera house—orchestra and all. Because Rome is one of our favorite cities, Marion and I and the children always look forward to June. That first one was memorable because I had Marion with me as a bride and because such close and dear friends as Licia and Joe, Jussi and Anna-Lisa were with us. Jussi was trying to call it off again, as he had the *Ballo* with Toscanini, and I was worried about him; but Joe wired him that we were all waiting and wanting him desperately, and he came, bringing Anna-Lisa and their delightful children, Lars and Anne-Charlotte.

The *Manon Lescaut* sessions went beautifully. One afternoon, after they were over, while we were all having lunch and drinking wine in the courtyard of the Grand Hotel, a few street musicians wandered in, and we all sang for the pleasure of it. Licia did the "Cor ingrate," and I sang "Sorrento." We were both in good voice and having fun. And then it was Jussi's turn, and he sang "O Sole Mio." It was the most unforgettable musical experience of my life.

I have never heard anyone sing the way Jussi sang that lovely day. He was an angel. Imagine—of all songs—"O Sole Mio." It was as if I'd never heard it before. Jussi's heart was in that song—that great heart that used to bang away so noticeably through his costume that I could actually take his pulse onstage just by looking at him. More than once in *Faust*, which was a particularly strenuous role for him after his first heart attack, I would run upstairs to his dressing room on the double to get the little white pills that stopped his palpitations.

I can still see Jussi's jolly, bottle-cork face. The kindness and sweetness of the man were in that voice that afternoon. It wasn't just that it was capable of wonderous gymnastics. It was more than *bel canto*. That magic day in Rome—Marion and I recall it often—Jussi Bjoerling sang as I have heard no other mortal sing. Whenever I sang with Jussi, I was more pleased with my own work. The greater the cast, the better I sing. Peerce, Milanov, and I did *Ballo* at the Met soon after this, and I not only remembered Toscanini's directions, but both Jan and Zinka were so magnificent that I surpassed myself. You just know that you're in the clear when you're working with voices like those. You've *got* to stay up there with them and be part of the excitement they create. My aria "Eri tu" even topped Milanov's triumph that night. Having always been lazy, I always rested on my laurels until they were in danger of being snatched from me.

There are nights that are impossible to forget. Leontyne Price and Franco Corelli made debuts together in *Trovatore*, and one was greater than the other that night. They were so glorious that I was thrilled to be making music with them.

Leontyne is a consummate artist. I had also sung with her four years before, in San Francisco, where she did her first *Aïda*. She was scared to death, and my heart broke as I recalled my own terrors. As Amonasro, I made the entrance I have made all these years, but instead of the forty or fifty Metropolitan men behind me, I had four seedy-looking extras at my side.

"*Padre!*" Leontyne sang as she rushed toward me.

"Don't betray me," I sang, and then seeing her shaking, I softly added, "No wonder I lost the war with *this* army."

Aïda relaxed. It is true she almost broke up, and she begged me not to make her laugh, but she got hold of herself. Leontyne was sensational that night, the greatest Aïda *I* have ever worked with. A very serious and dedicated musician, she keeps growing in this and other roles. That, of course, is the secret of a great artist.

A strange combination of insecurity and vanity, I am still surprised when my work is admired. I have no false modesty and my qualities do not escape me, but I find it difficult to believe my own life. I keep remembering the fat, stuttering kid who was so terrified of everybody.

Once, after an interview broadcast from the Waldorf's Peacock Alley with Tex and Jinx McCrary, I received a phone call from Connecticut. It was from an admirer who said that she owned all my recordings and truly appreciated *bel canto* singing. She hoped she had not disturbed me but just had to let me know what a fan she was. I was astonished: it was the great Geraldine Farrar.

Again, when Marion and I went to see Paul Muni in *Inherit the Wind,* I sent a note backstage, hoping the great actor would allow me to pay my respects. I couldn't believe the man's quick reply and eager invitation. It turned out that he too was a fan of *mine.* It's difficult for me to accept this.

Often mobbed on my concert tours by autograph hounds, I was surprised, on one occasion, in a high school, to find a young girl hidden in the classroom that had been transformed into a dressing room.

"All right, young lady," I said, buttoning my shirt, "What do you want my autograph on?"

"Nothing," the child answered. "I came in here to feed my snake."

Of course, my wife, with her *Positive Thinking* and the Italian primers she so subtly brought along to Europe on the first trip, has done more than anyone to give me real confidence. It is Marion who convinced me that there was no role I couldn't tackle and do well in, that hard work and challenge would not see me wanting and failing but more enriched and gratified. It is Marion who has dissipated many of my fears. By *not* working at full steam, I could always justify my not being as good as I wanted to be. She taught me, Marion did, the difference between vanity, of which I had too much, and ego, of which I had too little.

Gussie Rock should be canonized for finding me my wife. It is true that the life I've given Marion is a pretty good one—she didn't marry a shoe salesman—but she did give up her career for me. She had wanted to be a concert artist, and she could have made it. Instead, my wife has dedicated herself to me, and she is my fortress. Her advice is sounder than anyone else's; her honesty is brutal, but it's comforting too. Because when Marion approves, I know everything is all right.

Marion has changed me, oddly enough, not by browbeating

but by good example. That first summer abroad, she practiced the piano eight hours every single day! *Every* day! How amazing she was when I spoke of my insecurities.

"Of course, you're insecure, Bob, darling. You should be. You're ill-prepared. But that's easy to change."

It was all so simple to my Marion, and she was so right. I had been sent the score of Ernest Bloch's *Twenty-second Psalm*, which I was going to sing at the Hollywood Bowl, and Marion and I worked on it as I had never worked on anything in my life. This haunting Hebraic piece has no easy melodic line. Dissonant and exotic in the extreme, the marriage of words and music was anything but simple. Marion's musical interpretation was fascinating, and we worked hard on the piece in Paris, after my recording sessions were over; and we did more work on the way home on the *Queen Elizabeth*.

When I arrived in Hollywood, William Steinberg, the maestro, was astonished at my preparation; he even asked me which European coach I had worked with. Something new had been added to Mr. Merrill. It was Mrs. Merrill.

Unlike most opera wives, she does not hang around backstage with tissues, containers of coffee, throat lozenges, and false praise. She also never informs our friends that *"we're singing tonight,"* a favorite announcement of the Metropolitan spouse, second only to the nauseating, "Were we all right this evening?"

The bright eye and the glad hand are really depressing. Fedora Barbieri's husband always bravoed every member of the cast after a performance. He adored music. One night, when I too was in the audience and went backstage to visit, he waved furiously and squinted his eyes in gratitude. "Bravo! Merrill!" he screamed.

Bravo for what? I thought.

Marion has not built my ego on flattery. She seems to know when I will be responsive to criticism, and then she lets me have it with both barrels. At the theater during a performance, if she comes backstage for any reason, she says nothing negative. On the way home in the car, however, how often I have heard, "Bob, your second act—*oi!*"

There was no question about my luck in finding this girl.

And now I understood my mother's reactions to her. When we had returned from Europe and were in Hollywood for the Bloch concert, news reached me of my mother's remarriage. She was going to show me!

Lotza Balaban Miller was now Mrs. Conrad Leff, the wife of a silk salesman she had met at Grossinger's during the summer. Mr. Leff was bland and pale to the point of being practically nonexistent; and, indeed, he did not exist very long— as my mother's husband, anyway. But Momma would not be rejected and she had recognized in Marion my lifelong mate.

Mr. Leff now moved into Momma's house and escorted Momma to the opera. He was a nice enough fellow, Conrad, and didn't deserve the blow that life had just dealt him.

Momma nagged poor Conrad Leff horribly, and one night, at the Met, when Marion introduced her to someone as "Bob's mother, Mrs. Leff," she turned in a fury.

"My name is *Mrs. Merrill!*"

I think she actually believed that. It's certainly what my mother wanted, and that's what eventually killed her. She was quickly divorced from this gentle creature, who, she insisted, was "basking in our glory." And seeing that my new marriage was going to be a permanent one, she now escaped into illness.

You could almost see my mother willing herself sick. She could tear herself apart on cue. All you had to say was that it was impossible to make the trip out to Kew Gardens on Sunday because Marion had seen a house in New Rochelle that we might buy and Momma would start to disintegrate. She could pale and lose weight before your eyes. I cannot even say it was great acting; it was happening according to plan. She manufactured her ulcers, and then she made them bleed. She created her own suffering in order to inflict it on us. That is the greatest sickness of all.

Just as Momma had virtually given up singing once I was established, she gave up hope now that I was happily married. Marion thrilled me with the news that she was pregnant. It was all so wonderfully fast—correctly but wonderfully. To Momma, that sealed the bargain.

I returned to Las Vegas to appear with Louis Armstrong

in a great act written by Sid Kuller. What can I say about
Louis Armstrong? Our act was wonderful fun: opera versus
jazz, with Louis in a top hat singing "Vesti la giubba" and me in
a bop outfit singing "Honeysuckle Rose." It was a fantastic act,
and we were held over because of land-office business. In the
meantime, I fell madly in love with this man. Louis was never
tired, never depressed, and in his contract was a stipulation
that a case of beer always be backstage for him. He drank
gallons every day; and his wife, Lucille, would make wonderful
meals of kidney beans, rice, and pork shanks.

Louis made his own purgative, with special herbs, because his
beloved mother had told him, "You are only as healthy as your
stomach is clean!" He gave me some after the first show. Mr.
Armstrong was made of iron. I was not.

We had a ball, Louis and I. He's a great artist, and he never
says an unkind word about anybody. He is a beautiful human
being.

I've worked with quite a few wonderful people. With all
the wildness of the opera world and all its feuds, I've been
lucky. The tenors I kid; the other baritones are rarely in the
same operas; and the sopranos, all in all, have been delightful
to work with—although, as with everything else, I have special
favorites.

Temperament has never bothered me. The moods and super-
stitions of the opera world are understandable. After all, if my
own mother spit in the air and went to a Jewish gypsy on
Rivington Street, why shouldn't a basso keep a piece of torn
underwear on his dressing-room table for each performance; a
coloratura, her first dollar; a tenor, a yellowing and blurred
photograph of his great-grandmother? Not everyone is as cold-
blooded as the redoubtable Kirsten Flagstad, who would fall
asleep on her bier while Melchior sang away. She had to be
awakened from the nap just before her cue. The helplessness
and fears of most of us are things I understand well. Most
artists are highly strung, and their mates more so. There is
no one you know who can help you before a performance, so
you search for an intangible, some all-pervading power.

With some, like Corelli's wife, it is God. When Franco

approaches a high note, she crosses herself and freezes until it's all over. Every mirror in every dressing room has a telegram that wishes the singer a broken leg, a strep throat, or worse, in order to ward off the evil eye. To some, a talisman makes sense. But if I did have one and lost it before a performance, it would be my finish.

Every appearance is crucial, every debut Judgment Day. No people take their work more seriously—and have so much fun when things go wrong. You must, for you lose perspective if you consider your brief moment onstage earth-shattering. This is why lovable Kurt Baum always got into a mess. It was the end of the world if his C wasn't perfect. How much better to laugh. Stella Roman once demanded several extra mattresses to ensure a more comfortable landing when, as Tosca, she jumped from the parapet. One must never ask too much of this life: Miss Roman bounced back onstage.

In my cockier days, I came onstage as Escamillo and leaped *à la* Fairbanks on a table that was, unfortunately, on rollers. I sailed right across the stage and into the wings, scraping poor Risë Stevens en route. What do you do? You roar with laughter. What else?

Audiences in small towns think that La Scala or the Metropolitan give performances that are always impeccable. Nothing could be further from the truth, human beings—for the most part—being involved in the productions. Pressures and tensions and the commitments of the artists and conductors often see operas put on with no more than one full everybody-present rehearsal. And there are times when the left hand does not know what the stagehand is doing.

In one of my first *Ballo in Maschera's*, in which Marian Anderson had previously made a haunting debut as Ulrica, I assassinated the Count, sung on this occasion by Jussi. Renato was originally shot by Riccardo, but because of the difficulties with firearms, it had become traditional to use the more sinister and glamorous knife. Since a new production shatters tradition, Herbert Graf, our director, decided to return to the pistol. At the dress rehearsal, everything went well; but it was decided that it was still too risky, and we returned to the dagger. In the snafu that followed, my attack on Riccardo was miraculous: as I knifed him, a deafening report rang out, perfectly matching my stabbing action, confusing everyone in the theater but Jussi, who, having been massacred, had no choice but to die.

In case it is believed that I am amused only by other victims of the practical joke or the misfired dagger, let me note that in my very first *Forza del Destino*, as Don Carlo, I was looking for the seducer of my sister and murderer of my father. *Forza* is hardly a drawing-room comedy, and by this time it must be clear how apprehensive I am about *any* new role. The wounded tenor handed me a parcel to burn without opening. My recitative now debates the advisability of opening the box; and while I played with the packet, I discovered a photograph that absolutely stunned me. It was a French postcard so obscene that the vendor in the Place de l'Opéra in Paris would have hesitated to sell it to a drunken American tourist. It was the furthest thing from "my beloved sister Leonora," and it almost threw me. I had earned this from my fellow workers; it was reward for all *my* gags.

But the stress and strain of opera singing demands such outlets. Without such healthy release, anything can happen.

The next time I went to Venice, Marion was with me, and I sang at La Fenice Opera. Four performances of *Traviata* were being given with Anna Moffo as the Violetta. She had already done two, and I was making my debut in Italy with the third and fourth performances. Until now my commitments had been such and my love of all show business so time-consuming that it had been difficult to accept European offers; however, everything worked out for this short appearance at La Fenice. The audience was international, and there was worldwide press coverage. It was very important to me. After all, it was the first time Italy would hear me.

Moffo's husband, Mario Lanfranchi, was the stage director, and there was one perfunctory rehearsal and then the performance. Miss Moffo was a lovely Violetta. When the second act came and I made my entrance, I was greeted with a terrific ovation, and Miss Moffo and I began our duet. At the highly dramatic words, "*Ah! Morire preferiro!*" she collapsed.

I now sang the "E grave il sacrifizio" and bent down to lift her, but she was like lead. There was no response whatsoever. I tried to lift her once more, thinking, for the moment, she might be interpolating some action; but then my music cue was past, and my Violetta—supposedly a tubercular and not a cardiac case—was like a corpse. The curtain was, of course, rung down.

Within a fraction of a second, there appeared a couple of photographers and a doctor, who proclaimed that it was nothing serious but that the diva simply needed rest. The poor thing lay there like a drugged Juliet. This was not the first time the lady had passed out, and it wouldn't be the last. Tension can be a terrible thing.

It so happened that Dorothy Kirsten and her party were my guests for that performance, and Marion, having run backstage, now mentioned it. "How absolutely terrible!" Marion said, raising her voice noticeably. "I'm sure Dorothy would be glad to finish the performance."

A miracle now occurred that made the backstage of La Fenice a kind of Lourdes. Anna Moffo opened her eyes, rose with the help of her physician, and went on with the opera.

The next morning, even before I had time to read my excellent reviews or see the headlines and front-page photographs of her, Anna called me. She was terribly upset because rumor had it, she explained, that she had lost consciousness on purpose in order to ruin my debut. "You know how ridiculous that is, Bob. If it were true, I would have done it in the *first* act."

Yes, indeed. As she told her doctor, her portrayals were so real that she couldn't help being genuinely affected. I repeat that without a sense of humor—such involvement could end catastrophically. To take her explanation seriously, I can only assume that her Lucia would land her in Bellevue.

But it's all in the family: Anna and I have worked beautifully together since, and recently we recorded a lovely *Rigoletto;* her Gilda was beautiful.

God knows, there have been times when *I* have felt like fainting onstage, when the heart has gone out of me and I wanted desperately to be anyplace in the world but there.

It was in Minneapolis, while I was doing *Barber*, when—in the tradition of a B movie—I kept calling Doctor's Hospital in New York between the acts to find out whether I was a father yet. Almost a year after our marriage, Marion, the Dependable, was still as hardworking and devoted as ever: she was still laboring eight hours a day! And I was forced to be Figaro here, Figaro there, Figaro above, Figaro below, Figaro everywhere but at her side. I could have shot someone with my razor in the very best tradition of the opera.

What a night that was! The cornball scene of all time, but always fresh when you, personally, are cast in it.

I had an open line to the hospital in New York and kept reaching Mrs. Machno, who was not very communicative.

"How is Marion? What's happening?"

"*Oi!*" was her answer. "*Oi*, my daughter, my little girl."

My heart almost stopped. "Nothing's gone wrong has it? How's Marion? Listen to me! Is she all right? That's all I care about."

"*Oi!*" was her only answer. "My little girl is in labor. *Oi, oi, oi!*"

The stage manager was screaming at me, "You're onstage, Bob."

Every time I was offstage, this conversation was repeated, and it was impossible to get any more out of my mother-in-law. I'll never know how I got through that performance.

At last the opera was over, with stagehands and fellow singers asking, "Did she have it yet?"

At 2 A.M., I caught a plane, after calling Marion's father in Detroit and offering to pick him up. The switching of planes, the wait in the airport for Mr. Machno seemed interminable. Finally, at 5 A.M., we boarded the plane for New York. The flight to La Guardia Airport was endless. My car was parked there, and I drove like a madman, through stop signs and all, in the very worst father-versus-stork tradition.

When we arrived, my mother-in-law gave me the sweetest smile I've ever seen. "It's a boy, Bob. You have a son!"

There just isn't any music or poetry as beautiful as that combination of words. "You have a son!" I became dizzy with joy and was led like a child to the glass window, where I saw a crushed, shriveled, shrunken prune that was a replica of me. It was frightening how exactly like me he was.

"It can't be," I muttered. "He's gorgeous."

My early fears of marriage, my first childish terror of real responsibility had all combined to make me feel that I would never really know the beauty of marriage and children, although I wouldn't have admitted that to a living soul. After the fiasco with Roberta, I didn't see my future as anything but a succession of arias with no strong libretto to hold them together. My envy of Gil's wholesome and warm little family, his great little wife and wonderful kids, underlined the glittering emptiness of my life.

Marion changed all that. We now had a house and land in New Rochelle, and I was a solid citizen who didn't have to run all over the place in order to find something I couldn't even name. Marion had given me a home, and now, in my son, she had given me my greatest possession.

My mother obviously felt she was receding more and more from our lives. In the midst of a conversation about the family or opera or anything at all, she would now command the attention of the whole room and then ask whether her neckline was pleasing to the eye. Her pathetic attempts to be queen bee only resulted in her droning on and on, usually in a discourse on her ailments. But, unlike poor Tante Esther's rather sweet and plaintive fears, my mother's complaints were aggressive. The implication was clear: we were all killing her. Her sons had grown and left her for these strangers. She had sacrificed her talent, her youth, and now, indeed, her very life.

In self-defense, I would nap every time I visited her, leaving poor Marion the job of keeping her company and hearing her diatribes against the world. I could no longer bear her recriminations. I couldn't watch her blood pressure rise and see her ulcers gnawing at her. When she was well, she wasn't satisfied; when she was sick, there was no being near her. Gil and I did what we could. Certainly both our wives did as much and more. But Momma directed her health like a great conductor, laying the nerve ends bare so that we could all suffer. It was her overture to death, and it was a horrifying performance. All masks were dropped, and my mother looked at me with the expression of a victim of utter betrayal. Her eyes would burn into me accusingly. There was nothing I could do. Nothing.

We even tried having her live with us for a while, but with the baby, it proved impossible. The cries of little David, the general climate of a household revolving around the infant made it hardly the place for an ill-tempered old invalid, and that is what my bustling, energetic mother had become. Her lack of patience and tolerance, her bitterness and all the hate that was in her made it impossible. In a kind of ecstasy of spite, she now willed herself a stroke; I can almost swear it. I believe it, and so did the doctors. There was no other way for her to rule. The wheelchair became the throne, and a succession of private nurses either quit or were discharged by her before it became plain that a nursing home was the only answer. Even then, it was one nursing home after another.

She got along with no one, and she lived only for our visits, when she would bring herself back from the dead to see her boys and have them see her. She would then regale us with dark tales of the staff and the other patients. "Why should I get pills when she gets shots?" she would ask suspiciously. "Tell me *that* if you think I'm making it up. This is a butcher shop, not a hospital—you could beg for a glass of water and they laugh in your face. They come in the night and stare at me—then with the needles and pins they stick me. How they hate me!"

The last couple of years in my mother's life were terrible—senility the last straw. Her courage, her stamina, her independence all disappeared or, rather, were redirected in this awful self-destruction that would show us all our loss. Tante Lesser was right: my mother literally was eating herself up alive. It was a spectacle I wish on nobody. That vital woman was now reduced to a bitter, seething mass of regrets. She had done so much for me, given me everything. And now I was able to give her everything in the world but what she needed most. Despite my confusions, the toll was great.

Momma always knew what she was doing. After each visit to that Long Island nursing home, I became sicker and sicker. At the time, I was studying the role of Dr. Malatesta for the new production of Donizetti's *Don Pasquale,* and even with Marion's encouragement and cooperation, it became an impossibility. It was like voodoo. My mother, lying miles away in that nursing home, seemed to be controlling me. Like the young boy who refused to sing in the face of her demands, I now *couldn't* sing while she lay half paralyzed but filled with hatred. I couldn't digest my food. It lay on my chest, making it impossible for me to sing. My whole emotional state seemed to be a throwback to my childhood, and I was helpless. The management was furious when ten days before the production, I canceled. I knew that I could never do it justice under these conditions. It distressed me more than they realized, but I knew it was impossible. Frank Guerrera replaced me in the opera, which had Thomas Schippers debuting as conductor.

That same production sported the Met's first revolving stage, but my own *mise en scène* had to depend on the usual old-fashioned scene changes. They were familiar but rapid, and there was another addition to the cast of characters—my daughter, Lizanne, who was almost Italian.

Marion and I were back in Rome for another recording session, this one a *Rigoletto* with Jussi, Georgio Tozzi, Rosalind Elias, and Roberta, who was now remarried herself. Suzy Renardy came along with us this trip, to be with Marion, who wasn't due until August but who looked as if she were momentarily going to have the baby. I was petrified that she might slip on the polished marble floors at the Grand, and every time she didn't show for a session, everyone was sure she had given birth. Only Suzy, our private Azucena, knew it would be a girl and was certain she would be born at home.

Roberta and Marion avoided each other scrupulously, but one night at Passetto's Restaurant—with the whole cast; our director, Richard Mohr; George Marek, the president of RCA Victor's recording division; and our maestro, Jonel Perlea, all at one large table—it was unavoidable and inevitable that they be introduced.

"How do you do, Mrs. Fields?" Marion asked sweetly.

"How are you, Mrs. Merrill?" Roberta answered sweetly.

Nobody dropped dead, the earth remained in orbit, and we all ate heartily. Both Roberta and I had, at last, found the right person, and by this time we were happy for each other. She has a lovely family, Roberta, and we have all visited one another on occasion. One might say—not quite as Rabbi Putterman prophesied—that Roberta and I, after all, *have* lived happily ever after.

I now had everything—a wonderful wife, two beautiful children, and the opera *and* nightclub careers. My two worlds were balanced in heaven, with Marion managing my life. Everything in my universe was moving and dovetailing in perfect design. The only thing out of order was the falling star that now screamed its way across the sky, hurling curses at the gods that let her fire burn out to no use.

Marion called me in San Francisco, where I was singing with Leontyne Price, when my mother went into her last coma.

I flew home immediately, but Momma was dead before I could see her. A phone call announced coldly, formally, "Your mother has just expired." It was no surprise, certainly. She had been deathly sick for months, but she kept returning from death's door; and I half-expected her to go back and forth forever, commanding the Fates eternally. No matter what you are told, there is no proper preparation for a parent's death.

From the very beginning, I had always considered my mother larger than life, somehow above and beyond its petty demands. She had always inspired awe rather than love. She had been too strong to have known fear. In a rush, I saw her deterioration, her vulnerability, her failures, and then I cried for days.

Now that she was dead, I separated her from the rest of us and saw her for the first time as a special human being—not a wife, not a mother, but a woman who was born alone and was about to be buried, in the crazy rituals of our life, next to a complete stranger, my father. Between the beginning and the end was a space she never properly filled for herself.

My mother should have followed her own dream and nobody else's. She should have lived her own life and not mine. A dream is not transferable, though God knows she tried. We both resented her attempt, but certainly I was the luckier one. Without her—just exactly the way she was—my life would have been another story and not as happy a one.

With all its flaws, my world is the very finest one I know, and Lotza Balaban, Lillian Miller, "Mrs. Merrill," introduced me to it first by teaching me the music of the spheres. For that and for so much more, I will always be beholden. The respect and admiration for women that prepared me for my wife, I also, ironically, owe my mother. There are debts impossible to pay, though I tried my best.

At least, she lived to see us a permanent fixture at the Metropolitan Opera.

CURTAIN CALL

IN THIS RESTLESS WORLD, twenty years is permanent, and as I took my last bow and started for my dressing room, a feeling of elation pulled me upward. Sutherland's Lucia was incredible. The size and color of that voice and the accompanying agility dazzle me. She is like a giant running swiftly. While singing the second act duet, I took flight with her. You have no choice; she is divine.

My twentieth season! And during it, after all this time, I would do my first Scarpia. This scourge of Rome, this elegant sadist, Tosca's nemesis, in his powdered wig and black-satin knickers, had better have a voice that soars over the "Te Deum" in the first act or else. I had never dared to attack the role before, never believed I could meet its emotional demands. My present euphoria was dissipated as I remembered that I would have only one full rehearsal with the orchestra. *Every* night is opening night at the Met. After all, Scarpia would be another debut. And there had been a couple of great Scarpias: Scotti, Tibbett!

Did they go on with only one rehearsal?

Well, one thing was certain—they were as nervous as I.

What a challenge that role is! Your voice alone doesn't carry you. This one demands real characterization. There's rarely a complaint about my voice, but there's always the implication that I'm not Sir Laurence Olivier, which is true enough. But I'd like to hear *him* hit an A and hold it.

Shouts of congratulations followed me up the stairs.

"Thank you. It *did* go well! Thanks, I'll see you later at the party. Wasn't Sutherland glorious? . . . Yes, she'll be there."

And there was Mr. Bing. "Wonderful, Bob."

"You're coming to Voisin, Mr. Bing? You must!"

He laughed, shaking his head. "You can rest tomorrow. I have another opening."

"Please, Mr. Bing!"

"You're still young. Have your fun. I'm falling into bed."

"But it's my anniversary."

"I know, and I hope you're with us *another* twenty years. I promise I'll celebrate with you then."

Who would have dreamed way back then? It all came back to me: firing me when I was in Hollywood, snubbing me in Salzburg, avoiding me in New York. It was an international nightmare, that.

Was I really the same Bob Merrill who juggled his future as if it were some kind of garish little club meant to be thrown up into the air? What happened to the little boy who was too scared to sing for his relatives except from the bathroom? What happened to that cocky kid who was going to knock Bing Crosby off his Paramount throne? When did he change, the stuttering child, then the boastful playboy who dreaded responsibility and laughed his way through unstudied parts, not earning the bravos he loved so much?

How can I tell the young singers who come to see me the difference between the promise and the payoff, the many years between talent and real accomplishment? When Wilfred Pelletier flunked me out of the semifinals at those Met auditions years ago, he pleaded with me to work hard and not just settle for the gift that had gotten me past the preliminaries. Without discipline, there is no art. Take it from the laziest man alive.

But I wouldn't listen, and neither will the kids today. They will have to learn the hardest way there is—by living. What does it take to learn the difference between applause and the self-approval that is real fulfillment? It takes a lifetime and luck and someone who loves you enough to give you a kick in the pants when you need it.

Up in my dressing room, I took off my makeup and was surprised at how good I looked beneath it. I was exhilarated.

What a pity Momma couldn't have heard Sutherland. How she would have kvelled from that voice and from my singing with her.

She respected the gift, my mother! When she heard great music, she got a look that revealed a life she could share with no one—no one except me. And I had tried to refuse it.

How lucky that there are sometimes second chances. The gods have been very good to me. I love my work passionately, do it well, and can give the people I love everything they want. This is a lucky man, and I know it.

Strange, disjointed thoughts crowded my head as I dressed to leave for Voisin and my celebration. My position has enabled me to introduce my son and daughter to President Kennedy, to dine at the White House with President and Mrs. Johnson—to meet the great of my time. Life has been good to me. Usually, by the time you can afford the good things, your doctors won't allow you to enjoy them. I eat what I want, and Marion knows how to cook it.

As a matter of fact, I was starved now that the opera was over, and I was ready to welcome Voisin's long, beautiful buffet table, groaning under the weight of all the delicacies. A lot of people had been invited. In fact, half of tonight's audience, which was, even now, drifting across town to the midnight supper.

Alan Lerner was bringing Marion and Johnny Carson's wife, Joanne, to the party. London Records sent a limousine to pick me up, and when I arrived, Johnny, who had been taping his *Tonight Show* and couldn't hear the opera, was greeting the guests with that great charm of his. I joined Johnny, Marion, and Joanne on the receiving line, and I was thrilled to watch my past, present, and future flow by me.

My first leading lady, Licia Albanese, the Violetta of my debut, and Joan Sutherland, my Lucia of tonight, were there. We had made such music together. Everyone in the world seemed to be there.

I was chatting with two genuine Dames—Judith Anderson and Alicia Markova—at about one-thirty in the morning, when there was a commotion at the entrance and Hubert and Muriel Humphrey—all smiles, arms outstretched—came toward me. Fresh from two campaign speeches and a briefing at his hotel from party bigwigs, he had been advised to get to bed so that he could be fresh for the fray the next day. His schedule was worse than a concert singer's on a tour of one-night stands.

"But it's Bob Merrill's twentieth anniversary at the Met, and I said I'd be there," he had told his advisers.

Their response was unprintable, but my friend said good night, broke away from the smoke-filled room, collected his dear wife, and hustled over to Voisin, with security officers in hot pursuit.

Aside from all other considerations, the visit was relaxing. We had a great time, and his presence made everything else an anticlimax.

When everyone had gone and Marion and I were driving home to New Rochelle, I was still heady with the champagne and the excitement. I must have taken a catnap. When my eyes opened to slits, I was beautifully tired. I peeked at Marion as she drove, watching her face glow on and off like a beacon from the passing headlights of other cars. She was relaxed, assured, leaning slightly forward, facing what was ahead squarely, directly. Marion! All was right with my world.

The hum of the car, the soft music coming from the radio wrapped me in catlike contentment. I half woke myself from my half sleep with a great purr.

Marion spied me. "Well! Look who just woke up."

"Hi," I whispered.

"Hi."

"So? How do you like your date's friends, Miss Machno?"

"Very impressive. If it's true about birds of a feather and all that, it speaks pretty well for *him*."

"You're nice to go home with after a party."

"Thank you, kind sir."

"How would you like to be married to an opera singer who needs a nice Jewish girl to take care of him and make him chicken soup in the middle of the night?"

"Who wants to make chicken soup in the middle of the night? And I already have two kids by a nightclub entertainer."

"Oh? Is he attractive?"

"If you like the type. Personally . . ."

"You mustn't be disloyal to the father of your children," I objected. "Where is this Show Biz character now?"

"Lurking around somewhere. He's never far off, I'm afraid. *I* had to get involved with a Gemini!" She shook her head, not unhappily. "He's a far cry from the fellow who's doing his first Scarpia next week."

"Aren't you happy about that?"

"Very. There should be one every season. You know what I'd love to see next?"

"You're not starting with the Falstaff business again, Marion."

"But with your appetite, it's such type casting, Bob. I should think you'd jump at the chance."

"Ha!"

"What's 'ha'? You're eventually going to do it, darling. Why do you keep fighting it?"

"I haven't even done the Scarpia yet, Marion. What do you want from me?"

The conversation—the very track we were on—was so familiar that it continued softly, pleasantly. It was ground we had been over so often that it was smooth and polished and easy to slide over.

"You've got Falstaff in you, Bob, darling. Don't be scared of him."

"I'm glad *you* can see him there."

"Who didn't know he could do Scarpia?"

It was true. I had avoided him like the plague. I had once avoided Rigoletto. I avoided every new challenge.

"I'll think about it. Maybe next year. No, really, we'll talk about it, Marion. God knows I love the opera, but first things first. Let me get *Tosca* under my belt."

"All right, Bob."

"And then I'll think about it on one condition."

Marion prepared for a turn, and I saw that we were nearing

home. Familiar trees and bushes and mailboxes scurried by me.

"What's with the condition?" she said.

"I've worked like a demon on the Scarpia, Marion. When the season is over, if it comes through, I'd like to accept an offer that's in the air."

"Go on," Marion said wearily.

"Vegas wants me again, after all this time, and I'd love it. It's been so long since I've had that kind of fun."

"And *you* can't see yourself as pleasure-loving old Falstaff?"

"Would you mind terribly if it comes through?"

"I had to marry a Gemini," Marion repeated.

"What do you say, honey?"

The car slowed down. "So," Marion bargained, "first things first. We'll start with Las Vegas, 'singer mine.' "

We threw our heads back and roared with laughter as we slowly turned into our driveway.

INDEX

[279]